CONTEMPORARY

ONE

DISH

MEALS

MODERN INTERPRETATIONS OF CLASSIC ONE-POT COOKERY

NEW COUNTRY FARE

CONTEMPORARY
ONE
DISH
MEALS

MODERN INTERPRETATIONS OF CLASSIC ONE-POT COOKERY

MARA REID ROGERS

LAKE
ISLE
PRESS, INC.

Published by Lake Isle Press, Inc.,
2095 Broadway, New York, NY 10023.
Distributed by Publishers Group West,
Emeryville, CA

Grateful acknowledgment is made to the following for permission
to reprint previously published material:
Anne Disrude and *Food & Wine* for the recipes "Zucchini and Sun-Dried Tomato Pizza and
Quick Semolina Pizza Dough," (*Food & Wine*, May 1989, pp. 118 and 122)
Copyright © 1989 by Anne Disrude.
Phillip Stephen Schulz for the recipe "New-Fashioned Chicken Pot Pie with Phyllo Crust,"
from *As American As Apple Pie* (Simon & Schuster, 1990) by Phillip Stephen Schulz.
Copyright © 1988, 1990 by Phillip Stephen Schulz.

Photographs of Vegetable Cobbler, Autumn Vegetables, Pesto Minestrone,
Chili Con Carne Tequila, and Zucchini and Sun-Dried Tomato Skillet Pizza by
Jerry Simpson. Copyright © 1988, 1989, 1990 by Jerry Simpson.
Photographs of Bouillabaisse with Fennel and Chicken Pot Pie with Phyllo Crust by
Michael Skott. Copyright © 1988 by Michael Skott.

LIBRARY OF CONGRESS CATALOG CARD NUMBER 90-62524
ISBN 0-9627403-0-6

Book Design: Mary Moriarty

January 1991

10 9 8 7 6 5 4 3 2 1

Dedication

To Mark, a wonderful husband and my best friend.

Acknowledgments

With special thanks to Jane Ross and Hiroko Kiiffner, two very talented and inspirational women without whom this book never would have been;

Sarah (Sally) Belk, not only for her humor and friendship, but for her willingness to share her enthusiasm and love of food, and who taught me the importance of detail;

Nancy Kalish, whose friendship and belief in me has meant everything;

Jean Galton, for her steadfast culinary skill; Laura Lensgraf, the sister I never had, whose expert eye never let me down;

Grandparents Rogers for their antique cookbook collection that helped turn a passion into a career; and my mother, for her meatloaf.

Introduction

One-dish meals have never gone out of style. This cookbook is a collection of many recipes for one-dish meals—soups and stews, pastas and pot pies and casseroles—both old and new. Whether they are adaptations of classic recipes from around the world or entirely new, they all deliver hearty, visually appealing meals made with fresh, high-quality ingredients. These recipes are created to fit a modern life-style; all of them have in common a sense of bounty based on their use of a wide variety of ingredients, and a characteristic richness of flavor. The slow cooking called for in the preparation of many of these dishes provides for a distinctive development of flavor, giving them a uniquely full dimension and appeal.

Among the other chief virtues of the one-dish meal is its convenience. None of the recipes in this book requires elaborate cooking techniques. They are cooked in just one dish—baked in a casserole, braised in a Dutch oven or simmered in a pot. Presentation is simple: Dishes may be served family-style directly from the handsome oven-to-table cookware now available, or transferred to a serving platter or tureen.

These dishes are the ideal answer to the home cook's most pressing dilemma—how to prepare delicious dinners simply without the sacrifice of flavor and nutrition (to say nothing of the expense) common to take-out foods and store-bought packaged meals. The one-dish meal is both complete and well-balanced. It requires no appetizer or side dish. and may at most be accompanied by a tossed green salad and perhaps some hearty bread, followed, if you wish, by a dessert. The recipes call for easily available ingredients, rather than trendy, hard-to-find items that appear briefly on the shelves of the more fashionable purveyors of food and produce, and substitutions are offered wherever possible.

The preparation of the recipes has been adapted to the use of appliances like the food processor and microwave, in cases in which their use provides for real time-saving. There are notations in many recipes concerning the partial or complete preparation of the dish in advance, to be refrigerated or frozen. The entire meal may then be reheated by popping it into the oven or simmering it in a pot on the stove. Many familiar dishes have been given a "taste-lift"—the addition of a new and unexpected ingredient, the help of a modern appliance, or the use of a neglected but dearly loved piece of cookware. This book will prompt you to retrieve the wok, fondue pot, clay cooker, and other utensils from the back of the cupboard and put them once again to good use.

I have found that the appeal of the one-dish meal has never been so compelling. These foods satisfy everyone's craving for real home cooking, for wholesome, freshly made dishes that might have been served by our mothers and grandmothers. The simplicity of the last-minute preparation and serving of a meal -in-a-dish makes for a sense of relaxation that is a welcome relief from our too-busy lives. For we know that there is a world of difference between eating to appease hunger and truly enjoying food, and that the sharing of food with family and friends is one of life's greatest pleasures.

THE
BASICS

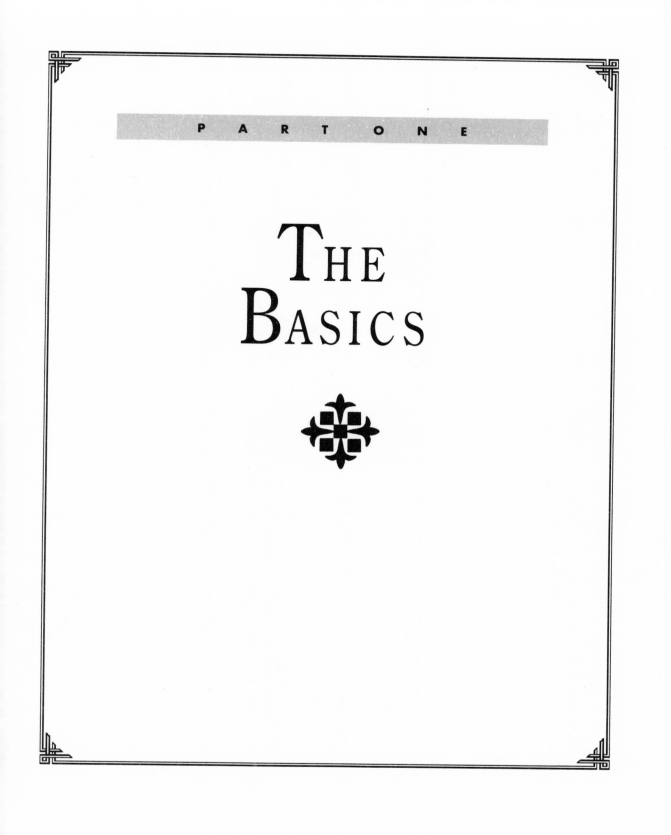

About the Recipes

I have been inspired to write this book for people who care about what they eat and who enjoy eating well. Most of us qualify as health-conscious lovers of good food and the recipes in this book reflect these concerns. They are delicious, easy to follow, visually attractive, and nutritious, too. For valuable guidelines and tips regarding ingredients, techniques, and equipment, please refer to this opening section.

PREPARATION OF INGREDIENTS

Within the recipes, certain assumptions have been made. Though most of the recipes do not specifically say to wash the fruits and vegetables called for, they should of course be washed before use. I will occasionally remind you of what you already know, such as when to peel or trim particular vegetables, and which ones take a more thorough rinse, such as leeks or spinach. But I will also give you less commonly known information, for example, how to prepare dried wild mushrooms or a fast method to peel pearl onions. Please read the entire recipe before beginning.

I also call for some vegetables to be left unpeeled. Just scrub the vegetables—such as eggplant and red boiling potatoes—very well; those with fairly thin skins, such as zucchini or yellow squash, may be left with their skins intact, too. It's better for you, and adds color to many dishes. Vegetables cooked in one-dish meals add valuable nutrients to the cooking liquid, too.

NUTRITIONAL CONCERNS

One of the ways I have modified recipes to make them more nutritionally sound without sacrificing flavor is to give substitutions or replacements for certain ingredients. In most recipes, I have called for (or you can substitute) unsalted margarine for butter, skim milk for whole milk, plain lowfat yogurt for sour cream, and half-and-half for heavy cream. When an oil is needed for cooking, I call for unsaturated fats such as olive oil and safflower oil versus the highly saturated oils. I also generally use less oil in dressings than the classic 3:1 ratio of oil to vinegar. I prefer to use olive oil for salad dressings, depending on the recipe, not only for its flavor, but because it is better for you than most other oils. I also call for safflower and corn oil for substitutions or alternatives. The recipes for homemade stocks on pages 184-187 use little salt, if any, and low-sodium canned broths are suggested as substitutes.

I have limited the use of canned products, opting for fresh ingredients whenever possible. Some ingredients are available fresh year-round; but although supermarkets and grocers are stretching the seasons, I find that tomatoes are just not very good year round, nor are strawberries, not to mention the expense! I do call for quality canned products such as Italian peeled plum tomatoes and tomato paste. Try to purchase the low-sodium versions if possible. When I call for prepared products that tend to contain a lot of salt, such as cooked beans, capers, anchovies, and olives, I suggest draining and rinsing them to rid them of as much salt as possible.

PREPARING PASTA AND RICE:

I omit adding salt to boiling water when cooking pasta. Just stir the pasta occasionally to prevent it from sticking together. Once it is cooked, drain and toss it lightly with olive oil to prevent sticking. Though you can substitute fresh pasta in any of the recipes, I don't list it as an alternative because of the high egg content of fresh compared to most commercial dried pasta, and because of the additional time it takes to make fresh pasta dough at home.

When directions are given to cook pasta or rice, it is usually to the al dente stage, which literally means "to the tooth." The pasta or rice should be slightly firm to the bite when tested;

this is the way it should be eaten and is especially important when the ingredient will be baked later. There is nothing worse than overcooked pasta or rice.

Note: If you want to substitute brown rice for white rice, you will need to lengthen the time the rice is simmered; brown rice can take up to 15 to 30 minutes longer than long-grain white rice to become tender. Alternatively, combine the brown rice with twice the amount of water needed to cook it and let it soak overnight. Drain, rinse, and proceed as usual with the recipe, treating it as you would white rice.

PREPARING MEAT:

Meat should be trimmed of any excess fat. I call for lean bacon and meat and for extra-lean ground meat whenever possible. Remove the skin from poultry before cooking it; there are only a few recipes in which the skin needs to be left intact to retain moisture during a "dry-heat" cooking process. Pour off excess fat when it is not needed for cooking. Also, skim the surface of soups and stews of excess fat. If you can make the dish ahead (preferably the day before serving) and refrigerate it long enough for the fat to rise to the surface and solidify, you can remove the fat easily and discard it.

Always rinse poultry before cooking it to help eliminate harmful bacteria. It is also good practice to rinse fish. Follow the specific cleaning instructions given in each recipe for shellfish. Also, always wash all cooking equipment and surfaces that come in contact with raw meats, seafood, and poultry with hot, soapy water. This includes your hands as well as the knife, cutting board, sink, etc.

Do try to be prudent when grocery shopping. Read the labels to make sure a product still contains the necessary nutritional elements after being nutritionally "modified." For example, when using skim milk, make sure it has been fortified with vitamins A and D, which are lost when the fat is removed.

Nutritional claims can be ambiguous. Just because the label uses the words "reduced," "free," or "low" doesn't mean that the product won't contain other potentially harmful ingredients, or that "light" or "lite" may actually refer to the consistency or taste of the product!

Be aware that some products contain excessive amounts of salt or sugar. Look closely at products you use all the time, such as peanut butter, and buy the brand with the least salt and sugar. Compare products from different manufacturers for fat and cholesterol content, too.

There are several schools of thought on the substitution of dried herbs for fresh. Some people believe the proportion should be 1:2; others recommend 1:3. I feel the proportion depends largely on the herb and the recipe, and I have given substitutions accordingly. I do not recommend using either commercially dried chives or basil, as neither has much flavor, and what flavor it does have is not reminiscent of its original state. Unless it is crucial to use fresh basil for a recipe, I will usually suggest a different herb as an alternative. The same applies to fresh chives, for which I sometimes use scallions as an alternative for their "oniony" flavor. All dried herbs should be crumbled before using, and some, such as rosemary, should be moistened in a little warm water before using. Please refer to Seasonings, pages 28-29.

Although I have tried to use other seasonings to take the place of extra salt and sometimes as an alternative to salt, it is important to remember that salt is a necessary seasoning. When you read "Salt and freshly ground pepper to taste," really taste the dish, season it with salt and pepper, give it some time for the flavors to blend, and then taste again before serving. As an experiment, try to season with more pepper than salt; you will be surprised at the magic of freshly ground black or white peppercorns. You won't miss the extra salt.

The "Dish" in One-Dish Meals

There is a tremendous variety of cookware to choose from in preparing a meal-in-a-dish. Since the techniques required for one-dish cookery are relatively easy, special equipment is not generally needed. The cookware called for in the recipes includes skillets, saucepans, pots, a stockpot, baking dishes, casseroles, and a Dutch oven. I generally specify a "heavy" utensil: This does not refer to its actual weight, but to the type of material from which it is made. A heavy-duty piece of equipment in general cooks more reliably because its surface heats more evenly.

In respect to the size of cooking utensils: The recipe specifies a small, medium, or large skillet. Though they can vary as to depth, a small skillet is on average 6 to 7 inches in diameter, medium 8 to 10 inches, and large 12 to 14 inches. I give approximate dimensions for the baking dishes, and quart sizes for other utensils.

Much oven-to-table ware is attractive enough to suit any occasion. When using cookware, just make sure that it is suited to the particular type of heat source you are using, flameproof for the stovetop and ovenproof for the conventional oven. This is especially important when transferring a utensil from the stove to the oven or vice versa: Make sure what is flameproof is also ovenproof! And check the handles, too!

FINDING THE RIGHT-SIZE COOKWARE

Cookware sizes may vary among manufacturers, but all can be measured by total volume in cups. If you are unsure about the volume of a container, and it is not marked, measure it. Fill a liquid measuring cup with water and pour it into the utensil, counting the number of cups and repeating until the container is full. All cookware in this book is listed in quart volume sizes: To translate into cups, you need only recall that there are 4 cups or 2 pints in a quart.

Baking pans and dishes vary widely in size and shape. A baking "pan" is made of metal, while a "dish" is made of glass. Baking pans and dishes are generally round, square, or rectangular. The majority of the recipes in this book call for standard baking dishes, usually shallow (to provide for faster and more even cooking) and rectangular.

If you don't have a baking dish of the exact measurements asked for, you can substitute a comparable dish with approximately the same surface area. To measure the surface area of a baking pan or dish, measure the length and width from the inside edges, then multiply the width by the length to determine the surface area in square inches.

Other utensils for one-dish-meal cookery are a little more specialized but very useful:

CASSEROLE:

The casserole is usually a deep dish with a lid and handles. It is important that the lid fit tightly. The handles are also important because the casserole and its contents can be very heavy: The handles need to be sturdy and large enough for you to lift the filled hot container easily. The shape of the dish may be round, oval, rectangular, or square. Round or square shapes are best for stove-top cooking because the utensil will heat more evenly. If the manufacturer indicates that the container is flameproof, ovenproof, or freezer-to-oven, make sure that the handles are, too. There are also individual casseroles for a single serving, with a typical volume of one cup.

SOUFFLÉ DISH:

A round, ovenproof soufflé dish is straight-sided and deep. The smaller, individual version is called a ramekin.

CAST-IRON SKILLET:

The cast-iron skillet is ideal for dishes that are cooked or partially cooked on the stove and then transferred to the oven.

SINGLE-PAN CHAFING DISH AND FONDUE POT:

Both the single-pan chafing dish and fondue pot can be used to cook food over direct heat provided by alcohol, electricity, or canned sources at the table or buffet. The fondue pot tends to be deeper than the single-pan chafing dish.

BAIN-MARIE CHAFING DISH:

This utensil contains two pans: the blazer pan for cooking over direct heat, and the bain-marie for cooking over water, double-boiler style. The bain-marie can also serve to gently warm foods already cooked.

GRATIN DISH:

The shallow, oval, slope-sided gratin dish is used to brown food in the oven or under the broiler. Usually made of porcelain bakeware, it is not meant for stove-top use.

Selecting the correct cookware is an essential part of outfitting any kitchen. Here is a brief outline of some of the pros and cons of specific materials that can help improve your cooking experience. Always read the manufacturer's instructions before using any new kitchen utensil.

ALUMINUM:

Aluminum is one of the best heat conducters, but it is not the most durable material for heavy use. Avoid thin-gauge in favor of heavy-gauge pots and pans that distribute heat more evenly. Aluminum can react chemically to certain foods, discoloring the finished dish and affecting its flavor. Recipes calling for a nonreactive cooking utensil indicate that you should not use aluminum. Avoid cooking acid-based foods, such as tomatoes, or dairy-based sauces made with milk, cream, or eggs in aluminum utensils. Avoid also cooking artichokes and asparagus in aluminum, and don't hard-cook eggs in an aluminum pot.

If you mistakenly use reactive cookware, you can remove the discoloration from the cookware with vinegar, then clean it thoroughly before using it again. (Note: Marinades, also acid-based, should never be placed in containers made of metals such as aluminum, copper, or cast iron; avoid plastic, too. Use only glass or glazed ceramic.) For the recipes for which I prefer to use glass cookware, I call for a "non-metal" container.

ANODIZED ALUMINUM:

This new type of aluminum product has a surface that has been sealed by a process called anodizing. Anodized aluminum pots are largely nonreactive, so they do not adversely affect food. If they are deeply scratched, however, you run the risk that they will react.

COPPER:

Copper utensils are beautiful and cook evenly: They conduct heat well. But they are not practical. Copper is difficult to keep clean, and the interior of the pot needs periodic re-tinning. Overall, copper cookware requires more upkeep than other types.

STAINLESS STEEL:

Stainless steel—I am not referring to carbon, enameled, tinned, or black steel—is a poor conductor of heat but is available combined with additional metals to improve conductivity. Stainless steel is nonreactive; it does not react to acidic or alkaline ingredients that discolor aluminum. Stainless steel rusts and must be scrubbed clean.

CAST IRON:

Cast-iron cookware conducts heat well. It is easy to clean and is very durable. Unfortunately, it is also very heavy. It is best used when cooking with little or no liquid, as it retains heat long after being removed from the stove or oven. Cast-iron cookware needs to be seasoned before use unless preseasoned or coated with a nonstick finish by the manufacturer (see the manufacturer's directions). For cleaning, never scour cast-iron ware; just wipe it with paper towels and a few tablespoons of salt, then rinse lightly in hot water and dry thoroughly. Avoid all detergents, soaps, or abrasives. If the utensil rusts, or if you find that food is sticking, then scrub and reseason the pan.

ENAMELED CAST IRON:

This material provides the heat conductivity of cast-iron cookware yet requires no seasoning of its surfaces. However, enameled cast iron is also very heavy and the enameled surface can crack or chip. Be careful not to overheat or heat when it is empty, to avoid damaging the enamel. Use a mild powdered cleanser to clean enameled cast iron, and avoid any cleanser that contains bleach, which can harm the surface.

CERAMICS:

Ceramic cookware includes glass, porcelain bakeware, and earthenware. Although it is not a good conductor of heat, glass retains heat very well. Glass will not react with food or impart any flavor. Not only is heatproof glassware excellent for the oven, it can also be used for microwave cooking, provided that it is certified by the manufacturer. Do not use glass under the broiler. Glass can crack with extreme temperature change, so let it cool down before washing it, and do not transfer it from the freezer to the oven unless the dish is specifically made for that use. Heatproof glass can be cleaned safely in the dishwasher; soak it first if necessary.

Most heavyweight porcelain can be safely placed in the oven or microwave: But always check the manufacturer's directions and double-check that there is no trace of metal in the glaze of any utensil to be used in the microwave, especially in any hand-painted decoration. Do not use porcelain for stove-top cooking. Most heavyweight porcelain can be washed in the dishwasher.

Earthenware includes many and various types of ceramics. It absorbs heat slowly but retains it well, and is therefore wonderful for cooking slowly at low oven temperatures, as it can enhance the development of flavors. When baking in earthenware, place the dish in a cold oven, then set the oven to the temperature desired. Avoid extreme changes in temperature, and never use earthenware for stove-top cooking. I recommend washing earthenware by hand with a mild soap.

Stoneware, a form of earthenware, is very durable and can be used in the oven. Avoid any sudden temperature change, however, and do not use stoneware for stove-top cooking. Most stoneware can be washed in the dishwasher.

Terracotta is another specialized form of earthenware. Only those terracotta dishes specially produced for baking should be used in the oven. A clay cooker is usually partially glazed terracotta that requires very special attention; the manufacturer's instructions should be read carefully and followed explicitly. Do not use terracotta on top of the stove. To wash terracotta cookware, rinse it quickly in warm water and baking soda.

NONSTICK COOKWARE:

Nonstick cookware allows you to cook using little or no fat. Food releases easily from the treated surfaces so that nonstick utensils are easy to clean. Never use abrasives that will scratch the surface, such as steel wool pads, cleansers, or metal utensils. Nonstick cookware should not be used over high heat.

Advance Preparation and Storage

The advance preparation and storage of delicious, robust, and healthy one-dish meals provides solutions to the major difficulties surrounding the getting of dinner on the table that we all face, whatever our immediate situation may be. I and my husband, for example, have professional businesses to manage that generally leave very little time for the preparation of dinner. Yet I am determined not to rely on take-out or prepared foods that are expensive, not particularly good for us, and lacking in flavor, leaving us finally unsatisfied.

I have committed myself, not only as a food professional but in the interest of living well, to eating home-cooked meals that are (1) appealing at the end of a long day; (2) nutritious; and (3) that will taste equally good whether refrigerated for a day or two or frozen and reheated months later. Add to this the concerns of using food in an economical fashion, and the need for an efficient way to plan meals flexible enough to get you through the week (particularly if you enjoy having friends for dinner on short notice, as we do) and you will have discovered the reasons for cooking or at least partially preparing one-dish meals ahead, with the intention of storing and using them for more than one meal.

The basic requirement of efficient meal preparation is, of course, to plan ahead. Very many of the recipes in this book can be partially or completely prepared a day ahead, and I have been careful to indicate the step to which a recipe may be thus prepared. All recipes in which a microwave oven may be used more efficiently than a stove-top or conventional oven to do part or all of the cooking have appropriate microwave instructions. And the majority of the recipes that can be successfully frozen have specific instructions on how to freeze, reheat, and serve without damage to the specific characteristics of the dish.

Even if you can't cook ahead, it is still critically important to plan ahead in order to shop for food and cook efficiently. Many of the recipes yield more than one meal, and planned leftovers make the speediest suppers. Do pay attention to the storage duration time, since foods refrigerated for too long a time lose important nutrients and can even become harmful. If you plan to freeze a dish or serve it and freeze leftovers, do so immediately after the food has cooled or as soon as it is removed from the table, and don't freeze it beyond the prescribed length of time. Once you thaw a dish that has been frozen, plan to cook or reheat it right way.

For a one-dish meal, you will be focusing your efforts on a single recipe incorporating all the required nutrients. Most important is the matter of strategy: It is essential to read the complete recipe before beginning and to plan how you're going to tackle it. It's possible that you or someone else can prepare some of the ingredients ahead—perhaps trimming green beans or rinsing and drying lettuce for storage in the refrigerator. Vegetables and fruits may be cut up in advance, and even as early as the day before you plan to cook them, although they should not be cut up more than a day ahead since they will start to lose important nutrients. Perhaps you can do some quick cooking ahead—the pasta or chicken for a composed salad, for example—or assemble a dish to be refrigerated and baked at some later point. Whatever you can do ahead will save valuable time later, when you're in a hurry. Think ahead also as to whether you're going to take advantage of an option to use a microwave in the preparation of a given recipe, or to freeze it, since the decision will affect the cooking or storage container you use.

Don't forget that one-dish meals are ideal for entertaining, allowing you to make ahead of time a dish that can be served at the most elegant dinner party or casual buffet, or as the main course of a picnic, a tailgate party, or other outdoor festivity. You may also want to plan holiday events around a one-dish meal rather than a traditional multi-course menu: There are plenty of other activities demanding your attention during the holidays, and cooking a one-dish dinner ahead of time will make for a far more relaxed meal to enjoy with family and friends—and less to clean up. So get out of the kitchen and congratulate yourself on your foresight and planning!

Microwave Basics

Microwave ovens are capable of much more than reheating a cup of coffee or melting butter. A microwave oven is a culinary tool that is meant to be user friendly.

Happily, many one-dish meals lend themselves to partial or complete preparation in a microwave oven* so I have therefore adapted as many of the recipes as possible to its use. What follows is a quick summary of microwave basics as they apply to the preparation of one-dish meals. I also believe it's a good idea to read and follow the manufacturer's instructions, as you would with any appliance.

*All recipes were tested in a microwave oven, *not* a microwave-convection oven.

POWER

All the recipes adapted to microwave preparation were tested in a large, full-power oven, operating at 700 watts. Some medium-power ovens operate at 500-600 watts, and low-power ovens at 400-500 watts. These distinctions are important because the power of an oven affects cooking time and the evenness with which food is microcooked; the higher the wattage, the faster and more evenly the food cooks.

If using a lower wattage oven, cook these recipes approximately 1 1/3 times longer than the microcook times specified in my instructions. This is a good rule of thumb, though subject to many variations. No two microwave ovens are exactly alike in their power outputs, even if they are of the same wattage and size, so it is best to work with your microwave and become familiar with its eccentricities. Ultimately, use your judgment as to how much time is required to achieve a great-looking dish cooked to your satisfaction in *your* oven.

Some recipes, by their nature, were not considered suitable for microwave adaptation for some of the following reasons:

- When the objective was a specific flavor or effect, e.g., sautéeing vegetables or browning a casserole, best achieved on top of the stove or in a conventional oven.
- When cooking a large quantity of food requiring an oversize container whose contents would cook unevenly or likely boil over.
- In some instances when foods of varying texture and density, e.g., a meat and a vegetable, had to be cooked at the same time.
- When microwaving was neither time-saving nor more convenient than a conventional oven, e.g., changing from conventional container to microproof containers or vice versa in the middle of a recipe.

For the recipes in this book, the terms LOW,

MEDIUM, and HIGH are used to describe power-setting levels in the microwave. Most of the microwave adaptations call for HIGH power, or "10," which is 100% power or full power.

As a general guide, the following terms apply:

- HIGH is 100% or full power

- MEDIUM may be 50% to 70% of the full power of your oven
- LOW is the lowest power setting on your oven, or 10% to 20% of full power.

However, please refer to your owner's manual for precise percentage equivalents for the power levels of your particular oven. To date, there is no industry standard.

MICROPROOF COOKING CONTAINERS

MATERIALS:

Use glass, paper, plastic, ceramic, porcelain, and earthenware dishes labeled for microwave use. Do not use any metal or enamelware. Be aware of metal-based glazes or cookware trimmed with metal that can damage your oven, and avoid using twist-ties sold with plastic bags that sometimes have a metal core. Microproof aluminum foil, however, can be safely used. When purchasing microproof plastic dishes, look for the words "suitable for microwave." Also, some plastic lids to microproof containers may not themselves be microproof. Always double-check your equipment before using.

SHAPE:

It is best to use round or oval-shaped dishes for optimal results. Food in the corners of square or rectangular dishes tends to cook first in a microwave, and as a result, is often overcooked. Also, straight-sided containers are preferable to angled ones, as the former cook more evenly and allow for easier stirring.

COVERS:

For most of the recipes in this book, instructions call for containers and dishes to be covered. In general, covering a dish distributes moisture and heat evenly and retains steam, allowing for faster cooking.

The following are useful tips regarding covers:

- A "tight cover," i.e., a microproof round glass or plastic lid, plate, or microproof plastic wrap will retain steam and allow the surface of the food to remain moist. Always open a tight cover away from you to avoid being scalded.
- When making a "tight seal" with plastic wrap, use a piece large enough to cover the top, side, and handles of a dish completely.
- "Vent" plastic wrap by slightly pulling back one corner before microwaving. This offers protection against scalding and allows you to stir freely without discarding the wrap. However, if much stirring is required, a microproof glass plate or lid would be far simpler to handle.
- If using plastic wrap, *always* pierce it immediately after cooking to allow steam to escape in controlled fashion.

- A "loose cover" is to lay a piece of micro-proof wax paper lightly on top of a dish. (If your oven has a turntable, partially tuck the wax paper under the dish to secure it.) Wax paper retains some steam, but also keeps moisture from settling on the surface of food, thereby preventing sogginess. It is also a good way to prevent splatters.
- A microwavable "paper towel cover" will absorb moisture and keep the surface of food dry. (If your oven has a turntable, partially tuck the paper towel under the dish to secure it.)

- An "uncovered" dish will allow moisture to evaporate.
- Use microproof "aluminum foil" to shield areas of food from cooking or to defrost certain sections more slowly.

DEPTH:

Follow specific recipe instructions in the selection of all cooking containers. Remember, the larger the exposed surface area, the faster food will cook in a microwave oven. A good rule of thumb is that the container be twice as high as the food it contains to avoid boiling over and to make stirring easier.

SOME MICROCOOK PRINCIPLES

COOKING AN ENTIRE DISH:

When an entire dish of food is micro-cooked, it cooks from the outer surfaces to the inside. Therefore, in order for food to cook evenly, it must be stirred from the outside of the dish toward the center. When stirring is impossible—as with a layered casserole or a cake, rotate the dish. If your microwave does not have a turntable, turn the dish clockwise or counterclockwise, and reposition it in the oven.

COOKING INDIVIDUAL FOOD(S):

If microcooking a variety or assortment of individual foods, arrange them in the dish, according to how slowly or quickly they cook. Those toward the outside of the dish will cook more quickly, relative to those in the center, so they may have to be rotated periodically for

best results. To microcook a large piece of food, turn it over and rotate the dish to ensure an even result. When microcooking a quiche or cake, elevate the food dish on an inverted microproof pie plate or custard cup to raise the food closer to the center of the oven where it seems to cook more evenly.

STANDING TIME:

The direction "let stand" that appears in the microwave recipes should be followed for best results. Since food continues to cook from residual heat after microwaving has ceased, the "standing time" has been factored into the recipes in anticipation of a perfectly cooked dish. The container itself is usually covered during this period of time and can remain inside or outside of the microwave while it "stands."

Here is a brief list of some flavors that become stronger in the microwave and others that diminish in intensity. Remember, it is prudent to season to taste just before serving.

BECOMES STRONGER:	BECOMES WEAKER:
Black pepper	Fresh garlic
White pepper	Fresh herbs (add after cooking)
Dried chilies	Alcohol and alcohol-based extracts
Szechuan pepper	Cumin
Cinnamon	Anise
Nutmeg	Caraway
Ground ginger	Allspice
Dried herbs	

Freezer Basics

Freeze it now and serve it later! Freezing is perfect for last-minute family suppers and entertaining. Like the microwave oven, the freezer is a time-saving appliance, ideal for storing one-dish meals.

PREPARATION FOR THE FREEZER

COOLING HOT FOODS:

Quickly cool hot liquids and foods to room temperature before freezing, taking care to do this as soon as possible after cooking. Ice-water baths can hasten the process. I set the pan containing the food in a larger pan of ice water, stirring occasionally. When the food has cooled to room temperature, ladle immediately into freezer containers or wrap and freeze as directed.

Tip: Do not freeze food in a single batch that would take up more than 10% of freezer's capacity.

CHOOSING A CONTAINER:

Try to package food in quantities sufficient for a single meal; *never refreeze thawed food* with the exception of raw foodstuffs taken from the freezer, cooked, and then returned to the freezer.

Only use containers specifically labeled "for freezer use," and *always read* specific package directions carefully. The containers I've listed here are those most readily available, easiest to use, and best for long-term storage. Try not to use deep containers that take a long time to thaw. Also, it's convenient to use wide-mouth containers that make it possible to remove food from the container without thawing, if needed. Just immerse container in hot water to loosen contents and remove.

Use moisture- and vaporproof containers of a size and shape appropriate to the food being frozen. They should seal airtight.

ALUMINUM CONTAINERS:

Aluminum containers are available in many sizes and styles and come complete with tight-fitting lids. They are not recommended for storing highly acidic foods that react unfavorably to aluminum (see following). Aluminum containers can be reused and can go from freezer to oven safely.

PLASTIC CONTAINERS:

In my opinion, plastic containers are the best, considering their variety and convenience of use. Most come with tight-fitting lids.

PLASTIC FREEZER BAGS:

These moisture- and vaporproof bags made from pliable plastic film are available in a variety of sizes and shapes. They are fine for solid foods, but not recommended for semisolid foods or liquids. Once the bag is filled, remove as much air as possible before sealing to prevent freezer burn. Freezer bags can be purchased with boxes for extra protection.

FREEZER-TO-OVEN AND FREEZER-TO-MICROWAVE BAKING DISHES:

These dishes are recommended for freezing foods that will later be baked or microwaved. This versatility makes them an attractive alternative to wraps and plastic containers in spite of their relatively high cost. They have the added advantage of being able to undergo extreme temperature changes without cracking or breaking.

WRAPPINGS:

Proper wrapping is essential to freezing foods successfully. Frozen foods that have been inadequately wrapped lose color, flavor, and vitamins; they will also surely dry out. Therefore, choose wrappings with the following qualities: moisture-and vaporproof, durable, oil- and grease-resistant, and easy-to-label. Only use wrappings and bags labeled "for freezer use," and always follow specific package directions.

HEAVY-DUTY ALUMINUM FOIL:

Heavy-duty aluminum foil gives better freez-er protection than regular aluminum foil. Wrap the item to be frozen in the foil and mold to seal. This foil does not require freezer tape, but the seal must be airtight. Be careful not to puncture the foil while wrapping and it is best to place a foil-wrapped parcel in a plastic freezer bag for added protection inside the freezer. When wrapping foods that react unfavorably to aluminum, such as acidic tomato products or cheese, wrap the food first in clear plastic freezer wrap, then in heavy-duty aluminum foil.

PLASTIC FREEZER WRAP:

This product gives better freezer protection than regular plastic wrap. It requires freezer tape, a special tape made to withstand very cold temperatures, for an air-tight seal. Freezer tape is available in most supermarkets.

LAMINATED WRAP:

I recommend this strong laminated paper, also called "heavy freezer paper." It, too, requires freezer tape to seal.

PACKING AND SEALING TO FREEZE

PACKING:

As a general rule, pack food solidly to keep air out, except for liquid or semisolid foods, such as soups and stews, that expand upon freezing. For such foods, leave about 1 inch of headspace below the rim in pint containers and about 1-1/2 inches in quart containers. All other foods should be sealed with as little air as possible.

SEALING:

Wrap food following the manufacturer's instructions for that product. Make sure to exclude all air, and seal packages and any loose-fitting lids with freezer tape.

LABELING:

Items to be frozen should be fully labeled to

ensure rapid turnover; the quality of frozen foods diminishes over time. Read the recipe for guidelines as to the "freezer life" of a specific dish, largely determined by its ingredients.

Use a freezer pen or wax crayon, not pencil, to label freezer foods. Write directly on the package or on an adhesive freezer label. Include the following information:
- Type of food
- Quantity or number of servings
- Date frozen
- Date to be consumed (refer to specific recipe for information)
- Any additional information relevant to future use, e.g., suggested garnishes, baking or cooking directions, etc.

FREEZING TIPS:

- Do not overcook foods to be frozen.
- Do not freeze toppings such as cheese, bread crumbs, and nuts. These should be added upon reheating.
- Do not freeze sauces that contain eggs, milk, or cheese; nor bacon or products containing fat, hard-cooked eggs, potatoes, rice, and pasta. These are best added later upon reheating.

- Seasonings such as chili powder and curry powder can lose some of their punch when frozen. Just add more while reheating, and adjust seasoning to taste prior to serving. Certain flavors tend to strengthen after having been frozen—pepper, garlic, cloves, and sage—so season accordingly.

THAWING:

For best results, I recommend thawing foods completely before attempting to cook or bake them. This method has several advantages, not the least of which is better control of cooking or reheating and minimal changes in the appearance, texture, and flavor of the food.

I find it easy to thaw food unattended in the refrigerator by simply leaving it in its freezer wrapper overnight or by setting the sealed, airtight freezer container in a bath of cold water until the food is sufficiently thawed for easy removal. I do not recommend using a microwave oven for thawing as the outer areas tend to get cooked by the time the center has defrosted.

Be careful not to leave thawed food at room temperature for a sustained period of time. Once thawed, use immediately!

Seasonings

Flavor. Everyone agrees it is one of the most important aspects of enjoying food. How our minds perceive flavor involves far more than our taste buds; all our senses are involved. Fragrance, texture, and visual presentation play a large role in determining our perception of how each bite tastes.

One-dish meals offer some of the most sophisticated flavors that you will find in any branch of cookery, in terms both of the development of the inherent flavors of the dish's major ingredients, and the opportunity for the effective use of seasonings. The long, slow cooking that is a feature of many of the recipes in the book—and in some cases the recommended preparation of the dish a day before serving it—allow for the distinctive seasonings of each dish to develop their fullest flavor potential.

I have taken advantage of several techniques available to the cook in making the most of the distinctive seasonings for each of the one-dish meals assembled here. Certain flavorings I find will add immeasurably to the taste of the finished dish without being themselves readily identifiable: The flavors of lamb and mashed potatoes in the Fragrant Shepherd's Pie (on pages 114-115), for example, are intensified and made more interesting by the inclusion of roasted garlic—undetectable in the finished dish—as the garlic becomes buttery and slightly nutty in flavor when roasted and then baked.

The use of very different or opposing flavors is another hallmark of the methods of seasoning exploited in the recipes which follow here. A case in point is the Watercress-Mint Spanakopita (pages 158-159), in which the strong, lingering flavor of watercress is successfully played against the sweet and cleansing flavor of mint. Certain complementary flavors, on the other hand, will combine to create a balanced taste with more distinction and depth than can be achieved otherwise. In the Curried Shrimp with Fruit, the sweetness of the fruit softens the full-flavored curry without diminishing any of the flavors; the cellophane noodles provide texture and a needed foil to the richness of the dish.

THE USE OF SEASONINGS

The goal of seasoning a dish is of course to intensify, balance, and selectively highlight its flavor through the addition and combination of specific herbs, spices, and other ingredients. The use of such seasonings can, in fact, promote good health as well as taste appeal through drastically reducing the addition of salt and sugar to many recipes. In the recipes that follow, I have in many instances added fresh lemon juice, a touch of hot chili pepper, or even vinegar to provide the taste boost otherwise achieved with salt. Although I occasionally add a very small quantity of sugar to a recipe, it is generally in the form of dark brown sugar, molasses, honey, or maple syrup, and is used not only to sweeten slightly

but also to lend its distinctive flavor to the dish. The rather surprising and distinctive result of this sort of flavoring can be tried in the making of Spicy Lamb Bobotie on page 136 or of Extra-Spicy Sloppy Joes on pages 112-113.

HERBS AND SPICES

The definition of herbs and spices differs slightly in the terminology of cooking: An herb is generally the leaf of a plant, while a spice is derived from the seeds, bark, roots, or other part of a plant.

It is important always to buy the highest quality and freshest possible herbs and spices. Fresh herbs should be a vivid green color without wilted, brown leaves or stem and with a strong, fresh rather than sour scent. They should be stored in the refrigerator, wrapped lightly in damp paper towels and sealed in a plastic bag, and used, if possible, within two days after you have purchased them. If you are fortunate enough to grow your own herbs, whether in a garden plot or on a windowsill, you can of course pick them immediately before their use.

I have indicated the appropriate substitution of dried herbs for fresh whenever possible; as noted in "About the Recipes," I do not recommend using commercial preparations of dried basil or chives. In general, dried herbs are two to three times stronger than fresh, although this rule of thumb fluctuates depending on the herb and how long it has been stored. Powdered herbs are significantly stronger than dried, so use them cautiously.

Dried herbs should be crumbled before using them. Some that are woody, like rosemary, need to be soaked in water to reconstitute them unless they are going to be cooked in liquid for a lengthy time; othewise they are

crunchy to the bite. If you are using whole herb stems or spices in soups or stews, you may wrap them in a square of fine-mesh cheesecloth, cook them submerged in the liquid, then discard them before serving the finished dish.

Spices should be purchased whole if you are willing to crush or grind them when necessary; they stay fresher much longer. They may be ground or pulverized as needed with a mortar and pestle, spice grinder, blender, or hand grater, which must then be cleaned thoroughly to avoid retaining the flavor of the spice. Also do grate your own nutmeg; you will be gratified at how much more fragrant it is than the commercially ground spice.

Dried herbs and spices should be stored in clean, dry, airtight glass containers and kept away from heat, light, or moisture. Always smell an herb or spice before using it to make sure that it has not lost significant flavor. An over-the-hill herb will smell rather like good-quality hay, while an old spice will lack its original intensity of fragrance. The ideal length of time for the storage of herbs and spices may vary from three to six months.

To read about the way some herbs and spices react to freezing and cooking in the microwave oven please see pages 27 and 24.

Freshness and quality are particularly important in the purchase of blended seasonings like chili powder and curry powder. If you don't have a good source near you, please refer to the list of mail-order sources folllowing.

Mail-Order Sources

AMERICAN SPOON FOODS
411 East Lake Street
Petoskey, MI 49770

616-347-9030

Dried mushrooms, such as morels, and many other products including a wide assortment of nuts, and delicious and unusual dried fruits such as blueberries and sour cherries. Catalog available.

APHRODISIA PRODUCTS
282 Bleecker Street
New York, NY 10014

212-989-6440

A huge supply of common and exotic herbs and spices, including marvelous Mexican oregano. Catalog available.

BALDUCCI'S
424 Avenue of the Americas
New York, NY 10011

212-673-2600
Outside of New York State:
1-800-822-1444

A large supply of sausages, including chorizo and seven kinds of Italian sausage. Also cured meats, cheeses, and many packaged gourmet items. Catalog available.

BRIDGE KITCHENWARE
214 East 52nd Street
New York, NY 10022

212-688-4220

Basic and specialized cookware. You name it, Bridge has it. Catalog available.

DEAN & DELUCA
560 Broadway
New York, NY 10012

212-431-1691
Outside of New York State:
1-800-221-7714

A very large selection of gourmet goods, including hard-to-find oils and vinegars. Great selection of dried pasta, grains, and beans. Catalog available.

THE EL PASO CHILI COMPANY
909 Texas Street
El Paso, TX 79901

915-544-3434

A large supply of southwestern goods. Catalog available.

PAPRIKAS WEISS
1546 Second Avenue
New York, NY 10028

212-288-6117

A fabulous source for many varieties of Hungarian paprika and other spices. Catalog available.

POTTERY BARN
Mail-Order Department
P. O. Box 7044
San Francisco, CA 94120-7044

415-421-3400

A wide variety of earthenware cookware, and glassware. Catalog available.

SANTA CRUZ CHILI AND SPICE COMPANY
P.O. Box 177
Tumacacori, AZ 85640

602-398-2591

Just as the name says—muchos chilies and spices. Catalog available.

WILLIAMS-SONOMA
Mail-Order Department
P. O. Box 7456
San Francisco CA 94120-7456

415-421-4242

Pretty casseroles, fondue pots, clay cookers and much more. Catalog available.

Garnishing and Presentation

One-dish meals have so much intrinsic visual appeal that they require only a deft finishing touch of color or arrangement to make them wonderfully appetizing. Chopped fresh parsley sprinkled on top of Beef Bourguignon, for example, is a garnish that adds flavor and color to the dish in the same way that cheese-covered croûtes, topping a bowl of onion soup, enhance the taste and appearance of the soup itself. Both the parsley and the cheese croûtes are excellent examples of garnishes for one-dish meals. They are simple, as they should be, and both are ingredients of the dish itself.

When other fresh herbs such as chives, tarragon, or basil are called for in a recipe, an extra quantity can be chopped or left whole (small basil leaves, for example) to be used for garnishing, too. Consider using freshly grated or shredded cheese in the same way or decorate with a brightly colored vegetable ingredient, cooked and arranged in a pattern of your choice or scattered in small pieces, confetti-like. Broccoli florets, julienned yellow crookneck squash, zucchini, or carrots, corn kernels, snow peas, artichoke hearts, pearl onions, and even miniature vegetables make eye-catching displays with little effort. Just plan to have a little extra of that garnish ingredient on hand for decorating.

Individual servings can be garnished appropriately with ingredients such as finely chopped or thin rings of raw red, yellow, or orange bell pepper, while cold one-dish meals can be served on platters lined with greens such as ornamental kale, watercress, bibb lettuce, red-leaf lettuce, radicchio, or endive, singly or in various assortments.

Though garnishes most frequently find their way to the centers and sides of a dish, there are many imaginative alternatives. Pureed vegetables or mashed, seasoned potatoes, for example, can be piped around the edges, echoing the outline of a dish or warm, homemade, miniature biscuits or dumplings can be placed on top of soups or stews before serving. Easier still, crustless sliced bread, cut into shapes with cookie cutters, lightly butttered and toasted in the oven, can decorate the tops of stews and other such fare appealingly.

- Coarsely chopped pimento
- Toasted slivered almonds or pine nuts (pignoli)
- Finely chopped hard-cooked egg white and/or yolk
- Brine-cured pitted black olives, whole or sliced lengthwise
- Scallion greens, sliced on the diagonal
- Bread crumbs or croutons made from flavorful and colorful breads such as corn bread or rye

When it comes to presenting one-dish meals at table modern cooks are particularly fortunate in the choice of available cookware. Oven (or stove-)-to-table cookware is now so attractively designed in a variety of styles that it can be used with confidence for entertaining, too. The convenience of these versatile pieces for one-dish meals is obvious.

Other accessories, also decorative elements of a kind, are the baking dish holders, fancy trivets, and heatproof tiles that can enliven a tabletop design. A plain serving dish can also be "dressed up" by wrapping the dish in a fetching cloth napkin and placing it in a sturdy basket for presentation, making sure to place a tile underneath.

One-dish meals, in short, lend themselves to imaginative, festive presentation that can make any cook look great.

ILLUSTRATIONS:

PART TWO

THE RECIPES

CHAPTER ONE

POULTRY

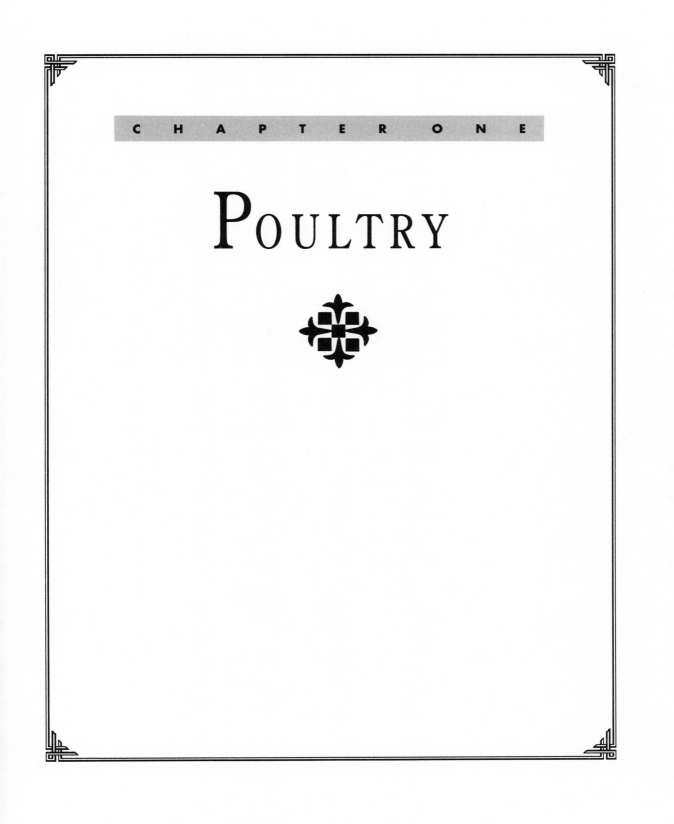

Chicken-Tortellini Soup

This is a modern version of classic chicken noodle soup, still the best cure for whatever ails you! It's easy to make and children love it. The multicolored tortellini bob to the surface and each bite tastes different.

2-1/2 *quarts chicken stock (page 186-187) or canned low-sodium chicken broth*

10 *ounces fresh chicken and prosciutto tortellini, preferably wrapped in different-flavored pastas such as egg, spinach, and tomato*

10 *ounces fresh cheese tortellini, preferably wrapped in different-flavored pastas such as egg, spinach, and tomato*

Half a *10-ounce package frozen green peas, thawed*

Half a *10-ounce package frozen chopped spinach, thawed*

4 *medium scallions, green part included, finely chopped*

1 *tablespoon finely chopped fresh oregano, or 1-1/2 teaspoons dried, crumbled*

1/4 *teaspoon salt*

1/2 *teaspoon freshly ground pepper*

2 *tablespoons finely chopped fresh parsley, preferably Italian flat-leaf*

3 *cups shredded cooked chicken, preferably breast meat*

PREPARATION

In a 6- to 8-quart pot over medium-high heat, bring stock to a boil. Add the tortellini, green peas, spinach, scallions, oregano, salt, and pepper. Cook the tortellini according to package directions or until they float to the surface and are al dente (slightly firm to the bite). Stir in the parsley and chicken, and season to taste with salt and pepper. Serve immediately.

Chicken Hominy with Cilantro and Jalapeño

Hominy is yet another of the gifts made by the American Indians to the European settlers. It consists of reconstituted corn kernels that can be cooked as a whole grain or dried again and ground to make grits.

ROASTED TOMATOES:

- 3 tablespoons olive oil
- 4 medium-sized ripe tomatoes, cored and cut into 1/2-inch-thick slices

FILLING:

- 6 strips lean slab bacon
- 1 medium yellow onion, minced
- 1 cup mild homemade or prepared salsa (chili-pepper-based sauce)
- 2 pounds skinless, boneless chicken breasts, rinsed, dried, and cut into 1/2-inch-wide strips
- 2 14-1/2-ounce cans whole golden hominy, drained (available in the supermarket)

SAUCE:

- 2 tablespoons unsalted butter or margarine
- 2 tablespoons all-purpose flour
- 1-1/2 cups milk, heated
- 2-1/2 tablespoons finely chopped fresh cilantro
- 1 4-ounce package cream cheese, diced, at room temperature
- 1 4-ounce jar chopped pimentos, drained
- 2 to 3 fresh jalapeño peppers, seeded, ribs removed, and minced (about 3 tablespoons) (page 109)

Salt and freshly ground white pepper to taste

PREPARATION

1. Preheat the oven to 375°F.

2. To roast the tomatoes: Lightly oil one or two large shallow baking pans. Arrange the tomato slices in rows. (*Note:* It is not necessary to leave space between the tomatoes, but they must be in a single layer.) Bake for 35 to 45 minutes or until the tomato slices have "puckered," but do not let the centers become dry or the edges brown. In the bowl of a food processor fitted with a metal blade, add the warm tomatoes and pulse 4 to 5 times or until coarsely chopped. Reserve until ready to use. (This can be done the day before, the chopped tomatoes cooled, transferred to an airtight container, and refrigerated.)

3. To make the filling: In a large heavy skillet over medium-high heat, fry the bacon 4 minutes or until it just begins to brown. Remove the skillet from the heat and transfer the bacon with a slotted spoon to a paper-towel-lined plate to drain. When bacon has drained, coarsely chop. Reserve the skillet with the drippings.

4. Return the skillet to medium-high heat, add the onion, and cook 3 to 4 minutes, stirring often, until onion is soft but not browned. Reduce heat to medium, add salsa and chicken pieces, and cook, stirring, 5 to 6 minutes or until chicken is just cooked. Set aside until ready to use.

5. To make the sauce: In a heavy 2- to 3-quart saucepan over low heat, melt the butter. Gradually whisk in the flour, whisking constantly until large bubbles appear, about 3 minutes. Cook 2 minutes, whisking constantly; do not let the roux brown. Remove from the heat and gradually pour in the hot milk, whisking constantly over bottom and sides of saucepan, until blended and smooth. Return the saucepan to low heat and stir until thickened, about 4 to 5 minutes. Stir in the cilantro and add the cream cheese a few pieces at a time. Add pimentos and jalapeños and cook for 3 minutes more, stirring constantly. Season with salt and pepper.

6. To assemble the casserole: Place a layer of the drained hominy on the bottom of a 3- to 4-quart baking dish or casserole. Top with the chicken mixture, cover evenly with the sauce, then top with pureed roasted tomatoes and sprinkle with cooked bacon. Bake for 40 to 50 minutes or until heated through. Let stand 5 minutes before serving.

TO MICROWAVE

Follow the recipe through step 5 as directed. At step 6, substitute a microproof dish. Cover, vent, and microcook on HIGH 8 to 9 minutes, turning once, or until bubbling. Uncover and cook 2 minutes more on HIGH. Let stand 3 minutes before serving.

Stir-Fried Chicken with Ginger and Sesame

SERVES 4

This recipe is an abbreviated version of the fabulous Chinese stir-fry technique that leaves meat and poultry succulent and vegetables crisp-tender with their natural, fresh flavor intact.

MARINADE:
- 3 scallions, green part included, finely sliced on the diagonal
- 2 tablespoons low-sodium soy sauce
- 2 teaspoons cornstarch, dissolved in 1 tablespoon water
- 1 teaspoon rice vinegar
- 1 teaspoon sugar
- 1/2 teaspoon ground ginger

- 1-1/2 pounds skinless, boneless chicken breasts, rinsed, dried, and cut into 1-inch-wide strips

- 2 tablespoons peanut oil
- 3 tablespoons finely chopped fresh ginger
- 3 medium cloves garlic, minced
- 1 small bunch broccoli, florets separated
- 1 medium red bell pepper, cored, seeded, and cut into 1-inch squares
- 1 8-ounce can sliced water chestnuts, drained
- 1/3 cup sesame seeds
- 1 tablespoon Oriental sesame oil (available at Oriental groceries or Chinese section of supermarket)

Freshly ground pepper to taste
Cooked brown or white rice

1. In a shallow non-metal baking dish, combine the marinade ingredients: scallions, soy sauce, cornstarch mixture, rice vinegar, sugar, and ginger. Stir in the chicken pieces until coated evenly with the marinade. Cover tightly and let stand for 15 minutes at room temperature. Stir once, re-cover, and marinate for 15 minutes more.

2. In a wok over high heat, heat the peanut oil until just smoking. Stir in the ginger and garlic and stir-fry, stirring vigorously, until aromatic but not browned, about 30 seconds.

3. Stir in the chicken (with the marinade) and the broccoli and stir-fry for 3 minutes, stirring vigorously. Add the bell pepper, water chestnuts, and sesame seeds. Stir-fry about 3 minutes more (adding up to 2 tablespoons water if needed to prevent sticking) or until the chicken is cooked when tested and no pink remains, and the broccoli is crisp-tender. Stir in the sesame oil to coat the mixture evenly, and season with pepper. Serve immediately over rice.

Coq au Vin avec Legumes

SERVES 4 TO 6

Coq au vin literally means "rooster with wine." I have added green beans to this classic French dish for heightened texture and nutritional value.

1/3 cup all-purpose flour
1/2 teaspoon salt
1/2 teaspoon freshly ground pepper
4 pounds chicken parts, rinsed and dried
2 tablespoons unsalted butter or margarine
3 tablespoons French brandy or Cognac
2 cups dry full-bodied red wine
Bouquet garni (place herbs in cheesecloth and tie bundle with string):
  • 3 medium cloves garlic
  • 5 sprigs fresh parsley
  • 4 sprigs fresh chervil or marjoram, or 2 teaspoons dried
  • 3 sprigs fresh thyme, or 1 teaspoon dried
  • 1 bay leaf

2 medium carrots, quartered
8 ounces white pearl onions, peeled (see below), or half a 16-ounce package frozen small white onions, thawed
6 ounces mushrooms, preferably short-stem, wiped clean with a damp paper towel
4 ounces green string beans, trimmed
Salt and freshly ground pepper to taste

1. In a large bowl combine the flour, salt, and pepper. Dredge the chicken pieces in the mixture, shaking off excess flour. Reserve chicken until ready to use.

2. In a heavy 6- to 8-quart pot over medium-high heat, melt the butter. Cook chicken pieces in batches about 5 minutes per batch, turning until pieces are browned evenly. Transfer the browned chicken to a medium bowl as pieces brown; then return all the chicken to the pot. Sprinkle with the brandy and carefully ignite. (Be careful—flames will be high, so stand back.) Shake pot gently until flames subside.

3. Stir in the wine, bouquet garni, and carrots. Bring to a boil. Reduce the heat, cover, and simmer for 25 to 30 minutes.

4. Add the onions, mushrooms, and string beans and simmer 10 minutes more.

5. Remove the chicken pieces and vegetables and keep warm until ready to serve. Remove and discard the bouquet garni.

6. Raise the heat to high and boil the cooking liquid about 4 to 5 minutes or until reduced to about 2 cups. Season with salt and pepper.

7. To serve, transfer the chicken pieces and vegetables to a warmed serving platter and ladle sauce over all.

TO PEEL PEARL ONIONS

Parboil pearl onions in boiling water for 1 minute. Drain and refresh under cold running water. Pinch onion at base of root and onion will "pop" out of its skin.

Chicken Marengo with Shrimp

SERVES 4

This famous dish was improvised by Napoleon's chef, Dunand, after Bonaparte's victory at Marengo in 1800. No food could be found except a hen, some crayfish, tomatoes, and garlic. It has been said that Dunand was so resourceful that he also cooked with some brandy from the general's own flask. In my adaptation, I have included brown sugar, fresh basil, and pitted prunes.

1/4 cup all-purpose flour
1/2 teaspoon salt
1/2 teaspoon freshly ground pepper
2 pounds chicken parts, rinsed and dried
2 tablespoons olive oil
1/4 cup dry vermouth or dry white wine
1 14-1/2-ounce can stewed tomatoes
1 tablespoon firmly packed light brown sugar
3 tablespoons fresh lemon juice

12 ounces mushrooms, preferably short-stem, wiped clean with a damp paper towel, trimmed, and thinly sliced
2 medium cloves garlic, minced
1-1/2 tablespoons finely chopped fresh basil
1/2 cup coarsely chopped pitted prunes
8 ounces medium shrimp, shelled, deveined, and rinsed thoroughly

1. In a large bowl combine the flour, salt, and pepper. Dredge the chicken parts in the mixture, shaking off excess flour.

2. In a heavy 6-quart Dutch oven or flameproof casserole over medium-high heat, heat the oil. Cook the chicken in batches, turning often so parts brown on all sides, about 7 to 9 minutes per batch. Transfer browned chicken to a medium bowl and reserve.

3. Add the vermouth to Dutch oven (be careful—liquid may splatter) and boil 1 minute, scraping drippings from bottom and sides. Add the tomatoes, brown sugar, lemon juice, mushrooms, garlic, basil, and prunes.

4. Reduce the heat to medium-low and add the reserved chicken. Cook, covered, 10 minutes, then turn chicken. Re-cover and cook for 20 minutes more, or until chicken tests done when pierced in thickest part and juices run clear.

5. Stir in the shrimp and cook, uncovered, for 2 to 3 minutes more, or until shrimp just turn opaque.

6. To serve, remove chicken with slotted spoon and place in the center of a serving platter with remaining sauce, while spooning a little over it.

Chicken Filé Gumbo with Okra

SERVES 6 TO 8

Gumbo is a classic one-dish Creole recipe from Louisiana. It is a soup—almost a stew—usually made with okra and a dark roux base. If you are squeamish when it comes to okra, use small whole okra and reduce the length of cooking time. I like to include filé, dried and powdered sassafras leaves, which is added to many Creole recipes for thickening. It has been said that filé is "relished by those accustomed to it." You try it and see. Also, this recipe can vary in "hotness"; be careful when adding the cayenne and Tabasco sauce as the heat from these ingredients gets hotter with time.

3 tablespoons all-purpose flour
1/2 teaspoon salt
1/2 teaspoon freshly ground pepper
12 ounces skinless, boneless chicken breasts, rinsed, dried, and cut into 3/4-inch-wide strips
2 tablespoons vegetable oil
3 tablespoons bacon drippings or vegetable oil
3 tablespoons all-purpose flour
1 medium yellow onion, finely chopped
1 medium green bell pepper, cored, seeded, and finely chopped
3 ribs celery, finely chopped
2 medium cloves garlic, minced
2 quarts chicken stock (page 186-187) or canned low-sodium chicken broth
1 14-1/2-ounce can stewed tomatoes
8 ounces fresh okra, stemmed and cut crosswise into 1/2-inch-long pieces, or 1 10-ounce package chopped frozen okra, thawed

2 cups fresh corn kernels, or 1 10-ounce package frozen, thawed
1 pound fresh spinach, stemmed, washed thoroughly, and coarsely chopped, or 1 10-ounce package frozen chopped spinach, thawed
1/4 cup finely chopped fresh parsley, preferably Italian flat-leaf
1/8 teaspoon cayenne pepper
1-1/2 teaspoons fresh lemon juice
Dash Tabasco sauce, or more to taste
Salt and freshly ground pepper to taste
1-1/2 to 2 teaspoons filé powder (available in gourmet specialty shops), moistened in 2 tablespoons water
Cooked white rice

PREPARATION

1. In a large bowl combine the flour, salt, and pepper. Dredge the chicken pieces in the seasoned flour, shaking off excess flour.

2. In a large heavy skillet over medium-high heat, heat the 2 tablespoons oil. Cook chicken in batches, about 4 to 5 minutes per batch, turning pieces so that they brown evenly. Transfer browned chicken to a medium bowl in between batches and reserve.

3. To make the roux: In a heavy 6- to 8-quart pot over medium-high heat, heat the bacon drippings to just below smoking. Add the 3 tablespoons flour and whisk vigorously until mixture turns a rusty dark brown, almost black, about 10 minutes. (*Note:* Be careful not to let roux burn. If roux is burned you will see tiny black specks.)

4. Remove pot from heat and add the onion, bell pepper, celery, and garlic. Return pot to medium-low heat and cook, stirring often, until onion is soft but

not browned, about 4 minutes. Gradually stir in the chicken stock, then add the tomatoes (with their liquid), okra, corn, spinach, parsley, and cayenne.

5. Bring mixture to a simmer and add the reserved chicken. Simmer for 25 minutes, uncovered, stirring occasionally. Stir in the lemon juice and Tabasco. Season with salt and pepper. (This recipe can be prepared up to this point 1 day ahead. Let cool, cover, and refrigerate. Reheat gently before proceeding with recipe.)

6. To serve, remove pot from heat and stir in moistened filé powder. Serve warm over rice.

COOK'S NOTE

Making a dark roux is tricky. Have all the ingredients ready before starting roux.

Follow recipe, except do not add filé powder. When gumbo has cooled to room temperature, wrap, seal, and label. Freeze up to 3 months.

To Serve: Thaw and reheat gently, stirring occasionally until warmed through. Remove pot from heat and stir in moistened filé powder. Adjust seasoning with salt, cayenne, and Tabasco. Serve warm over rice. To serve leftovers, reheat gently; boiling causes filé powder to become "stringy."

Vegetable-Stuffed Chicken Breasts

SERVES 4

This is the answer to the ever-present what's-for-dinner? dilemma, and it's quick, easy, and scrumptious. To quickly shred the vegetables, cut them into inch-long pieces and use the food processor fitted with a shredding disc. Shred the vegetables first, squeezing out extra moisture with your hands, before preparing the rest of the recipe. This recipe also works wonderfully with slices of veal!

4 boneless, skinless chicken breasts (about 2-1/2 pounds), rinsed and dried
1 medium zucchini, coarsely shredded
2 medium carrots, coarsely shredded
1 cup shredded provolone cheese
2 teaspoons finely chopped fresh oregano, or 1 teaspoon dried, crumbled
1 teaspoon finely chopped fresh thyme, or 1/2 teaspoon dried, crumbled
1/2 teaspoon salt
1/2 teaspoon freshly ground pepper
2 cups homemade or canned tomato sauce
1/4 cup finely chopped fresh parsley, preferably Italian flat-leaf, to garnish

PREPARATION

1. On a work surface, place a breast half between two sheets of plastic wrap. With a meat mallet or wooden rolling pin, pound from the center of the breast toward the outer edge until the breast half is flattened to about 1/4 inch thick; rotate 180 degrees frequently, every 5 strikes. (*Note:* Chicken should not be so thin that you can see through it.) Repeat with remaining breast halves, reusing plastic wrap if not punctured. Set aside chicken until ready to use.

2. Preheat the oven to 375° F.

3. In a medium bowl combine shredded zucchini, carrots, and cheese. Stir in the oregano, thyme, salt, and pepper until well blended.

4. Place the 8 pounded chicken breast halves on a sheet of wax paper. Depending on the size of the breast, place 1/4 to 1/3 cup filling down the center of each breast, leaving about a 3/4-inch margin on each edge. Roll up each chicken breast tightly, leaving ends open.

5. Place the rolls seam side down in a shallow 13-by-9-by-2-inch baking dish or casserole. (*Note:* The pan needs to be large enough to accommodate all of the chicken rolls in a single layer.)

6. Drizzle the rolls evenly with the tomato sauce. Bake, covered, for 40 to 50 minutes.

7. To serve, transfer the rolls to a warmed serving platter, ladle with sauce, and sprinkle with the chopped parsley.

Clay Pot Chicken

SERVES 4

The clay cooking pot makes an ideal vessel for roasting, as it virtually steams the chicken and vegetables in their own juices. This treatment, along with the noteworthy technique of rubbing tarragon-flavored butter beneath the skin of the breast, keeps the chicken moist and succulent while imbuing it with the distinctive flavor of parsnips, carrots, and cabbage with which it cooks. By removing the top of the cooker in the final stages of roasting, you are still able to achieve a light golden skin. The versatile 3-1/2 quart clay cooker can accommodate a whole chicken weighing up to six pounds, and is fine for this recipe.

1   *tablespoon dried tarragon, crumbled*
1/2   *teaspoon salt*
1/2   *teaspoon freshly ground pepper*
5   *tablespoons plus 1 teaspoon unsalted butter or margarine, at room temperature*
1   *3-pound chicken, rinsed and dried inside and out*
1   *large red onion, quartered*

3/4   *pound green cabbage, tough outer leaves removed, cored and shredded*
2   *medium carrots, cut into 1/2-inch-thick slices*
3   *medium parsnips, peeled and cut into 1/2-inch-thick slices*
1-1/2   *cups homemade or canned tomato sauce*

1. Immerse the top and bottom of a 3-1/2 quart clay cooker in cold water and soak at least 15 minutes, or until ready to use, then drain.

2. In a small bowl, with a fork, cut the tarragon, salt, and pepper into 5 tablespoons of the softened butter until well blended.

3. With your fingers, gently pull the skin away from the breast of the chicken. Run your fingers along the breast to release the membrane holding the skin to the breast. (*Note:* The objective is not to puncture or remove the skin, but to form a "pocket" where you can rub the butter between the meat and the skin.)

4. Rub the tarragon butter between the chicken and the skin. Press the skin against the breast and lightly rub the surface of the skin to smooth the butter underneath evenly.

5. Stuff the cavity with the pieces of quartered onion. Truss the chicken and place breast side up in the center of the bottom of the drained clay cooker. Rub the remaining teaspoon softened butter on the skin of the chicken.

6. In a medium bowl combine the shredded cab-bage, carrots, parsnips, and tomato sauce, stirring until blended. Arrange around the chicken.

7. Place the clay cooker, covered, in a cold oven. Set the oven temperature to 450° F, and bake for 50 minutes. Remove the cover and bake for 30 to 35 minutes more or until the skin is a light golden brown and chicken juices run clear when pierced with a fork in the thickest part. Let stand 10 minutes before carving.

CLAY COOKER TIPS

- Soak pot (top and bottom), immersed in cold water, 15 minutes prior to cooking.

- Place clay cooker in a *cold* oven, *never* preheated.

- Avoid a sudden temperature change. Once food is in the oven, set the oven at a lower temperature and gradually raise it to desired temperature.

- To avoid sudden breakage of clay cooker, never remove the clay cooker from a hot oven to a cold counter. Place something between the cooker and the counter, such as a thick wooden cutting board.

- Never use a clay cooker for stove-top cooking.

Turkey with Mole

SERVES 8

Turkey cooked in *mole poblano*—a chili sauce with almonds, spices, and chocolate—
is one of the most famous dishes in Mexican cuisine. Its origins date back to early Spanish
colonial times, and it was supposedly invented by nuns in the Convent of Santa Rosa in the
city of Puebla. The word *mole* comes from an Indian word meaning "concoction," and some
versions of the sauce contain over two dozen ingredients! Traditionally, the recipe calls
for several types of chilies: *ancho, mulato, pasilla*, and *chipotle*. Since these peppers
can be difficult to find outside of places with a Mexican-American population,
this recipe calls for the more readily available dried hot red chilies. Serve
Turkey with Mole over rice or rolled up in corn or flour tortillas.

6 pounds turkey parts, preferably all dark meat such as drumsticks and thighs, rinsed and dried	1 teaspoon ground cinnamon
	5 black peppercorns
	1/4 cup sesame seeds
1 medium yellow onion, quartered	1 teaspoon dried hot red pepper flakes, crushed
2 ribs celery, quartered	3/4 teaspoon salt
2 medium carrots, quartered	3 medium yellow onions, halved
2 tablespoons vegetable oil	4 medium cloves garlic
3/4 cup blanched almonds	1-1/2 ounces unsweetened chocolate, coarsely chopped
1 cup unsalted peanuts	
1/2 cup seedless raisins	1 14-1/2-ounce can stewed tomatoes
1/2 teaspoon aniseed	Salt and freshly ground pepper to taste
1/2 teaspoon ground cloves	Cooked rice, or warmed flour or corn tortillas

PREPARATION

1. In a heavy 8- to 10-quart pot over high heat, add
the turkey, onion, celery, carrots, and enough cold
water to cover by about 3 inches. Bring to a boil,
then reduce heat to low and simmer, partially covered, 2 to 2-1/2 hours or until turkey is tender.

2. Preheat the oven to 350° F.

3. In a medium skillet over medium heat, heat the oil
and add the almonds, peanuts, raisins, aniseed, cloves,
cinnamon, and peppercorns. Toast 4 to 6 minutes, stirring constantly. Add the sesame seeds, stirring 2 minutes more or until seeds are toasted also.

4. In the container of a blender or the bowl of a
food processor fitted with a metal blade, blend the
chili peppers and toasted almond mixture until finely ground. Add the salt, onions, and garlic, and
blend until finely chopped and well blended. Force
mixture through the finest blade of a food mill or

coarse sieve into a medium bowl. The mixture should be as smooth as possible; set aside until ready to use.

5. Strain the turkey stock into a large bowl, discarding the vegetables. Reserve 2 cups of the stock; save remaining stock for another use. Remove the meat from the bones and discard the bones and skin.

6. Add the turkey meat to the bottom of a 6-quart ovenproof Dutch oven or casserole. Stir the chocolate into the reserved 2 cups warm turkey stock until the chocolate is melted. Add the chocolate mixture to the Dutch oven. Stir in the stewed tomatoes and reserved almond and chili mixture. Season with salt and pepper.

7. Bake, covered, for 45 to 50 minutes or until hot throughout.

Chicken à la King

SERVES 4

There are many diverse legends as to the origin of this great American dish. But no matter its ancestry, this medley of cream, chicken, and pimentos will always be popular!

CHICKEN:
2-1/2 *pounds whole chicken breasts, rinsed and*
        skinned, or 3 cups 1-inch-wide pieces of
        cooked chicken, preferably white meat,
        with 1 cup chicken stock (page 186-187)
        or low-sodium broth, heated
   1 *medium yellow onion, quartered*
   2 *medium carrots, quartered*
   3 *ribs celery, quartered*
   2 *medium leeks, green part included,*
       washed thoroughly, tough outer leaves
       removed and quartered
   8 *black peppercorns*
   1 *bay leaf*
1/2 *teaspoon salt*

SAUCE:
   1 *tablespoon unsalted butter or margarine*
   4 *ounces mushrooms, preferably short-stem,*
       wiped clean with a damp paper towel,
       trimmed, and thinly sliced
1-1/2 *tablespoons unsalted butter or margarine*
1-1/2 *tablespoons all-purpose flour*
   1 *cup milk, heated*
   2 *egg yolks, lightly beaten, at room*
       temperature
   3 *tablespoons dry sherry*
   2 *dashes Tabasco sauce, or more to taste*
   1 *tablespoon fresh lemon juice*
   1 *4-ounce jar chopped pimentos, drained*
Salt and freshly ground white pepper to taste
Toast triangles, cooked rice, or baked puff pastry
        shells

1. To prepare the chicken: In a 6- to 8-quart pot over medium-high heat, add the chicken parts, onion, carrots, celery, leeks, peppercorns, bay leaf, salt, and enough cold water to cover by 3 inches. Bring to a boil. Reduce heat to low and simmer, partially covered, 30 minutes or until chicken is tender, occasionally skimming the foam from the surface.

2. Remove the chicken and reserve. Raise the heat to high and bring the stock to a boil, skimming the foam from the surface occasionally. Boil for 30 minutes or until liquid is approximately reduced by half.

3. Meanwhile, remove the meat from the chicken and discard the bones. Cut the chicken into 1-inch-wide pieces. Set aside the chicken meat until ready to use. Strain the reduced chicken stock, discarding the vegetables and all solid particles from the broth. Reserve 1 cup of the warm stock and save the remaining stock for another use. (This recipe can be made up to this point 1 day ahead. Let cool, wrap, and refrigerate the chicken and stock separately.)

4. To make the sauce: In a large skillet over high heat, melt the 1 tablespoon butter and add the mushrooms. Raise the heat to high and sauté about 4 minutes or until lightly browned and tender.

Remove the skillet from the heat and reserve mushrooms and their juice.

5. In a heavy 3- to 4-quart saucepan over low heat, melt the 1-1/2 tablespoons butter. Whisk in the flour, whisking constantly until large bubbles appear, about 3 minutes. Cook, 2 minutes more, whisking constantly; do not let roux brown.

6. Remove the saucepan from the heat and gradually add the 1 cup reserved warm stock, whisking constantly over the bottom and sides of saucepan until blended and smooth. Return saucepan to low heat and stir in the hot milk. Cook 4 to 5 minutes, stirring frequently, until slightly thickened.

7. Off the heat, whisk 1/4 cup of the hot sauce into the beaten egg yolks, then whisk this mixture back into the saucepan. Whisk in the sherry, Tabasco, and lemon juice. Add the reserved chicken, pimentos, and mushrooms with their juice to the saucepan.

8. To serve, heat mixture, stirring frequently, over low heat for 5 minutes or until chicken is heated through. Season with salt, freshly ground white pepper, and more Tabasco if desired. Serve hot over toast triangles, rice, or in baked puff-pastry shells.

Chicken Paprikash with Egg Dumplings

This Hungarian meal is equally delectable with 1 pound of flaked poached halibut added in place of the chicken, just before serving.

CHICKEN:
- 2 tablespoons unsalted butter or margarine
- 4 pounds chicken parts, rinsed and dried
- 2 medium yellow onions, finely chopped
- 2-1/2 cups chicken stock (page 186-187) or canned low-sodium chicken broth
- 2 medium-sized ripe tomatoes, seeded and chopped
- 1 medium green bell pepper, cored, seeded, and cut into 1/4-inch wide strips
- 1-1/2 to 2 tablespoons Hungarian semisweet or hot paprika (See Source List, page 30)
- Salt and freshly ground pepper to taste

DUMPLINGS:
- 2 eggs, lightly beaten
- 1/8 teaspoon salt
- 2 cups all-purpose flour
- 1 cup milk
- 1 cup sour cream, at room temperature

PREPARATION

1. Preheat the oven to 350° F.

2. To prepare the chicken: In a heavy 6-quart oven-proof Dutch oven or flameproof casserole set over high heat, melt the butter and sauté the chicken pieces in batches just until yellow, not browned, about 4 to 6 minutes. Remove the chicken and set aside until ready to use.

3. Add the onions to the Dutch oven and sauté until lightly browned, about 5 minutes. Stir in 1/2 cup of the chicken stock, reduce heat to low, and cover. Cook onions for 25 to 30 minutes, stirring occasionally, or until they fall apart.

4. Add the tomatoes, bell pepper, paprika, the remaining 2 cups stock, and reserved chicken. Raise the heat to high and bring to a boil.

5. Transfer the Dutch oven to the preheated oven, cover, and bake for 30 minutes or until chicken juices run clear when pierced in the thickest part.

Season with salt and pepper.

6. To make the dumplings: In a medium bowl combine the eggs with the salt. Stir in the flour until well blended. Add the milk, 1/4 cup at a time, and mix until smooth.

7. Transfer the Dutch oven from the oven to the stove over medium-high heat. Remove the chicken and keep warm until ready to use. When the broth is simmering, using a colander, place the dumpling dough inside and with the back of a wooden spoon, press the dough through the holes until about 1 inch long. Cut the strands of dough from the colander base with a knife, to release the dumplings into the simmering broth. Repeat with the remaining dumpling dough. Cook the dumplings until they float to the surface, about 2 minutes. Mix 1/2 cup of the liquid into the sour cream and then stir back into the Dutch oven along with the reserved chicken. Season with salt and pepper, serve immediately.

Creamy Chicken Pot Pie with Herbed Crust

SERVES 4

Though this recipe has long been called a pie, it is actually a casserole with a top crust. To add a touch of whimsy, make the steam vent with a cookie cutter shaped like a chicken. For an elegant presentation, bake this pie in individual casserole dishes with a puff-pastry crust, per the instructions in Variation 1 on page 59.

CRUST:

1-1/2 cups sifted all-purpose flour
   1 teaspoon salt
   1 tablespoon finely chopped fresh dillweed, or 2 teaspoons dried, crumbled
 1/2 cup lard or unsalted butter (1 stick), cut into 8 pieces, chilled
   1 egg yolk beaten with 2 tablespoons water
   3 to 4 tablespoons ice water

FILLING:

   4 tablespoons (1/2 stick) unsalted butter or margarine
   1 large red onion, finely chopped
 1/4 cup all-purpose flour
 1/2 cup chicken stock (page 186-187) or canned low-sodium chicken broth, heated
 3/4 cup half-and-half, heated

   2 teaspoons finely chopped fresh rosemary, or 1 teaspoon dried, crumbled
   1 teaspoon dried savory, crumbled
   1 teaspoon salt
 1/2 teaspoon freshly ground pepper
   2 tablespoons dry sherry
   3 ribs celery, finely chopped
   2 medium carrots, cut into 1/4-inch-thick slices
   8 ounces mushrooms, preferably short-stem, wiped clean with a damp paper towel, trimmed, and thinly sliced
   3 cups cooked chicken, cut into 1/2-inch-wide strips

GLAZE:

   1 egg yolk beaten with 1 tablespoon milk or cream

PREPARATION

1. To make the crust: In a medium bowl sift together the flour and salt. Stir in the dillweed. Using a pastry blender or fork, cut in the chilled lard or butter, a few pieces at a time, until mixture resembles coarse cornmeal. Stir in the egg yolk beaten with water. Then add the ice water, a tablespoon at a time, as needed to allow dough to form but not become sticky. Form into a flat disk. Wrap in wax paper and chill at least a half hour or until ready to use.

To make the crust in a food processor: In the bowl of a food processor fitted with a metal blade,

combine the flour, salt, and dillweed and pulse to mix. Add the lard or butter and pulse until the mixture is the consistency of coarse cornmeal. Pulse in the egg yolk beaten with water. Then, while pulsing machine, add the ice water through the feed tube a tablespoon at a time. Process until dough is moist and just hangs together. (Do not let dough form into a ball in the processor.) Remove dough from the bowl, form into a flat disk, wrap in wax paper, and refrigerate at least a half hour or until ready to use. (The dough can be prepared ahead, wrapped, and refrigerated for up to 2 days. Bring the dough to room temperature before proceeding.)

2. Preheat the oven to 375° F.

3. To make the filling: Melt the butter in a heavy 3- to 4-quart saucepan over medium heat. Raise the heat to medium-high and cook the onion, stirring often, for 3 to 4 minutes, until soft but not browned. Reduce the heat to medium and whisk in the flour, a little at a time, until smooth. Cook, stirring constantly, for 4 minutes.

4. Add the hot chicken stock, hot half-and-half, rosemary, savory, salt, and pepper and whisk until blended. Stir in the sherry, celery, carrots, mushrooms, and chicken. Simmer, partially covered, until the vegetables are just tender, about 8 minutes. Remove the saucepan from the heat, transfer contents to a deep 2- to 3-quart baking dish or casserole (preferably oval), and reserve.

5. On a lightly floured work surface, roll out the dough 1/4 inch thick. Trim to fit the top of the baking dish with a 1-inch overhang. Lightly moisten the edges of the baking dish with water. Place the crust gently on top of the dish and crimp the edges to seal. Either cut a steam vent with a cookie cutter or make 2 diagonal slashes in the crust to expose the filling. Brush crust lightly with the egg glaze.

6. Bake the pie for 35 to 40 minutes or until crust is golden brown.

FREEZING TIPS

Omit the egg glaze until ready to bake. Carefully wrap unbaked pie in two layers of freezer wrap, place in a moistureproof plastic bag, seal, and label. Freeze up to two months.

*To Serve***:** Thaw. Brush pie with glaze. Place in a preheated 375° F oven and proceed with step 6.

VARIATION 1

Substitute 1 sheet of frozen, pre-rolled puff pastry (half a 17-1/4-ounce package*) for the herbed crust. Trim the thawed puff pastry to fit the top of the baking dish with a 1/2-inch overhang and crimp. Cut a steam vent to expose the filling and brush with a glaze of 1 egg yolk lightly beaten with 1 teaspoon water. Bake in a preheated 375° F oven for 20 to 25 minutes or until crust is puffed and golden brown.

*Available in freezer section of supermarket. Follow package directions for thawing tips.

VARIATION 2

Substitute turkey for the chicken and thyme for the dillweed.

Chicken Pot Pie with Phyllo Crust

This updated version of a favorite traditional recipe uses jicama, a sweet, crisp tuber usually found in Mexican cuisine. This version is crowned with thin layers of flaky phyllo dough instead of the denser crust we are accustomed to.

FILLING:

1 3-1/2 pound chicken, rinsed and dried inside and out

1 large yellow onion, unpeeled

3 medium carrots, 1 coarsely chopped, 2 cut into 1/4-inch dice

1 rib celery, coarsely chopped

1 medium turnip, peeled and coarsely chopped

1 medium parsnip, peeled and coarsely chopped

4 sprigs fresh parsley, preferably Italian flat-leaf

4 cups chicken stock (page 186-187) or canned low-sodium chicken broth

1 teaspoon apple cider vinegar

1 large leek, including green part, tough outer leaves removed, washed thoroughly and finely chopped

1 small jicama, peeled and cut into 1/4-inch dice

5 tablespoons unsalted butter or margarine, at room temperature

2 tablespoons all-purpose flour

1 cup half-and-half, heated

Pinch ground allspice

Pinch ground nutmeg, preferably freshly grated

1/2 teaspoon salt

1/4 teaspoon freshly ground pepper

CRUST:

8 sheets frozen phyllo dough, available at supermarkets, thawed according to package directions

1 tablespoon unseasoned dried bread crumbs

PREPARATION

1. To make the filling: In an 8- to 10-quart pot over high heat, combine the chicken, onion, chopped carrot, celery, turnip, parsnip, parsley, chicken stock, and vinegar. Add enough cold water to cover the chicken by 3 inches. Bring to a boil. Reduce the heat to medium and simmer, partially covered, until no more pink remains when tested in the thickest part and the chicken is very tender, about 50 minutes. Remove from the heat and transfer the chicken to a plate. Let cool for 30 minutes or until cool enough to handle.

2. When the chicken is cool enough to handle, remove and discard the skin and bones, and cut the meat into bite-sized pieces. Strain the cooking liquid, discarding all solid particles, and reserve 1-1/2 cups, saving the remainder for another use.

3. In a heavy 2- to 3-quart saucepan over high heat cover the leek with the 1-1/2 cups of reserved cooking liquid and bring to a boil. Reduce the heat to medium-low and add the diced carrot and cook, stirring occasionally until tender, about 10 minutes. Add the jicama and cook stirring occasionally about 5 minutes more or until just tender. Using a slotted spoon, transfer the vegetables to a medium bowl and reserve. Reserve 1 cup of the cooking liquid in the saucepan and set aside; discard remaining liquid.

4. In a heavy 2- to 3-quart saucepan over low heat, melt 2 tablespoons of the butter. Whisk in the flour and cook, stirring constantly, for 2 minutes; do not let roux brown. Whisk in the reserved cup of cooking liquid and bring to a boil, stirring occasionally. Boil, stirring frequently, for 3 minutes. Whisk in the heated half-and-half, allspice, and nutmeg and return to a boil, stirring occasionally. Cook, stirring frequently, until thick, about 8 minutes. Remove the saucepan from the heat and let cool, stirring occasionally. Stir in the chicken, reserved vegetables, salt, and pepper. Transfer the filling to a shallow 10-inch round baking dish.

5. Preheat the oven to 425° F. Melt the remaining 3 tablespoons butter.

6. To prepare the crust: On a work surface, lightly brush 2 sheets of the phyllo dough with some melted butter and sprinkle each with 1 teaspoon of the bread crumbs. Repeat twice more with the remaining phyllo (two sheets at a time), melted butter, and bread crumbs, reserving a little of the butter. Place the last 2 sheets of phyllo on top and brush with butter. Invert the phyllo dough onto the baking dish and trim the sides to a 1/2-inch overhang. Brush the top and sides lightly with the remaining butter. Tuck under the sides. Cut a hole in the center of the pie to expose the filling and bake for 30 minutes, or until the top is golden brown and crisp.

Hoppin' John with Shredded Chicken and Scallions

SERVES 4 TO 6

Serving Hoppin' John is a New Year's Day tradition in the South. There are many rituals concerning its presentation: Served with a platter of greens, it will bring financial success for the coming year. When cooked with a dime, it will assure the lucky finder good fortune. And the original ritual is surely the hoppin' of the children round the table when they found out Hoppin' John was being served! Make up your own rituals. I suggest plenty of corn bread to sop up the potlikker.

2 cups dried black-eyed peas, picked over
6 strips lean slab bacon
2 medium yellow onions, minced
2 ribs celery, finely chopped
3 medium cloves garlic, minced
3 sprigs fresh thyme, or 1 teaspoon dried,
    crumbled
1 bay leaf
1/4 teaspoon dried hot red pepper flakes, crushed

1 cup long-grain white rice
Salt and freshly ground pepper to taste

CONDIMENTS:
Shredded cooked chicken
Grated sharp Cheddar cheese
Finely chopped tomatoes
Minced red onion
Thinly sliced scallions

1. Soak the peas overnight in enough cold water to cover by 2 inches. Or place the peas in a saucepan with enough cold water to cover by 2 inches and bring to a boil. Remove the saucepan from the heat, cover, and let stand 1 hour at room temperature. Drain and rinse.

2. In a heavy 6- to 8-quart pot over medium heat, add the bacon and cook about 7 minutes, turning often, until the bacon is crisp and browned. Remove bacon with a slotted spoon and transfer to a paper-towel-lined plate to drain. Reserve about 2 tablespoons of bacon drippings in pot; pour off remainder.

3. Add the minced onion, celery, and garlic to the pot with bacon drippings. Cook, stirring, for 4 minutes or until the onion is soft but not browned.

4. Stir in the reserved bacon, black-eyed peas, thyme, bay leaf, and red pepper flakes. Add 2 quarts water and bring to a boil. Reduce the heat to very low and simmer for 15 to 20 minutes or until the black-eyed peas are just tender.

5. Remove and discard the sprigs of thyme and the bay leaf. Set the pot over low heat.

6. Add the rice and simmer, covered, about 15 minutes or until the rice is tender. (*Note:* The Hoppin' John should not be completely dry; it should still have some liquid.) Season with salt and pepper. Serve hot topped with condiments.

FREEZING TIPS

Let cool. Do not top with condiments. Wrap, seal, label, and freeze up to 3 months.

To Serve: Thaw. Reheat gently over low heat, stirring often until heated through. Serve hot with condiments.

Turkey Tetrazzini with Corn Bread Topping

This soothing dish, originally made with chicken, was invented in the early twentieth century and named in honor of the opera star Luisa Tetrazzini, whose love of good food was legendary. Turkey Tetrazzini can be served (or may be frozen) in individual casserole dishes.

PASTA:
- 8 ounces spaghetti
- 1 tablespoon olive oil

SAUCE:
- 2 tablespoons unsalted butter or margarine, at room temperature
- 1 medium yellow onion, minced
- 6 ounces mushrooms, preferably short-stem, wiped clean with a damp paper towel, trimmed, and thinly sliced
- 2 medium green bell peppers, cored, seeded, and finely chopped
- 2 ribs celery, finely chopped
- 3 tablespoons unsalted butter or margarine, at room temperature
- 3 tablespoons all-purpose flour
- 1-1/2 cups chicken stock (page 186-187) or canned low-sodium chicken broth, heated
- 1/2 cup milk, heated
- 2 dashes Tabasco, or more to taste
- 1/8 teaspoon cayenne pepper, or more (up to 1/4 teaspoon) to taste
- 2 tablespoons dry sherry
- 1/4 teaspoon salt
- 1/2 teaspoon freshly ground white pepper
- 4 cups cooked turkey, cut into 1/2-inch-wide strips
- 3 scallions, including green part, thinly sliced

TOPPING:
- 3/4 cup dried crumbs from day-old corn bread or sugarless corn bread muffin
- 1/4 cup freshly grated Parmesan cheese
- 2 tablespoons unsalted butter or margarine

PREPARATION

1. Preheat the oven to 375° F.

2. To prepare the pasta: To a 6- to 8-quart pot of boiling water, add the spaghetti and stir occasionally. Return to a boil and boil 7 to 9 minutes or until al dente (slightly firm to the bite). Drain and transfer to a 3- to 4-quart baking dish. Toss pasta with the olive oil to coat, and reserve at room temperature.

3. To make the sauce: In a large heavy skillet over high heat, heat the 2 tablespoons butter and sauté the onion, mushrooms, bell peppers, and celery for 5 to 7 minutes or until tender. Remove from heat but reserve in pan until ready to use.

4. In a 2- to 3-quart saucepan over low heat, melt the 3 tablespoons butter and gradually whisk in the flour, whisking constantly until large bubbles appear, about 3 minutes. Cook 2 minutes more, whisking constantly; do not let the roux brown. Remove from the heat, gradually pour in the hot stock, then add the hot milk, whisking constantly over bottom and sides of saucepan until well blended and smooth. Return saucepan to low heat and stir until thickened, about 4 to 5 minutes. Remove saucepan from heat and stir in Tabasco, cayenne, sherry, salt, and pepper. Remove saucepan from heat and stir in the turkey and scallions. Stir sauce mixture into skillet with reserved vegetables.

5. Ladle the sauce mixture over the pasta and toss together gently until well blended. (This recipe can be made up to this point 1 day ahead. Let cool, wrap, and refrigerate. Bring to room temperature before proceeding with recipe.) Sprinkle evenly with the bread crumbs and Parmesan cheese, and dot with the butter. Bake for 40 to 45 minutes or until heated through and lightly browned.

TO MICROWAVE

Follow recipe through step 5, substituting a lightly buttered 3-quart microproof baking dish and with-holding the topping. Microcook, covered and vented, on HIGH 4 minutes, stir once, then re-cover and microcook 4 minutes more. Sprinkle with topping and microcook on HIGH 3 minutes more or until heated through. Let stand, covered, 3 minutes before serving.

FREEZING TIPS

Proceed with recipe through step 4, then spoon sauce over pasta and gently toss together until well blended. Omit topping. Let cool to room temperature, wrap, seal, and label. Freeze up to 2 months.

To Serve: Thaw. Sprinkle with topping and bake in preheated 375°F oven for 40 to 45 minutes or until heated through and top is lightly browned.

VARIATION

Substitute cooked chicken for turkey and French bread crumbs for corn bread crumbs.

Creamed Chicken with Wild Rice and Artichoke Hearts

SERVES 4

I have tasted many variations of creamed chicken, but I have finally created what I think to be the most interesting and elegant—ivory chicken against mahogany-colored rice. A mouthwatering sauce with a hint of tarragon and sherry complements the marinated artichoke hearts. Experiment when you choose a mold for the rice, as it shapes well and can be presented in many ways.

RICE:

- 4 cups cooked wild rice (follow directions on a 6-ounce package wild rice)
- 2 tablespoons unsalted butter or margarine, melted
- 1/4 cup finely chopped fresh chives or Italian flat-leaf parsley
- 1/4 teaspoon salt
- 1/4 teaspoon freshly ground white pepper

CREAMED CHICKEN:

- 2 tablespoons unsalted butter or margarine
- 1 medium yellow onion, finely chopped
- 3 ribs celery, finely chopped
- 1 cup chicken stock (page 186-187) or canned low-sodium chicken broth
- 2-1/2 cups cooked chicken (preferably breast meat), cut into 1/2-inch dice
- 1 6-ounce jar marinated artichoke hearts, drained and cut lengthwise into eighths

SAUCE:

- 2 tablespoons unsalted butter or margarine
- 2 tablespoons all-purpose flour
- 1 cup milk, heated
- 1 tablespoon dry sherry or vermouth
- 2 teaspoons finely chopped fresh tarragon, or 1/2 teaspoon dried, crumbled

Salt and freshly ground white pepper to taste

PREPARATION

1. To make the rice: Liberally grease the bottom and sides of a 1-1/2 quart ring mold. In a medium bowl gently combine warm rice, melted butter, chives, salt, and pepper. With the back of a spoon press the rice into the mold until tightly packed. Keep warm until ready to use. (The rice mold can be prepared 1 day ahead, covered, and refrigerated. Bring to room temperature and keep warm until ready to use.)

2. To make the creamed chicken: In a large skillet over medium-high heat, melt the butter and add the onion and celery. Cook 4 to 5 minutes, stirring occasionally, or until soft but not browned. Reduce the heat to low, add the stock, chicken, and artichoke hearts, and stir to blend. Drain, discarding the cooking liquid, and reserving the chicken and vegetables until ready to use.

3. To make the sauce: In a heavy 2- to 3-quart saucepan over low heat, melt the butter, then whisk in the flour until large bubbles appear, about 3 minutes. Cook 2 minutes more, whisking constantly; do not allow the roux to brown. Remove pan from heat and gradually add the hot milk while whisking over bottom and sides of saucepan, until well blended and smooth.

4. Return the saucepan to low heat and add the sherry. Cook until thickened, stirring frequently, about 4 to 5 minutes. Pour sauce into skillet with chicken mixture and gently stir to combine. Stir in the tarragon and season with salt and pepper.

5. To serve, place warmed serving plate on top of rice mold. Invert, tap top of mold, and gently lift to release rice ring. Fill center of rice ring with warm creamed chicken and serve immediately.

Chicken Tortilla Pie with Refried Beans and Tomatillo Sauce

SERVES 4

Layers of corn tortillas, two cheeses, tomatillos, and jalapeños make this Mexican-inspired meal a delight! This is one dish I recommend that you eat the day you cook it, as the tortillas become soggy over time and do not reheat well.

CHICKEN FILLING:
- 2 pounds skinless, boneless chicken breasts (about 3 whole breasts), rinsed and dried
- 2 medium unpeeled yellow onions, quartered
- 2 medium unpeeled carrots, quartered
- 1 teaspoon salt
- 1 cup sour cream
- 1 cup shredded sharp Cheddar cheese
- 1 cup shredded Monterey Jack cheese
- 1 medium red bell pepper, cored, seeded, and finely chopped
- 3 scallions, green part included, thinly sliced
- 1-1/2 tablespoons chili powder
- 1/8 teaspoon cayenne pepper
- Salt and freshly ground pepper to taste

GREEN SAUCE:
- 2 medium cloves garlic, minced
- 8 ounces fresh tomatillos (Mexican green tomatoes), husked and quartered (about 2 cups)

- 2 to 3 fresh jalapeño peppers, seeded, ribs removed, and finely chopped (page 109) or 2 tablespoons drained chopped pickled jalapeños
- 12 6-inch corn or flour tortillas

BEAN FILLING:
- 1 16-ounce can refried beans (available in Mexican section of supermarket), at room temperature

GARNISH:
- 1/2 cup shredded sharp Cheddar cheese
- 1/2 cup shredded Monterey Jack cheese
- 1 medium-sized ripe avocado, peeled, pitted, and sliced lengthwise into 8 slices (rub lightly with lemon or lime juice to prevent discoloration)
- 1/4 cup sliced black olives
- Sour cream

PREPARATION

1. To make the filling: Place the chicken in a 6- to 8-quart pot over medium heat, add the onions, carrots, salt, and enough cold water to cover by about 3 inches. Bring to a boil. Reduce heat to medium-low and simmer 10 to 15 minutes or until chicken is very tender but not falling apart. Remove from heat and strain, reserving chicken but discarding cooking liquid, onions, and carrots.

2. Preheat the oven to 350° F. Liberally grease the bottom of an 8-inch round cake pan, preferably springform.

3. In the bowl of a food processor fitted with a metal blade, add the hot chicken in batches. Pulse 3 times or until coarsely chopped. Transfer the chicken to a medium bowl and combine with the sour cream, Cheddar cheese, Monterey Jack cheese, bell pepper, scallions, chili powder, and cayenne. Season with salt and pepper. Reserve until ready to use.

4. To make the sauce: In the same processor bowl, pulse the garlic until minced. Add the tomatillos and jalapeños and process until pureed.

5. To assemble the pie: Place a tortilla on the bottom of the prepared springform pan. Spread a sec-ond tortilla with one third of the refried beans and place bean side down on the tortilla in the pan. Stack with a third and then a fourth tortilla and spread the fourth tortilla with one third of the chicken mixture and drizzle with one third of the sauce. Repeat twice with remaining tortillas ending with the twelfth and final tortilla spread with the final third of the chicken mixture and green sauce. Press down pie gently to make flat. Sprinkle with 2 tablespoons each of the grated sharp Cheddar and Monterey Jack cheese.

6. Bake for 50 minutes to 1 hour or until heated through and cheese is melted but not brown.

7. To serve, garnish with avocado slices, sliced black olives, and remaining shredded Cheddar and Monterey Jack. Serve with sour cream.

Kentucky Burgoo

SERVES 8 TO 10

I first saw a recipe for burgoo in an old cookbook. It went like this:

100 pounds beef	30 tomatoes
12 chickens	12 cans corn
1-1/2 bushels potatoes	3 boxes oatmeal
1 peck turnips	4 pounds salt
1 peck carrots	3/4 pounds pepper
1 gallon onions	12 heads cabbage

A recipe of this magnitude fed an entire church congregation on Sunday or perhaps the crowd at the Kentucky Derby! What went into the burgoo sometimes depended on what animal happened to go by the cook's window at the time. The list of possible meats used in burgoo included squirrel, rabbit, and possum, plus a wide assortment of vegetables and seasonings. Though I spared the possum, I did include chicken, beef, and ham hock for an added dimension.

2 tablespoons vegetable oil
1 pound lean boneless beef, preferably chuck, trimmed and cut into 1-inch cubes
2 pounds chicken parts, preferably stewing chicken, skinned
4 cups chicken stock (page 186-187) or canned low-sodium chicken broth
4 cups beef stock (page 185-186) or canned low-sodium beef broth
1 smoked pork hock (about 8 ounces)
3 medium yellow onions, unpeeled but ends trimmed
1 medium head garlic, unpeeled but ends trimmed
5 medium carrots, peeled and cut into 1-inch-long pieces

2 medium boiling potatoes, scrubbed but unpeeled, cut into 1-inch cubes
1 29-ounce can unseasoned tomato sauce
1/3 cup bourbon
1 to 2 small whole dried hot red peppers, or 1/2 teaspoon dried hot red pepper flakes, crushed
1/4 cup fresh lemon juice
2 cups shelled fresh lima beans, or 1 10-ounce package frozen, thawed
2 cups fresh corn kernels, or 1 10-ounce package frozen, thawed
1 teaspoon salt
1/2 teaspoon freshly ground pepper

PREPARATION

1. In a heavy 8- to 10-quart pot over medium-high heat, heat the vegetable oil. Add the beef and sear in batches, turning often so cubes brown evenly, about 7 to 9 minutes per batch. Transfer seared meat to a medium bowl in between batches and reserve.

2. Return the meat to the pot. Add the chicken parts, chicken and beef stock, smoked pork hock, onions, garlic, and carrots. Bring to a boil (will take about 30 minutes). Boil for 20 minutes or until stock is reduced by about one sixth.

3. Reduce heat to low, cover, and simmer until meat is very tender and chicken begins to fall from bones, about 30 minutes. (*Note:* Skim off foam from stock as it rises to the surface.)

4. With a slotted spoon, remove chicken, pork hock, and onions and any onion skin. Discard pork hock, onions, and onion skin. When chicken is cool enough to handle, remove the meat from the chicken, discarding the bones and skin.

5. Return the chicken to the pot and add the potatoes, tomato sauce, bourbon, red peppers, lemon juice, lima beans, and corn. Simmer, uncovered, stirring occasionally, for 30 minutes or until potatoes are soft but not falling apart. Adjust seasoning with salt and pepper.

COOK'S NOTE

This stew is best if served the day after it is made, which allows the flavors to meld. The garlic peel and onion skin are left on to impart extra body and color to the stock. Any that does not dissolve can be discarded at step 4.

FREEZING TIPS

Let cool, wrap, seal, and label. Freeze up to 2 months.
To Serve: Thaw. Reheat burgoo gently over low heat, stirring often, until heated through.

Chicken Cacciatore

Chicken cacciatore, always a favorite in my home, is derived from the Italian *pollo alla cacciatora*, "chicken in the hunter's style," a hearty dish of chicken cooked in a robust sauce of tomatoes and peppers. Black olives and capers add a special flavor to this version.

3 tablespoons all-purpose flour
1/2 teaspoon salt
1/4 teaspoon freshly ground pepper
3 pounds chicken parts, rinsed and dried
2 tablespoon olive oil
2 medium cloves garlic, minced
2 medium shallots, finely chopped
2 medium green bell peppers, cored, seeded, and cut into 1/2-inch dice
1 14-1/2 ounce can whole peeled Italian plum tomatoes, crushed, with juice

2 tablespoons tomato paste, preferably Italian
8 ounces mushrooms, preferably short-stem, wiped clean with a damp paper towel, trimmed, and thinly sliced
3 tablespoons dry white wine
2 tablespoons white wine vinegar
2 tablespoons finely chopped fresh basil or 1 teaspoon dried thyme, crumbled
1/2 cup pitted oil-cured black olives
2 tablespoons drained capers
1 teaspoon grated lemon zest

PREPARATION

1. Preheat the oven to 350° F.

2. In a large bowl combine the flour, salt, and pepper. Dredge the chicken pieces in the mixture, shaking off excess flour.

3. In a large skillet over medium-high heat, heat the olive oil. Cook chicken in batches, about 5 minutes per batch, turning until pieces are browned evenly. Transfer the browned chicken to a medium bowl and reserve until ready to use.

4. Reduce heat to low and add the garlic, shallots, bell peppers, tomatoes, tomato paste, and mushrooms. Then add the wine, vinegar, and basil, and cover. Stirring occasionally, cook vegetables for about 15 minutes or until just tender. Remove the skillet from the heat and stir in the olives, capers, lemon zest, and reserved chicken.

5. Transfer the mixture to a 3- to 4-quart baking dish and bake, covered, for 1 hour or until chicken juices run clear when chicken is pierced in thickest part.

TO MICROWAVE

Follow recipe through step 4. Transfer mixture to a 3-quart microproof dish. Cover, vent, and microcook on HIGH 5 minutes. Stir, re-cover, and microcook on HIGH 4 minutes. Stir re-cover, and microcook on HIGH 4 minutes more or until chicken is cooked. Let stand 4 minutes, covered, before serving.

Chicken with Pine Nuts, Saffron, and Whole-Wheat Pasta

SERVES 6 TO 8

The keynote ingredient of this exotic, slightly hot dish is saffron. Highly prized saffron gives a color and flavor that is unique, and turmeric is no substitute! Saffron is obtained from the stigmas of a species of crocus and the 4,000 flowers needed to make a single ounce of saffron powder must be processed by hand. Fortunately, a small amount of this unique and most expensive spice flavors an entire dish, as proven by this delicately perfumed recipe.

2   tablespoons olive oil or safflower oil
1/3   cup pine nuts (pignoli)
2   pounds skinless, boneless chicken breasts, rinsed, dried, and cut into 1/2-inch dice
4   medium cloves garlic, minced
1   large red onion, finely chopped
1   large green bell pepper, cored, seeded, and finely chopped
8   ounces mushrooms, preferably short-stem, wiped clean with a damp paper towel, trimmed, and thinly sliced

1/2   cup dry white wine
8   ounces whole-wheat spaghetti
1   lightly packed teaspoon saffron threads
1-1/2   cups chicken stock (page 186-187) or canned low-sodium chicken broth, heated
2   tablespoons unsalted butter or margarine
2   tablespoons all-purpose flour
1/2   cup milk, heated
3/4   teaspoon dried hot red pepper flakes
Salt and freshly ground pepper to taste

PREPARATION

1. To make the filling: In a large skillet over medium-high heat, heat the olive oil and add the pine nuts. Cook, stirring often, until toasted and lightly golden brown, about 2 minutes. (*Note:* Do not let pine nuts become dark brown.) Remove the skillet from the heat, and using a slotted spoon, transfer pine nuts to a medium bowl and reserve.

2. In the same skillet over high heat, add the chicken and sauté in batches about 4 minutes per batch, or until lightly browned. Transfer chicken to the bowl with the pine nuts as it is browned and reserve.

3. Add the garlic, onion, bell pepper, mushrooms, and white wine to the skillet. Cook, stirring often, for 7 to 8 minutes or until vegetables are tender. Transfer, with the juices, to the bowl with the chicken and pine nuts and reserve.

4. Preheat the oven to 350°F. Lightly butter a 13-by-9-by-2-inch baking dish.

5. To prepare the pasta: To a 6- to 8-quart pot of boiling water, add the spaghetti. Return to a boil, stirring occasionally, and cook for 6 to 8 minutes or until al dente (slightly firm to the bite). Drain and transfer to the prepared baking dish. Toss the spaghetti with the chicken mixture and reserve at room temperature.

6. To make the sauce: Place the saffron threads in the hot stock to soak. In a heavy 2- to 3-quart saucepan over low heat, melt the butter. Add the flour, whisking constantly until large bubbles appear, about 3 minutes. Cook for 2 minutes more, whisking constantly; do not let the roux brown. Remove the saucepan from the heat and gradually pour in the hot milk, whisking constantly across the bottom and along the sides until blended and smooth. Stir in the stock with the softened saffron and the red pepper flakes. Return the saucepan to low heat, stirring until thickened, about 4 to 5 minutes. Season with salt and pepper.

7. Ladle the sauce over the mixture in the baking dish and toss gently until well blended. Cover and bake for 35 to 40 minutes or until heated through. Serve directly from the baking dish.

COOK'S NOTE:

The recipe can be made up to 1 day before serving. Cool, wrap, and refrigerate. Reheat, covered, in a preheated 350°F oven until heated through.

Cassoulet with Duck and Garlic Sausage

SERVES 8 TO 10

Cassoulet is the celebrated casserole of southwest France. There are many regional variations, though the primary ingredient is always white beans. One recipe may specify pig's tail, another uses leg of lamb and confit (preserved goose or duck), and the list goes on and on. According to several authorities, before white haricot beans were cultivated in France—they came originally from Spain—fava beans were used. I opt for navy beans because not only are they more readily available, they make for a more creamy texture. Duck is included in this recipe for flavor, but it is not preserved, a change that will avoid additional fat. Traditionally, the crust is broken up to seven or eight times and allowed to re-form, making a thicker crust. In this recipe the crust is broken only once, but if you want a thicker crust, try the time-honored French technique.

2 cups dried white navy beans, picked over
2 teaspoons dried thyme, crumbled
2 teaspoons dried rosemary, crumbled
2 bay leaves
1 pound duck drumsticks, skinned, rinsed, and dried
1 pound garlic sausage, pricked all over with a fork, or other unsmoked fresh sausage
8 ounces lean boneless pork, cut into 1/2-inch dice

1 pound pork knuckle
4 ounces pork fatback, cut into 1/2-inch dice
1 can whole peeled Italian plum tomatoes, drained and chopped
10 small white boiling onions
1/2 cup unseasoned dried bread crumbs, preferably made from day-old French bread
2 tablespoons unsalted butter or margarine

PREPARATION

1. Soak the beans in enough cold water to cover by about 2 inches; cover and let stand overnight at room temperature. Or place the beans in a saucepan with enough cold water to cover by 2 inches and bring to a boil. Remove the saucepan from the heat, cover, and let stand 1 hour at room temperature. Drain and rinse.

2. In a heavy 8- to 10-quart ovenproof pot over high heat, add the beans, thyme, rosemary, bay leaves, duck, and sausage. Add enough cold water to cover by 2 inches. Bring to a boil. Reduce heat to low and simmer, partially covered, for 30 minutes. Remove the sausage and duck and reserve until ready to use. Continue to cook the beans for 30 minutes more.

3. Meanwhile, in a 3- to 4-quart saucepan over high heat, add the pork, pork knuckle, fatback, and enough cold water to cover by 2 inches. Bring the mixture to a boil, then boil for 10 minutes. Drain the mixture, discarding the cooking liquid.

4. Preheat the oven to 375° F.

5. Strain the beans and reserve the cooking liquid, adding water if needed to make 4 cups. Then return the beans and 4 cups cooking liquid to the pot; add the pork, pork knuckle, fatback, tomatoes, and onions. Cut the reserved sausage into 1/2-inch-thick slices. Remove the meat from the duck, discarding the bones. Add the sausage and duck meat to the

pot with the bean mixture and set over medium-low heat. Simmer for 30 minutes. Remove the knuckle and discard.

6. Sprinkle the cassoulet with the bread crumbs and dot with the butter. Transfer the pot to the top third of the oven and bake the cassoulet for 20 minutes or until the top is browned; a crust should form on the top of the casserole.

7. Break the crust once with a spoon, and allow the liquid to flow from beneath over the top of the crust. Then return to the oven for 30 minutes more or until lightly browned and a thin crust has re-formed. If a thicker crust is desired, repeat step 7, adding more liquid if needed. Remove from the oven and let stand for 10 minutes before serving.

COOK'S NOTE

This recipe can be made up to 2 days ahead. Reheat in a preheated 375°F oven until heated through.

FREEZING TIPS

Follow the recipe through step 5. Cool, wrap, seal, and label. Freeze up to 2 months.

To Serve: Thaw and proceed with steps 6 and 7.

SEAFOOD

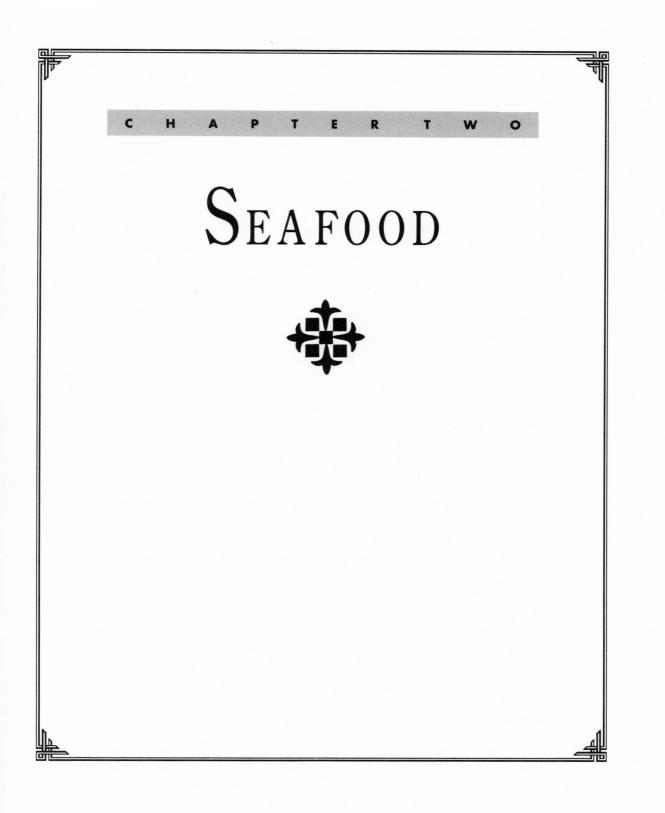

New England Clam Chowder

I am from Boston, the true home of New England clam chowder. I will never forget
when I first moved to Manhattan and went to dinner with some new friends. The restaurant's
specialty was clam chowder and, feeling homesick, I ordered it, dreaming of creamy
clam essence. Much to my dismay, I was served what I now know as Manhattan
clam chowder— no cream, and lots of tomatoes—absolute heresy!
Recently a friend informed me that someone in Maine once tried to introduce a bill
to prevent the marriage of clams and tomatoes. I am not surprised.

3 tablespoons unsalted butter
2 medium yellow onions, finely chopped
1/2 cup finely chopped fresh fennel
3 medium cloves garlic, minced
3 ounces salt pork, finely chopped (about
    1/2 cup)
3-1/2 tablespoons all-purpose flour
1 pound boiling potatoes, preferably red-
    skinned, scrubbed but unpeeled, cut into
    1/4-inch dice
1/2 cup dry white wine
1/3 cup finely chopped fresh chervil or
    2 teaspoons dried, crumbled
1/4 cup finely chopped fresh parsley, preferably
    Italian flat-leaf

2 cups fish stock (page 187)
3 dozen clams, scrubbed, soaked, shucked
    (page 87), and finely chopped (about
    1/4 cups) with clam liquor reserved.
    (Note: Chopped clams are available from
    fishmonger or supermarket.)
2 cups half-and-half, at room temperature
2 cups milk, at room temperature
1/2 cup heavy cream, at room temperature
2 cups fresh corn kernels, or 1 10-ounce
    package frozen, thawed
2 dashes Tabasco sauce, or more to taste
Salt and freshly ground white pepper to taste
1/2 cup crushed unsalted soda or milk crackers

PREPARATION

1. In a heavy 6- to 8-quart pot over medium-high heat, melt the butter and cook the onions, fennel, garlic, and salt pork, stirring often, for 4 minutes or until onions are soft but not browned. Stir in the flour, potatoes, wine, reserved clam liquor, chervil, and parsley.

2. Reduce the heat to low and add the stock. Simmer, covered, 7 to 9 minutes or until the potatoes are tender but not soft.

3. Stir in the clams. Mix 1/2 cup of the stock with the half-and-half, then return to the pot. Stir in milk, heavy cream, corn, and Tabasco. Season with salt and more Tabasco if desired. Stir in the crushed soda crackers, 1/4 cup at time, until desired consistency is reached. Simmer for 5 minutes more, stirring often, just until clams are opaque and chowder hot throughout. Do not let boil. Serve immediately.

Shrimp and Crabmeat Quiche

SERVES 6

MAKES 1 9-INCH QUICHE

This is a very satisfying quiche, as it contains more filling than custard.

CRUST:

1 sheet frozen, pre-rolled puff pastry (half a 17-1/4-ounce package), thawed (follow package directions for thawing tips)

1 tablespoon Dijon-style mustard

FILLING:

2 tablespoons unsalted butter or margarine

1 medium yellow onion, thinly sliced

3 medium leeks, white part only, washed thoroughly and thinly sliced

8 ounces cooked crabmeat, picked over

4 ounces cooked fillets of lemon or gray sole, or other mild, sweet-flavored fish, cut into 1-inch-wide strips

8 ounces cooked medium shrimp, shelled, deveined, and rinsed thoroughly

4 eggs

1 cup milk

1 cup half-and-half

1/2 cup shredded Swiss Gruyère cheese

2 teaspoons finely chopped fresh thyme, or 1/2 teaspoon dried, crumbled

2 tablespoons finely chopped fresh chives or scallions, green part included

1/4 teaspoon ground nutmeg, preferably freshly grated

1 tablespoon finely chopped fresh parsley, preferably Italian flat-leaf

1 teaspoon salt

1/2 teaspoon freshly ground white pepper to taste

PREPARATION

1. Preheat the oven to 400° F.

2. To prepare the crust: On a lightly floured work surface roll out the puff pastry large enough to fit a 9-inch pie plate or quiche pan with a 1-inch overhang. Cut to fit and gently press into edges and up sides of pan and crimp. Brush the bottom of pastry shell with the mustard. Lightly cover with plastic wrap and refrigerate until ready to use.

3. To make the filling: In a large skillet over medium heat, melt the butter and add the onion and leeks. Cover and cook 15 minutes or until tender, stirring occasionally. Gently stir in the crabmeat, fish, and

shrimp just to coat. Reserve until ready to use.

4. In a medium bowl whisk together the eggs, milk, half-and-half, cheese, thyme, chives, nutmeg, parsley, salt, and pepper until well blended.

5. Ladle the seafood mixture into the pastry shell and pour the egg mixture on top.

6. Bake the quiche for 10 minutes. Then reduce temperature to 350° F and bake for 35 to 40 minutes more or until filling is set and crust is light golden brown. (*Note:* Quiche filling will become firmer as it cools.) Serve quiche warm or at room temperature.

The Classic Tuna-Noodle Casserole

SERVES 4

Here is a comfort food guaranteed to evoke only the best childhood memories.

PASTA:
8 ounces medium egg noodles
Olive Oil

SAUCE:
1 tablespoon unsalted butter or margarine
1/4 cup finely chopped yellow onion
1/4 cup diced celery
1/4 cup diced green bell pepper

1 10-3/4-ounce can condensed cream of mushroom soup
1 4-ounce jar chopped pimentos, drained
1/2 cup milk
1 6-1/2-ounce can water-packed white tuna, drained and flaked
1/4 teaspoon salt
1/4 teaspoon freshly ground pepper
1 cup slightly crumbled potato chips

PREPARATION

1. Preheat the oven to 425° F.

2. To prepare the pasta: To a 6- to 8-quart pot of boiling water, add noodles and stir occasionally. Return to a boil and boil 7 to 9 minutes or until al dente (slightly firm to the bite). Drain, toss with some olive oil, and set aside.

3. In the same pot over medium-high heat, melt the butter. Add the onion, celery, and bell pepper. Cook, stirring often, for 5 minutes or just until tender.

4. Combine onion mixture, soup, pimentos, milk, tuna, salt, and pepper with the noodles in a 3- to 4-quart baking dish or casserole, tossing to coat evenly. Sprinkle top evenly with potato chips. (This dish can be prepared up to this point 1 day ahead, but omit the potato chips. Let cool, wrap, and refrigerate. Bring to room temperature before proceeding.)

5. Bake for 20 to 25 minutes or until casserole is heat-ed through and potato chips are lightly browned.

TO MICROWAVE

Combine all ingredients except potato chips in a microproof 3-quart baking dish, cover, and vent. Microcook on HIGH 8 minutes, stirring twice, or until heated through. Uncover, sprinkle evenly with potato chips and microcook on HIGH 1 to 2 minutes more. Let stand 10 minutes before serving.

FREEZING TIPS

Omit potato chips until ready to reheat. Let casserole cool, then wrap, seal, label, and freeze up to 3 months.
   To Serve: Thaw. Sprinkle evenly with potato chips and reheat, covered, in a preheated 425° F oven for 20 to 25 minutes or until heated through and potato chips are lightly browned.

A Contemporary Tuna Noodle Casserole

SERVES 4

This recipe adds grated lemon zest to the marinade and topping, but for extra flavor, substitute your own lemon pasta for the conchiglie. Just add one teaspoon grated zest to the flour before mixing the dough for half a pound of homemade pasta! Also, try using fresh orange in place of lemon for a variation on this theme.

MARINADE:

1/2 cup dry white wine
2 tablespoons olive oil
1/2 cup fresh lemon juice
2 tablespoons finely chopped fresh dillweed, or 2 teaspoons dried, crumbled
1 tablespoon grated lemon zest
1/2 teaspoon salt
1/2 teaspoon freshly ground white pepper
1 pound tuna steaks, rinsed, boned, skinned, and cut into 1-inch cubes

PASTA:

8 ounces conchiglie (shells) or other medium-shaped pasta
Olive oil

SAUCE:

2 tablespoons unsalted butter or margarine, at room temperature
1 medium yellow onion, minced
3 scallions, including green part, thinly sliced
8 ounces mushrooms, preferably short-stem, wiped clean with a damp paper towel, trimmed, and thinly sliced
3 tablespoons unsalted butter or margarine, at room temperature
3 tablespoons all-purpose flour
1-1/2 cups chicken stock (page 186-187) or canned low-sodium chicken broth, heated
1/2 cup half-and-half, heated
1 tablespoon finely chopped fresh dillweed, or 2 teaspoons dried, crumbled
6 ounces fresh snow peas, trimmed and washed, or 1 6-ounce package frozen, thawed
Salt and freshly ground white pepper to taste

TOPPING:

1/3 cup unseasoned dried bread crumbs, preferably made from day-old French bread
1 teaspoon grated lemon zest
1/2 teaspoon salt
1/2 teaspoon freshly ground white pepper
2 tablespoons unsalted butter or margarine, diced

PREPARATION

1. To prepare marinade: In a shallow non-metal baking dish, combine marinade ingredients: the wine, olive oil, lemon juice, dillweed, lemon zest, salt, and pepper. Add the tuna and coat evenly with the marinade. Cover and marinate at room temperature at least 30 minutes or up to 1 hour, turning fish after 15 minutes. Drain, discarding marinade.

2. Meanwhile, prepare the pasta: To a 6- to 8-quart pot of boiling water, add the conchiglie and stir occasionally. Return to a boil and boil 5 to 6 minutes or until al dente (slightly firm to the bite). Drain and transfer to a shallow 13-by-9-by-2-inch baking dish or casserole. Toss pasta with a little olive oil to coat and reserve.

3. Preheat the oven to 375° F.

4. To make the sauce: In a large skillet over high heat, heat the 2 tablespoons butter and sauté the onion, scallions, and mushrooms for 3 to 4 minutes or until tender. Remove from heat but reserve in skillet until ready to use.

5. In a heavy 2- to 3-quart saucepan over low heat, melt the 3 tablespoons butter and gradually whisk in the flour, whisking constantly until large bubbles appear, about 3 minutes. Cook 2 minutes more, whisking constantly: do not let roux brown. Remove saucepan from the heat and gradually pour in the hot stock, then the hot half-and-half, whisking constantly over the bottom and sides of the saucepan until well blended and smooth. Return saucepan to low heat and stir until thickened, about 4 to 5 min-utes. Remove saucepan from heat and stir in the drained tuna, dillweed, and snow peas, and season with salt and pepper. Stir sauce mixture into skillet with reserved vegetables.

6. Ladle the sauce mixture over the pasta and toss together gently until well blended. (This recipe can be made up to this point 1 day ahead. Let cool, wrap, and refrigerate. Bring to room temperature before proceeding with recipe.)

7. To prepare the topping: In a small bowl toss together the bread crumbs, lemon zest, salt, and pepper. Sprinkle pasta mixture evenly with topping mixture and dot with the butter. Bake for 40 to 45 minutes or until heated through and the top is a light golden brown.

FREEZING TIPS

Proceed with recipe through step 6. Let cool to room temperature, wrap, seal, and label. Freeze up to 2 months.

To Serve: Thaw and proceed with step 7.

Coulibiac of Salmon

This is a marvelous Russian pie: a narrow pastry filled with layers of salmon, vegetables, rice, and eggs. I have omitted the traditional pancakes that are part of the layered filling, and the dried sturgeon backbone.

2 tablespoons unsalted butter or margarine
1 medium yellow onion, finely chopped
8 ounces mushrooms, wiped clean with a damp paper towel, trimmed, and minced
2 tablespoons fresh lemon juice
1/4 cup dry vermouth
2 pounds fresh spinach, stemmed, washed, and finely chopped, or 1 10-ounce package frozen chopped spinach, thawed
2 tablespoons finely chopped fresh dillweed, or 2 teaspoons dried, crumbled

Salt and freshly ground white pepper to taste
1 pound skinless, boneless salmon fillets
1 17-1/4-ounce package frozen puff pastry, thawed (follow package directions for thawing procedure)
2 cups cooked rice or other grain, such as couscous or barley
5 hard-cooked eggs, cut into 1/4-inch-thick slices

GLAZE
1 egg yolk beaten with 1 tablespoon milk

PREPARATION

1. Preheat the oven to 400° F.

2. In a large skillet over medium-high heat, melt the butter and add the onion and mushrooms. Cook, stirring often, about 4 minutes or until mushrooms are browned. Stir in the lemon juice, vermouth, spinach, and dillweed. Season with salt and pepper.

3. Reduce heat to low, top the spinach mixture with the salmon fillets, and cook, covered, 10 to 12 minutes or until spinach has wilted and salmon is just opaque. (Be careful not to overcook salmon.) Remove and reserve the salmon. Raise the heat to high and bring to a boil. Boil the spinach mixture 1 to 2 minutes, stirring, to reduce slightly, and then reserve. Let cool to room temperature and drain.

4. On a lightly floured work surface, roll out each pastry sheet (there will be 2) to a 13-by-10-inch rectangle. Lay a sheet of puff pastry on an ungreased shallow baking pan. Spread half the rice in a 3-inch-wide strip down the center of the pastry, leaving space on the sides and a 2-inch margin of dough at either end. On top of the rice spread half the drained spinach mixture, then half the egg slices. Top with all the salmon fillets, keeping them in one layer.

5. Now reverse the order: top the salmon with the remaining egg slices, spinach mixture, and rice. Press down on the filling gently to mold into a narrow, elongated shape. With a pastry brush, paint some of the glaze on the dough along the edges of the filling. Lay the second sheet of puff pastry over the filling and press the edges of the dough together to encase the filling; seal tightly. Fold over the excess dough back on top of itself and crimp to seal. Brush dough with remaining glaze.

6. Bake for 25 to 30 minutes or until puffed and a light golden brown. Serve immediately.

Kedgeree

Kedgeree is originally an Indian dish comprised mainly of rice, lentils, eggs, and onions. Embellished with lightly smoked haddock (finnan haddie) by the British, kedgeree was and still is a staple of English country fare. Served in a covered silver dish, it is a traditional part of the hearty English breakfast enjoyed by hungry riders home from the hunt. Smoked whitefish or sturgeon substitutes for finnan haddie in this recipe.

2 cups milk
1 center-cut salmon steak (about 8 ounces)
3 tablespoons olive oil
1 medium yellow onion, finely chopped
2 cups cleaned and washed raw basmati rice (available in gourmet section of supermarket), soaked in 4 cups cold water for 30 minutes, then drained (see page 89), or Texmati (long-grain American basmati) or long-grain white rice
2-1/2 teaspoons curry powder
1 tablespoon fresh lemon juice
1/8 teaspoon cayenne pepper
1 teaspoon turmeric
1-1/2 tablespoons peeled fresh grated gingerroot

1/2 teaspoon salt
1/4 teaspoon freshly ground pepper
1/2 cup dry white wine
1/2 cup heavy cream, at room temperature
6 ounces fresh asparagus spears (about 5 medium), trimmed and cut into 1-inch-long pieces, crosswise, optional
8 ounces smoked whitefish or sturgeon, skinned, boned, flaked, and any dark meat removed
1-1/2 cups shelled fresh green peas, or 1 10-ounce package frozen, thawed
3 tablespoons unsalted butter or margarine, at room temperature
4 hard-cooked eggs, thinly sliced

PREPARATION

1. In a medium skillet over high heat, bring the milk and 1/2 cup water to a simmer. As soon as you see steam rise, reduce the heat to low. Do not let boil. Add the salmon steak and poach, covered, for 7 to 8 minutes or until fish is just opaque. Be careful not to overcook the fish: it should not be dry enough to flake easily from the bones.

2. Remove salmon with a slotted spoon and set aside at room temperature until ready to use. When cool enough to handle, remove bones, skin, gray fat, and break into 1-inch-long pieces and reserve.

Strain the poaching liquid and add water to make 3-1/4 cups. Set aside.

3. In a heavy 3- to 4-quart saucepan over medium-high heat, heat the olive oil, add the onion, and cook, stirring often, until soft but not browned, about 3 to 4 minutes. Stir in the rice and cook, stirring constantly, 4 minutes more. Stir in curry powder, lemon juice, cayenne, turmeric, ginger, salt, and pepper, stirring vigorously 1 minute.

4. Reduce the heat to low, then add 3 cups of the

reserved poaching liquid and the wine (be careful—the liquid may splatter). Mix the heavy cream with the remaining 1/4 cup of the reserved poaching liquid and return to the saucepan. Gently stir in the asparagus if using. Cook, covered, for 10 to 15 minutes or until the liquid is absorbed and the rice is tender.

5. Remove the saucepan from the heat and stir in the salmon, whitefish or sturgeon, peas, and butter. Transfer to a warmed serving platter, garnish with egg slices, and serve immediately.

HINTS FOR PERFECT HARD-COOKED EGGS

- Never use an iron or aluminum-lined pot to cook eggs.

- To avoid a green "ring" around yolks, don't overcook hard-cooked eggs.

- The best way to hard-cook eggs is to never allow them to boil. Bring water to a boil, gently add eggs, and immediately lower heat. Simmer eggs 12 to 15 minutes. Remove eggs and place in a basin of cold water for 1 minute to stop cooking and facilitate peeling.

COOK'S NOTE

If you want to use finnan haddie (partially smoked haddock), poach it with the salmon very briefly to just finish cooking it. Then proceed with recipe.

Spinach and Mussel Soup

SERVES 4 TO 6

The rosemary, cilantro, and mussels make for an unusual but very pleasant combination in this Spanish-style soup.

1 large red onion, finely chopped
1 pound spinach, stemmed, washed thoroughly, and finely chopped, or 1 10-ounce package frozen chopped spinach, thawed
3 large ripe tomatoes, peeled, seeded, and finely chopped
2 tablespoons tomato paste, preferably Italian

2 cups fish stock (page 187) or 2 8-ounce bottles clam juice
1/4 cup Cognac
1 teaspoon finely chopped fresh rosemary, or 1/2 teaspoon dried, crumbled
2 pounds mussels, scrubbed, soaked (page 87) and debearded
1 tablespoon finely chopped fresh cilantro

1. In a heavy 6- to 8-quart pot over high heat, add the onion, spinach, tomatoes, tomato paste, stock, Cognac, and rosemary. Bring to a boil, and then reduce heat to medium-low. Cover and simmer 30 minutes, stirring occasionally.

2. Add the mussels and simmer, covered, for 2 minutes longer or until all mussels have opened. Discard any mussels that have not opened. Stir in the cilantro and serve immediately.

Quick Fish Soup with Orzo

SERVES 4

This is a great year-round soup, but it's especially good for summer, as it makes a light but satisfying meal. A surprising ingredient is cucumbers, which are wonderful when cooked. For a nice variation, try the soup with some chopped Swiss chard, added with the orzo pasta.

1 tablespoon olive oil
1 medium yellow onion, thinly sliced
1 medium clove garlic, minced
2 ribs celery, very thinly sliced
2 medium carrots, cut into 1/4-inch dice
2 medium cucumbers, peeled, trimmed, seeded, and finely chopped
1 medium-sized ripe tomato, peeled (page 92), seeded, and finely chopped

3-1/2 cups fish stock (page 187) or 1 8-ounce bottle clam juice and 2-1/2 cups water
2 teaspoons finely chopped fresh dillweed, or 1 teaspoon dried, crumbled
1/2 cup orzo (rice-shaped pasta)
1 pound cod or haddock fillets, cut into 1/2-inch-wide strips
Salt and freshly ground pepper to taste

1. In a heavy 4- to 6-quart pot over medium-high heat, heat the oil. Add the onion and sauté about 4 minutes or until a light golden brown.

2. Reduce heat to medium-low and add the garlic, celery, carrots, cucumbers, and tomato. Stir in the fish stock and dillweed and simmer, partially covered, stirring occasionally, for 15 minutes or until the vegetables are tender.

3. Add the orzo, re-cover, and cook 10 minutes more, stirring occasionally, or until orzo is tender and triple its original size.

4. Add the cod and simmer, uncovered, 3 to 4 minutes more, or just until fish is opaque. Season with salt and pepper. Serve immediately.

Oyster Loaves

Here's an English specialty, perfect to serve for a brunch.
I have added corn and peas to create a more balanced meal, while complementing the oysters.

2 tablespoons unsalted butter (Note: Do not substitute margarine in this recipe.)
2 cups shelled green peas, or 1 10-ounce package frozen, thawed
2 cups corn kernels, or 1 10-ounce package frozen, thawed
1 tablespoon fresh lemon juice
1/8 teaspoon cayenne pepper

1 dozen oysters, scrubbed and shucked, liquor reserved
4 large soft rolls, preferably a slightly rich roll, such as brioche, cut in half and half the interior scooped out
2 tablespoons unsalted butter, melted
1/2 cup sour cream, at room temperature
2 tablespoons finely chopped fresh chervil, to garnish

PREPARATION

1. Preheat the oven to 325° F.

2. In a large skillet over medium heat, melt the 2 tablespoons butter. Add the peas, corn, reserved oyster liquor, lemon juice, and cayenne. Bring to a simmer and add the oysters. Simmer the oysters for 2 minutes, stirring, or until the oysters loosely curl and just turn opaque. Be careful not to overcook the oysters. Transfer oysters to a bowl with a slotted spoon and cover to keep warm until ready to use. Reserve skillet with liquid until ready to use.

3. Spread each roll and lid inside with the melted butter and toast in the oven for 5 minutes. Keep the rolls warm until ready to serve.

4. When the rolls are toasted, add the sour cream to the liquid in the skillet. Set over low heat, stirring constantly, and add the oysters. Heat, stirring, for 1 minute or just until warmed through. Ladle sauce and oysters evenly among rolls, garnish with chervil, and cap with roll lids. Serve immediately.

COOK'S NOTE

I don't recommend using the oven method to steam open oysters. Your fishmonger will happily (and quickly) shuck oysters for you; just ask him to reserve the liquor also. If you are going to shuck them at home, first place the oysters in the freezer for 15 minutes; this relaxes the adductor muscle. If you need to clean the oysters after shucking, do not rinse; just pick any broken pieces of shell off with your fingers.

Curried Shrimp with Fruit

SERVES 4

This meal will take you to the tropics!

1 tablespoon vegetable oil
1 medium yellow onion, finely chopped
2 tablespoons curry powder
1/2 teaspoon ground ginger
2 cups chicken stock (page 186-187) or canned
   low-sodium chicken broth
1 medium-sized unpeeled tart apple, preferably
   Granny Smith, cut into 1/4-inch dice
1 cup fresh pineapple cut into 1/2-inch dice, or
   1 8-ounce can unsweetened pineapple
   chunks, drained, and halved into 1/2-inch
   chunks

1 3-3/4-ounce package bean thread
   (cellophane) noodles (available in Oriental
   grocery stores or the Oriental food section of
   the supermarket)
1-1/2 pounds medium shrimp, shelled, deveined,
   and rinsed thoroughly
Salt and freshly ground pepper to taste
1 medium-sized ripe but firm banana, thinly
   sliced, to garnish
1/2 cup julienned fresh coconut or shredded
   unsweetened coconut (available at health
   food stores), to garnish

PREPARATION

1. In a heavy 2- to 3-quart saucepan over medium-high heat, heat the oil. Add the onion, curry, and ginger and cook, stirring often, 3 to 4 minutes or until soft but not browned.

2. Add the stock, apple, and pineapple. Simmer, covered, stirring occasionally, for 15 minutes or until fruits are just tender.

3. Meanwhile, break each bundle of cellophane noodles in half and soak in cold water to cover for 10 minutes or until pliable, then drain.

4. Strain the curry mixture, reserving the fruit and

keeping it warm until ready to serve. Return the cooking liquid to the saucepan over low heat. Add the shrimp to the saucepan and cook for 2 to 3 minutes or until shrimp are just opaque.

5. Remove the saucepan from the heat and add the drained noodles. Stir until just heated through. Season with salt and pepper.

6. To serve, distribute the curried noodles and shrimp among 4 shallow soup bowls, top with reserved fruit, and garnish with banana and julienned coconut.

Sea Scallop and Corn Casserole

This casserole has tender sea scallops nestled in fresh spinach and corn kernels, topped with a cloud of fluffy corn spoonbread. Use only young, fresh spinach, not frozen, as it is more delicate and compatible with the texture of the other ingredients.

4 tablespoons (1/2 stick) unsalted butter or margarine

1 medium clove garlic, minced

2 medium scallions, including green part, finely chopped

2 cups fresh corn kernels, or 1 10-ounce package frozen, thawed

1 pound spinach, stemmed, rinsed thoroughly, and finely chopped

1/8 teaspoon cayenne pepper

1 pound sea scallops, rinsed

1 cup yellow cornmeal

1/2 teaspoon salt

1/4 teaspoon freshly ground pepper

1 cup lowfat buttermilk

3 eggs, separated, yolks lightly beaten

PREPARATION

1. Preheat the oven to 350°F.

2. In a large heavy skillet over medium heat, melt 2 tablespoons of the butter. Add the garlic, scallions, corn, spinach, and cayenne. Cook, stirring often, for 4 minutes. Stir in the scallops until just coated. Using a slotted spoon, transfer the spinach mixture to a 9-by-9-by-2-inch baking dish, spread evenly, and reserve until ready to use.

3. Stir the cornmeal into 1/2 cup cold water (to help prevent lumping). In a heavy 3- to 4-quart saucepan over medium-high heat, combine 1-1/2 cups water with the salt and pepper. Bring to a boil. Gradually add the cornmeal-water mixture, whisking vigorously and constantly to prevent lumping. Cook, whisking vigorously, 1 to 2 minutes or just until corn meal

is thick and pulls away from the sides of the saucepan. Remove from the heat, and stir in the remaining 2 tablespoons butter and the buttermilk. Stir in the beaten egg yolks until well blended and transfer to a large bowl.

4. In a medium mixing bowl, beat the egg whites until stiff but not dry. Working quickly, stir one quarter of the egg whites into the cornmeal mixture to lighten it, then gently fold in the remaining whites.

5. Spoon the batter over the spinach mixture, spreading evenly. Bake in the middle of the oven for 55 to 60 minutes, until puffed and lightly browned. The spoonbread will be soft in the center and crusty on the top and edges. Serve immediately.

Cacciucco

SERVES 6 TO 8

This is my favorite of all the international fish soups. According to legend, this Tuscan soup was first made by the widow of a fisherman lost at sea from the leavings her children begged from the neighbors' fish nets. I have been told that it should contain at least five types of seafood, including lobster, squid, shellfish, and several varieties of saltwater fish. In the traditional preparation, the squids' ink sacs make the soup black in color. In this version the ink sacs are discarded, and the soup is served on toasted slices of garlic bread in large and (if you have them) colorful bowls.

2 tablespoons olive oil

8 ounces small squid (about 4) (ask your fishmonger to clean the squid for you and discard the ink sacs), cut crosswise into 1/4-inch-wide rings

3 medium cloves garlic, minced

1/4 to 1/2 teaspoon hot dried red pepper flakes, crushed

1 large red onion, finely chopped

3 ribs celery, finely chopped

2 medium carrots, finely chopped

1 cup dry red wine

1 16-ounce can whole, peeled Italian plum tomatoes, chopped, with juice

1 uncooked lobster tail (about 8 ounces), cut into 1-inch-wide pieces

1 pound medium shrimp, shelled, deveined, and rinsed thoroughly

1 swordfish steak (about 8 ounces), cut into 1/2-inch-wide pieces

1 dozen clams, soaked, scrubbed and shucked (see directions following page), liquor reserved

1 pound mussels, soaked, scrubbed, debearded, and shucked (see directions following page), liquor reserved

1 small sea bass (about 1 pound) (ask your fishmonger to fillet), cut into 1-inch-wide pieces

8 ounces lemon or gray sole fillets, cut into 1-inch-wide pieces

1/2 cup finely chopped fresh parsley, preferably Italian flat-leaf

Salt and freshly ground pepper to taste

PREPARATION

1. In a heavy 6- to 8-quart pot over high heat, heat the oil. Add the squid and cook for 30 seconds, stirring frequently, until just opaque. Remove and reserve.

2. In the same pot stir in the garlic, red pepper flakes, onion, celery, and carrots and cook, stirring often, for 4 to 5 minutes or until vegetables are tender.

3. Reduce the heat to medium and add the wine, tomatoes, and reserved clam and mussel liquor. Cover and cook for 10 minutes more. Add the lobster, shrimp, and swordfish and cook, covered, 2 minutes more. Then add the clams, mussels, sea bass, and sole and cook for 2 to 3 minutes more or until seafood is just opaque. Stir in the parsley, season with salt and pepper, add the reserved squid, and serve immediately.

HOW TO PREPARE CLAMS AND MUSSELS:

Cleaning and Soaking Instructions: Soak the clams or mussels immersed in cold salted water in the refrigerator for at least 2 hours, up to 6 hours. This cleansing process helps get rid of sand and intestinal waste. Drain and rinse, and discard any shellfish that float to the surface, or whose shells are open and won't close when tapped several times. A trick is to sprinkle the water with fine corn meal. Sometimes the shellfish eat it and then they expel previously digested food.

To steam open the clams and mussels: Scrub the clams and mussels, and debeard the mussels. Arrange on a baking sheet and bake in a preheated 500° F oven for 1 to 2 minutes or just until the shells open slightly. Remove carefully so as not to spill the clam and mussel liquor. Discard any shellfish that do not open. Proceed with shucking.

Fish Florentine with Couscous

SERVES 4

The French term "Florentine" refers to the use of fresh spinach.
You can substitute skinless boneless chicken breasts for the fish if you like; just pound them
lightly with a mallet before proceeding with the recipe (see instructions on page 51).
I have used couscous for a grain, but rice, brown or white, is also divine. (I don't recommend
substituting frozen spinach for this dish; you'll want the more delicate texture of fresh.)

FISH AND FILLING:
- 1 tablespoon olive oil or vegetable oil
- 1 large red onion, finely chopped
- 2 medium cloves garlic, minced
- 2 ounces mushrooms, preferably short-stem, wiped clean with a damp paper towel, trimmed, and finely chopped
- 1 pound fresh spinach, stemmed, rinsed thoroughly, and finely chopped
- 1 cup cooked couscous (made from about 1/3 cup uncooked)
- 3 tablespoons finely chopped fresh basil or 2 teaspoons dried thyme, crumbled
- 2 tablespoons dry white wine
- Salt and freshly ground pepper to taste
- 4 fillets of sole, flounder, or other mild, firm-fleshed fish (about 8 ounces each)
- 1 14-1/2-ounce can whole peeled Italian plum tomatoes, chopped, with juice

MORNAY SAUCE:
- 2 tablespoons unsalted butter or margarine
- 2 tablespoons all-purpose flour
- 3/4 cup milk, heated

- 1/2 cup half-and-half, heated
- 2/3 cup shredded French Gruyère or Swiss Gruyère cheese
- Salt and freshly ground white pepper to taste

PREPARATION

1. To prepare the filling: In a large skillet over high heat, heat the oil. Add the onion, garlic, and mushrooms and sauté for 3 to 4 minutes or until mushrooms are browned. Stir in the spinach and sauté for 1 to 2 minutes more or until wilted. Stir in the cooked couscous, basil, and wine. Season with salt and pepper.

2. To prepare the fish:Lay out the fish fillets on a work surface. Spoon 1/2 cup of the filling down the center of each fillet and starting with the narrower end of the fillet, roll up tightly, leaving the ends open. Tie each bundle crosswise in 2 places with kitchen twine.

3. Place the fish bundles in the skillet and set over low heat. Top the fish bundles with the tomatoes. Cook, covered, for 4 minutes, then turn the bundles over, re-cover, and cook for 5 minutes more or until the fillets are just opaque throughout. Keep warm until ready to serve.

4. To make the sauce: In a heavy 1- to 2-quart saucepan over low heat, melt the butter. Whisk in the flour and cook, whisking vigorously, for 4 minutes; do not let the roux brown. Remove the saucepan from the heat and gradually whisk in the hot milk and the hot half-and-half, whisking vigorously until blended and smooth. Add the shredded cheese and cook, stirring, for 2 minutes or until cheese is melted. Season with salt and pepper.

5. To serve, untie the fish bundles, transfer to a warmed serving platter, spoon tomatoes over, and top with the Mornay sauce. Serve immediately.

Saffron-Shrimp Pilau

SERVES 4 TO 6

Pilau, a favored Asian method of cooking seasoned rice, can be served plain or with other foods. Of all the international types, I prefer to use the aromatic, nutty basmati rice from India and Pakistan, but Texmati rice from the United States, another aromatic long-grain rice, would also be delicious. The secret to this meal is to have the correct amount of liquid so the rice turns out moist and fluffy, not mushy.

1 pound medium shrimp, shelled, deveined,
and rinsed thoroughly
1 lightly packed teaspoon saffron threads
2 tablespoons olive oil
1 medium yellow onion, minced
2 medium cloves garlic, minced
1 tablespoon unsalted butter or margarine
2 tablespoons peeled fresh grated gingerroot
1-1/2 tablespoons curry powder
1/4 teaspoon ground cinnamon
1/4 teaspoon ground ginger
1/4 teaspoon ground cloves
1/4 teaspoon ground cardamom, optional
1/2 teaspoon freshly ground pepper
2 cups cleaned and rinsed raw basmati rice
(available in gourmet section of
supermarket) or Texmati
1/2 cup dry white wine
1 teaspoon salt
1 10-ounce package frozen green peas, thawed
1/4 cup dried currants or seedless raisins
3/4 cup salted cashews, coarsely chopped, to
garnish

PREPARATION

1. In a 2- to 3-quart saucepan over medium heat, add 4 cups cold water, and bring to a simmer. Add the shrimp and poach about 1 minute or just until opaque. (Be careful not to overcook shrimp.) Remove shrimp with a slotted spoon, reserve half the cooking liquid, and keep shrimp at room temperature until ready to use. Put saffron threads in reserved shrimp cooking liquid, crush with back of spoon, and let soak.

2. In a heavy 6- to 8-quart pot over medium-high heat, heat the olive oil. Add the minced onion. Cook onion, stirring, about 4 minutes, until light golden brown, being careful not to let the onion burn. Add the garlic, butter, ginger, curry powder, cinnamon, ground ginger, cloves, cardamom, and pepper. Cook, stirring, up to 1 minute more or until spices are lightly toasted and release their aroma, but do not let garlic brown.

3. Add the rice to the pot and cook, stirring constantly, until rice begins to brown, about 4 minutes. Add the wine (be careful—liquid may splatter), bring to a boil, and boil 2 minutes. Stir in the reserved cooking liquid with the saffron and add the salt. Bring to a boil. Reduce the heat to very low and cover, cooking the rice mixture undisturbed (do not lift off the lid or stir) for 10 minutes or until the rice is just tender but not mushy.

4. Remove pot from the heat and gently toss the shrimp, peas, and currants together with the rice mixture. (Combine ingredients gently with a fork: the rice and peas will be fragile.) Season with salt to taste. Recover and let rest undisturbed 5 minutes more.

5. Transfer to a warmed serving platter, garnish with cashews, and serve immediately.

TO PREPARE BASMATI RICE FOR COOKING

Clean rice by picking out any foreign particles (such as pieces of pebble, twig, or unhulled rice). Then rinse rice to remove lighter foreign particles and starch, which makes rice sticky when cooked. To rinse, place rice in a bowl and fill with cold water to cover and let stand for 5 minutes so that foreign particles rise to the surface. Drain and repeat until water is clear. (If using Texmati rice, clean and rinse but do not soak. Soaking is an essential step unique to basmati rice and the Persian rice domsia, though domsia needs a longer soaking period, usually overnight.) Soaking helps prevent the rice grains from cracking or breaking during cooking.

Soak the basmati while proceeding with recipe. To soak rice, combine in a medium bowl with 4 cups cold water and let soak for 30 minutes, and drain.

Lobster Newburg with Asparagus

SERVES 4

As the story goes, the elegant old Delmonico's restaurant in New York honored a favorite patron, the sea captain Wenberg, by naming this dish for him. After a falling-out, his connection with the dish was severed by reordering the first three letters of its name to read "Newburg." I've added mushrooms, asparagus, and cauliflower to the original recipe for additional color and texture (not to mention nutrition). It makes a wonderful meal served hot over rice, enclosed in crepes, or spooned into baked puff-pastry shells.

3 tablespoons unsalted butter or margarine
2 medium shallots, minced
6 ounces mushrooms, preferably short-stem, wiped clean with a damp paper towel, trimmed, and thinly sliced
2 cups cooked fresh lobster meat, cut into 1-inch julienne or 1 11.3-ounce package frozen cooked lobster meat, thawed, and rinsed
2 tablespoons Madeira
1/8 teaspoon cayenne pepper

2 egg yolks, lightly beaten, at room temperature
1 cup half-and-half, at room temperature
8 ounces thin asparagus, cut into 1-inch-long pieces on the diagonal, cooked until just tender
8 ounces cauliflower or broccoli florets (about half a small head), broken into very small florets with 1/4 inch of stem left on, cooked until just tender
Salt and freshly ground white pepper to taste
Warm crepes, cooked rice, or baked puff pastry shells

PREPARATION

1. In a heavy 4- to 6-quart pot over medium-high heat, melt the butter. Add the shallots and mushrooms and cook 3 to 4 minutes, stirring often, or until soft. Add the lobster, Madeira, and cayenne and cook, stirring often, for 2 minutes more.

2. Beat the egg yolks into the half-and-half and stir into the saucepan. Cook, stirring often, for 2 minutes. Add the asparagus and cauliflower and cook for 2 minutes or until hot throughout. Season with salt and pepper. Serve immediately rolled in crepes, over rice, or in baked puff pastry shells.

Bouillabaisse with Fennel

SERVES 6

This simple Mediterranean fisherman's stew was made from the day's catch.
The casualness of the presentation makes it stunning—the contrasting heap of scarlet
lobster shells, ink-colored mussels, and luminous shrimp and scallops.
The finished dish is garnished with *rouille* (literally "rust"), a spicy Provençal mayonnaise
from which I have omitted the egg, which gives the bouillabaisse its red intensity.
Serve with garlic and herb croutons or your favorite homemade crusty bread.

2 tablespoons olive oil

4 medium leeks, white part only, washed thoroughly and thinly sliced

2 medium red onions, thinly sliced

3 cups fish stock (page 187) or bottled clam juice

3/4 cup dry white wine

5 large ripe tomatoes, peeled (page 92), seeded, and cut into 1/2-inch dice

1 teaspoon grated orange zest

1 teaspoon loosely packed saffron threads, moistened in 1/4 cup stock or clam juice

Bouquet garni (place ingredients in cheesecloth and tie bundle with string):
- 1/2 teaspoon fennel seeds
- 1 bay leaf
- 3 sprigs fresh tarragon, or 1-1/2 teaspoons dried
- 10 black peppercorns

1/8 teaspoon cayenne pepper

1 dozen clams, soaked and scrubbed (page 87)

1 uncooked lobster tail, shell intact (about 8 ounces), cut into 1-inch-thick pieces

1 pound mussels, soaked, scrubbed, and debearded (page 87)

12 ounces firm-fleshed fish fillets such as red snapper, sea bass, or halibut, cut into 1-inch-wide pieces

4 ounces medium shrimp, shelled with tail left on, deveined, and rinsed thoroughly

3 ounces sea scallops

1 tablespoon Pernod, optional

Rouille (recipe on following page)

1/4 cup finely chopped fresh parsley, preferably Italian flat-leaf, to garnish

---

PREPARATION

1. In a heavy 8- to 10-quart pot over medium heat, heat the oil. Add the leeks and onions and cook for 10 minutes, stirring often, or until onions are soft but not browned. Add the stock, wine, tomatoes, orange zest, saffron, bouquet garni, and cayenne. Bring to a boil.

2. Reduce the heat to low and simmer 10 minutes, stirring occasionally. Add the clams and sliced lobster tail and simmer 5 minutes. Add the mussels and fish pieces and cook 3 minutes. (Do not stir or the fish will fall apart.) Add the shrimp, scallops, and Pernod if using, and simmer 1 minute more or until shrimp are just opaque and all shellfish are opened.

Remove and discard the bouquet garni. Discard any shellfish that have not opened.

3. To serve, remove seafood with a slotted spoon to large soup bowls, ladle broth over it, and garnish with *rouille* (recipe follows) and parsley. Serve immediately.

ROUILLE

MAKES 1-1/4 CUPS

 5 medium cloves garlic, halved
 1 tablespoon fresh lemon juice
1/8 teaspoon cayenne pepper
 2 medium roasted red bell peppers, cored, seeded, peeled (note this page), and quartered
1/2 cup olive oil, preferably extra virgin
Salt and freshly ground pepper to taste

In a blender, at medium speed, process the garlic, lemon juice, cayenne, and peppers until pureed, about 1 minute. Through the opening in the center of the cover, very slowly add the olive oil, a teaspoon at a time, while blender is running at low speed, until all the oil is incorporated and well blended. Remove the container and season with salt and pepper. Keep refrigerated until ready to use. *Rouille* can be made 1 day in advance, stored in an airtight container, and refrigerated.

HOW TO ROAST PEPPERS

Place a whole pepper directly on the burner or medium-low flame of a stove, with stem pointed away from flame. Roast, using tongs to rotate every few minutes, until charred and beginning to blister. Remove the pepper with tongs and transfer to a brown paper bag or wrap loosely in foil and seal, to allow pepper to steam, about 5 to 6 minutes. When pepper is cool enough to handle, using a sharp paring knife, remove and discard the skin, core, and seeds. Wipe pepper with a damp paper towel to remove any excess skin.

HOW TO PEEL TOMATOES

Drop whole tomatoes into a pot of boiling water for 10 to 12 seconds. Drain immediately, and refresh under cold running water. When cool enough to handle, carefully remove skin with a sharp paring knife.

CHAPTER THREE

BEEF, VEAL, AND GAME

Chili Con Carne Tequila

SERVES 4

This recipe was given to me by Greg Spence of Austin, Texas. He uses both fresh and dried chilies, including the fiery serrano and the milder ancho chilies. Since chili peppers can be hard to find, this recipe calls for a combination of fresh and dried chilies and chili powder. (For mail-order sources for premium chili powder and Mexican oregano, see page 30.) Though a purist's chili does not contain beans, this version, which everyone loves, uses red kidney beans. Although the recipe takes little time to prepare, it does require a long cooking time and in fact is best made the day before, to allow time for the flavor of the chili powder to blend with the chocolate.

2 tablespoons vegetable oil

2 pounds lean boneless beef, preferably round, cut into 1-inch cubes

2 medium yellow onions, finely chopped

1 to 2 fresh jalapeño peppers, seeded, ribs removed, and minced (page 109)

1 4-ounce can mild peeled chopped green chilies, drained

4 medium cloves garlic, minced

3 to 4 tablespoons chili powder, depending on strength

2 teaspoons paprika, preferably Hungarian hot (page 30)

2 teaspoons ground cumin

1 tablespoon dried oregano, preferably Mexican (page 30), crumbled

1 large ripe tomato, finely chopped

1 14-1/2-ounce can whole peeled Italian plum tomatoes, chopped, with juice

1 12-ounce bottle dark ale or beer, preferably Mexican

3 tablespoons tequila

1 cup beef stock (page 185-186), or canned low-sodium beef broth

1 ounce unsweetened chocolate, coarsely chopped

1/2 teaspoon ground cinnamon

1 15-ounce can red kidney beans, drained and rinsed

Shredded sharp Cheddar cheese, to garnish, optional

Green bell pepper strips, to garnish, optional

Minced white onion, to garnish, optional

Sliced sweet or sour pickles, to garnish, optional

PREPARATION

1. In a 6- to 8-quart pot over medium-high heat, heat the oil and sear the beef in batches, turning cubes often so they brown evenly on all sides, about 7 to 9 minutes per batch. Transfer meat to a medium bowl as it is browned and reserve. Add the onion and cook, stirring often, 3 to 4 minutes or until soft but not browned.

2. Raise the heat to high, and add the reserved meat, jalapeños, green chilies, garlic, chili powder, paprika, cumin, oregano, fresh tomato, and canned tomatoes. Then stir in the beer, tequila, stock, chocolate, and cinnamon. Bring to a boil. Reduce heat to low and simmer 4 hours, stirring occasionally.

3. Just before serving, stir in the kidney beans and cook, stirring often, until just heated through, about 5 minutes. To serve, distribute among 4 shallow soup bowls and garnish with cheddar cheese, green pepper, onions, and pickles if desired.

Picadillo-Stuffed Peppers

SERVES 4

Picadillo is a spicy, stewlike dish that varies throughout Mexico and the Caribbean. *Picadillo* is delicious over rice, or you can use it to fill tacos. Stuffed in green chilies that are dipped in batter and deep-fried, you have the traditional Mexican chiles rellenos. In this recipe, *picadillo* graces large red, orange, or yellow bell peppers, which do double duty; not only are the peppers good to eat, they serve as colorful bowls for the *picadillo*.

PICADILLO:
- 1 pound lean boneless pork, preferably from a Boston butt, trimmed and cut into 1-1/2-inch chunks
- 1 pound lean boneless beef, preferably chuck, trimmed and cut into 1-1/2-inch chunks
- 1 medium yellow onion, quartered
- 4 medium cloves garlic
- 2 tablespoons olive oil
- 1 medium red onion, finely chopped
- 2 medium cloves garlic, minced
- 1 teaspoon ground cumin
- 1/2 teaspoon ground cloves
- 1/2 teaspoon freshly ground black pepper
- 1/2 teaspoon ground cinnamon
- 1 tablespoon chili powder
- 1/4 teaspoon cayenne pepper
- 1 16-ounce can whole peeled Italian plum tomatoes, drained and chopped (reserve liquid)
- 1 tablespoon packed dark brown sugar
- 1-1/2 tablespoons red wine vinegar
- 1 medium Granny Smith apple, peeled, cored, and coarsely chopped
- 1/3 cup dried currants or seedless raisins
- 1/2 cup slivered blanched almonds, toasted (see note, following page)

Salt and freshly ground pepper to taste

SAUCE:
- 1 large ripe tomato, peeled (page 92), halved, and seeded
- 1 small clove garlic, minced
- 1/3 cup finely chopped red onion
- 1/4 cup dry white wine
- 1 fresh jalapeño pepper, seeded, ribs removed, and minced (page 109)
- 2 whole red, yellow, or orange bell peppers, halved lengthwise, ribs removed, and seeded (do not remove stems)

1. To make the filling: In a heavy 6- to 8-quart pot over medium-high heat, add the pork, beef, onion, and garlic. Add enough cold water to cover by 3-inches and bring to a boil. Reduce the heat to medium-low and simmer 15 minutes.

2. Remove pot from heat and strain, discarding the onion, garlic, and cooking liquid. Transfer the pork and beef to the bowl of a food processor fitted with a metal blade; pulse 4 to 5 times or until the meat is finely chopped.

3. In a heavy 3- to 4-quart saucepan over medium-high heat, heat the olive oil. Add the red onion and minced garlic. Cook, stirring often, 3 to 4 minutes or until onion is soft but not browned. Add the cumin, cloves, black pepper, cinnamon, chili powder, and cayenne. Cook, stirring frequently, 1 minute or until spices are lightly toasted and release their aroma.

4. Preheat the oven to 350°F.

5. Reduce the heat to very low and add the finely chopped meat, tomatoes, brown sugar, vinegar, apple, and currants. Simmer, covered, stirring occasionally, for 10 minutes. (*Note:* If picadillo becomes dry, add some of the reserved tomato liquid.)

6. Stir in the toasted almonds and season with salt and pepper. Remove saucepan from the heat and reserve.

7. To make the sauce: In the container of a blender, add the tomato and blend until pureed. Add the garlic, onion, wine, and jalapeño. Blend until well combined.

8. Arrange bell peppers cut side up in an 8-by-8-by-2-inch baking dish. Fill each pepper with the meat mixture. (Recipe can be prepared up to this point 1 day ahead. Cool, cover, and refrigerate the peppers and sauce separately.)

9. Surround the peppers with the tomato sauce and bake, covered, for 20 to 30 minutes or until the peppers are tender.

TO MICROWAVE

Follow recipe through step 7. At step 8, substitute a microproof dish, and microcook, covered and vented, 5 minutes on HIGH, turning once. Microcook 5 minutes more on HIGH, vented. Let stand 3 minutes before serving.

FREEZING TIPS

Follow recipe through step 8. Let cool, wrap the Picadillo-Stuffed Peppers and sauce separately, seal, and label. Freeze up to 1 month.

To Serve: Thaw peppers and sauce and proceed with step 9.

VARIATION

Add 1 cup canned, drained, cooked black beans with other ingredients in step 5.

TO TOAST ALMONDS

Place almonds on a baking sheet and toast in a preheated 350°F oven for about 10 minutes, stirring often. (Be careful not to let the almonds burn; they should be a light brown when toasted properly.) Transfer immediately to a fine-meshed rack or paper-towel-lined plate to cool.

Red Flannel Corned Beef Hash

SERVES 4

The beets that are the main ingredient of red flannel hash, when added to corned
beef hash, create a vividly colored and delicious meal that even purists will find hard to resist.
If there is a secret to this dish, it is to avoid overcooking or overmixing the potatoes.
I prefer to use boiling potatoes, rather than baking potatoes, and I don't peel them;
they cook better and don't become mushy.

5   strips lean slab bacon
2   medium boiling potatoes, scrubbed but
    unpeeled, cooked and quartered
2   medium cooked fresh beets, quartered,
    or 2 8-1/2-ounce cans, drained
3   medium yellow onions, finely chopped
1   pound cooked corned beef, cut into 1/4-inch
    dice (about 3 cups)
1/4 cup finely chopped fresh parsley, preferably
    Italian flat-leaf

Dash Tabasco sauce, or more to taste
1   tablespoon Worcestershire sauce
2   teaspoons Dijon-style mustard
1/3 cup heavy cream
Salt and freshly ground pepper to taste

TOPPING:
4   eggs

PREPARATION

1. Preheat the oven to 425° F.

2. In a large, heavy ovenproof skillet over medium-high heat, fry the bacon until brown and crisp. Remove the skillet from the heat and transfer the bacon to a paper-towel-lined plate to drain. Carefully wipe out the skillet, leaving about 1/2 teaspoon bacon drippings in the skillet and reserve.

3. In the bowl of a food processor fitted with a metal blade, pulse the potatoes about 4 times or until finely chopped (about 1/8-inch dice). Repeat the process with the beets. Set aside until ready to use.

4. Return the skillet with the bacon drippings to medium heat. Add the onions and cook 3 to 4 min-

utes, stirring often, or until soft but not browned. Stir in the corned beef, beets, potatoes, parsley, Tabasco, Worcestershire sauce, mustard, and heavy cream. Season with salt and pepper.

5. Cook, stirring gently, for 4 minutes. Remove the skillet from the heat and press the bottom of a 1/2-cup measure into the hash to make four evenly spaced indentations. (This recipe can be made up to this point 1 day ahead. Let cool, wrap, and refrigerate. Bring to room temperature before proceeding with recipe.)

6. Bake the hash in the upper third of the oven for 15 minutes or until the top is crisp. Remove from the oven and carefully break an egg into each indentation. Return the skillet to the oven and bake for 6 to 10 minutes, depending on desired doneness of the eggs.

7. To serve, cut the hash into quarters, one egg per wedge. Crumble reserved bacon, sprinkle on the hash, and serve.

Corned beef is classically made from beef brisket (though sometimes other cuts and meats are used) that has been cured in salt. The name is derived from the term "corn," meaning to preserve in brine. Corn is an old English word for small particles, such as the salt grains used in the curing process—hence, "corned beef."

Southwestern Beef Stew with Quinoa

SERVES 4 TO 6

Quinoa is a grain with a squashlike flavor that expands up to five times its original size. It is the highest in protein of all the grains, and is now available in North America. You can purchase it at most supermarkets and health-food stores.

2 tablespoons olive oil
2 pounds lean, boneless beef, preferably chuck, trimmed and cut into 1-inch cubes
1 medium onion, finely chopped
3 medium cloves garlic, minced
3 medium zucchini, cut into 1/2-inch-thick slices
1 medium acorn squash, (about 1-1/4 pounds) cut into 1/2-inch-dice
2 tablespoons tomato paste, preferably Italian
3/4 cup dry red wine
3-2/3 cups beef stock (page 185-186), or canned low-sodium beef broth

2 medium red bell peppers, cored, seeded, and cut into 1/2-inch wide strips
1/4 to 1/2 teaspoon dried hot red pepper flakes, crushed
1/2 teaspoon ground cumin
1 teaspoon chili powder
1/2 teaspoon ground allspice
1/4 teaspoon ground cinnamon
1 teaspoon dried oregano, crumbled
1 cup quinoa, picked over and rinsed
Salt and freshly ground pepper to taste

1. In a heavy 6- to 8-quart pot over medium-high heat, heat the oil. Add beef in batches and sear, turning often so cubes brown evenly on all sides, about 7 to 9 minutes per batch. Transfer meat to a medium bowl as it is browned and reserve.

2. Add the onion to the pot and cook 3 to 4 minutes, stirring often, until soft but not browned. Add the garlic, zucchini, and squash and cook 4 to 5 minutes, stirring occasionally, until just tender. Add to bowl with reserved meat.

3. Stir in the tomato paste and wine. Bring to a boil and boil for 1 minute, scraping up browned bits from bottom and sides of kettle.

4. Reduce heat to low and add the stock, bell peppers, red pepper flakes, cumin, chili powder, allspice, cinnamon, oregano, and reserved meat and vegetables. Add water to cover by about 2 inches. Simmer, partially covered, for 50 to 60 minutes, stirring occasionally, until meat is tender but not falling apart.

5. Stir in quinoa and simmer, uncovered, stirring occasionally, 20 minutes more or until about 5 times its original size. Season to taste with salt and pepper. Just before serving, skim or use a single layer of paper towel to blot any grease that has risen to the surface.

Philadelphia Cheese-Steak Supper Sandwiches

SERVES 4

My husband recently visited Philadelphia for the first time and came back a different person, yearning to go back to the very same luncheonette to have another fabulous "cheese-with" (in Philadelphia lingo, a cheese-steak with sautéed onions). I have kept the "cheese-with" in re-creating this dish, but have substituted Swiss cheese for the American and added Russian dressing to make a dinner version of this special sandwich.

CONDIMENT:
Russian Dressing (recipe on following page),
at room temperature

SANDWICH:
1 tablespoon unsalted butter or margarine
2 medium yellow onions, thinly sliced

4 cube steaks (about 1 pound), both sides seasoned
liberally with salt and freshly ground pepper
4 Italian-style hero rolls, approximately 8 to 9
inches long
2 tablespoons unsalted butter or margarine, melted
8 ounces thinly sliced Swiss cheese or muenster
cheese, at room temperature

1. Preheat the broiler.

2. Prepare recipe for Russian Dressing.

3. To prepare the sandwich: In a large skillet over medium-high heat, melt the butter, add the sliced onions, and cook, stirring often, 5 minutes or until soft and lightly golden brown. Remove onions with a slotted spoon and reserve until ready to use.

4. Add the seasoned cube steaks to skillet with onion juices and cook 2 to 3 minutes per side to desired doneness (2 minutes each side for medium-rare). Reserve.

5. Slice the rolls in half lengthwise. Brush each roll with 1/2 tablespoon melted butter and broil cut side up 5 to 6 inches from the heat for about 1 to 2 minutes or until lightly browned.

6. Distribute the onions, cube steaks (with pan juices), and Swiss cheese evenly among the rolls.

7. Place the rolls under the broiler and broil 30 to 40 seconds or until cheese has melted but not browned.

8. To serve, spread the Russian Dressing evenly over the roll tops and cover sandwiches. Serve warm.

TO MICROWAVE

Follow recipe through step 6. Place sandwiches on a large microproof platter. Microcook on HIGH 1-1/2 to 2 minutes until cheese melts. Spread with Russian Dressing and serve.

VARIATION

This recipe gives you two sandwiches in one. Just substitute rye bread for the Italian rolls, cooked corned beef for the cube steaks, and top with drained sauerkraut—a Reuben!

RUSSIAN DRESSING
MAKES 1-2/3 CUPS

1 egg, at room temperature
1 egg yolk, at room temperature
1 teaspoon fresh lemon juice
1/2 teaspoon salt
1/4 teaspoon freshly ground pepper
1/2 cup olive oil, at room temperature
3 tablespoons minced onion
2 tablespoons ketchup
2 tablespoons grated fresh horseradish, or
   1 tablespoon prepared horseradish, drained
1 tablespoon fresh lemon juice
1/2 tablespoon chili powder
Dash Worcestershire sauce, or more to taste
Salt and freshly ground pepper to taste
1/4 cup finely chopped green bell pepper
1 medium-sized ripe tomato, seeded and finely chopped

1. In a blender container, blend at medium speed the egg, egg yolk, 1 teaspoon lemon juice, salt, and pepper for 15 seconds, or until mixture becomes lemon-colored and thick. With the blender running constantly at medium speed, gradually pour the oil through the opening in the center of the cover into the egg mixture in a thin, steady stream until well blended. (*Note:* Do not pour the oil in all at once or mixture may separate.)

2. With the machine running at low speed, add the minced onion, ketchup, horseradish, 1 tablespoon lemon juice, chili powder, and Worcestershire sauce through the opening in the center of the cover. Remove container from blender and season dressing with salt and pepper.

3. Fold the chopped pepper and tomato into the dressing and set aside until ready to use.

Savory Steak and Kidney Pie

Even those not enamored of kidneys will relish this traditional dish from Great Britain. The ingredients are very basic: beef, kidneys, red wine, and onions. I have added sage to the crust, and wild mushrooms and thyme to the filling.

CRUST:

1-1/2 cups all-purpose flour
1 teaspoon salt
1 tablespoon finely chopped fresh sage, or
   1-1/2 teaspoons dried, crumbled
1/4 teaspoon freshly ground pepper
1/2 cup lard or unsalted butter (1 stick), cut
   into 8 pieces, chilled
1 egg yolk beaten with 2 tablespoons water
3 to 4 tablespoons ice water

FILLING:

1/4 cup all-purpose flour
1 teaspoon salt
1/2 teaspoon freshly ground pepper
1-1/2 pounds lean boneless beef, preferably
   round steak, trimmed and cut into
   1-1/2-inch pieces
8 ounces veal kidneys, cleaned, trimmed, and
   cut into 1/2-inch-wide pieces, crosswise

3 tablespoons unsalted butter or margarine
8 ounces white pearl onions, peeled, trimmed
   (page 48), or half a 16-ounce package frozen
   small white onions, thawed
4 ounces mushrooms, preferably short-stem,
   wiped clean with a damp paper towel,
   trimmed, and quartered
1 ounce dried wild mushrooms, such as cepes
   or porcini, soaked in 1 cup hot water
   (page 149), reserving soaking liquid
1/2 cup dry red wine
1/2 cup beef stock (page 185-186) or canned
   low-sodium beef broth
1 bay leaf
3 sprigs fresh thyme, or 1/2 teaspoon dried,
   crumbled

GLAZE:

1 egg yolk beaten with 1 tablespoon milk,
   cream, or water

PREPARATION

1. To make the crust: In a medium bowl sift together the flour and salt. Stir in the sage and pepper. Using a pastry blender or fork, cut in the chilled lard or butter, a few pieces at a time, until mixture resembles coarse cornmeal. Stir in the egg yolk beaten with water. Then add the ice water, a tablespoon at a time, as needed to allow the dough to form but not become sticky. Form into a flat disk. Wrap in wax paper and chill at least a half hour or until ready to use.

To make the crust in a food processor: In the bowl of a food processor fitted with a metal blade, combine the flour, salt, sage, and pepper and pulse to mix. Add the lard or butter and pulse until the mixture is the consistency of coarse cornmeal. Pulse in the egg yolk beaten with water. Then, while pulsing machine, add the ice water through the feed tube a tablespoon at a time. Process until dough is moist and just hangs together. (Do not let dough form into a ball in the processor.) Remove dough from bowl, form into a flat disk, wrap in wax paper, and refrigerate until ready to use. (The dough can be prepared ahead, wrapped, and refrigerated for up to 2 days. Bring dough to room temperature before proceeding.)

2. Preheat the oven to 425° F.

3. To make the filling: In a large bowl combine the flour, salt, and pepper. Dredge the beef and kidney pieces in the flour mixture, shaking off excess flour. Reserve until ready to use.

4. In a heavy 3- to 4-quart saucepan over medium-high heat, melt the butter. Add the onions and fresh mushrooms and cook for 5 to 8 minutes, stirring frequently, until onions are soft but not browned and mushrooms are tender. Transfer the onion mixture to a large bowl and reserve until ready to use.

5. Set the same saucepan over medium-high heat and sear the beef and kidney pieces in batches for 7 to 9 minutes, turning, until browned evenly. Transfer meat to the large bowl with the onion mixture, as it is browned and reserve.

6. To the same saucepan add the wild mushrooms and their liquid and bring to a boil, scraping the bottom and sides of the saucepan. Return the reserved vegetables and meats to the saucepan. Stir in the wine and stock. Bring to a boil. Boil for 1 minute. Reduce the heat to medium-low, add the bay leaf and thyme, and simmer, covered, about 45 minutes or until the meat is cooked. Remove the saucepan from heat. Remove and discard the bay leaf and thyme sprigs. Transfer the meat mixture to a 3- to 4-quart baking dish or casserole, (preferably oval) and set aside until ready to use.

7. On a lightly floured work surface, roll out the dough about 1/4 inch thick. Trim to fit the top of the baking dish with a 1-inch overhang. Lightly moisten the edges of the baking dish with water. Place the crust gently on top of the dish and crimp the edges to seal. Either cut a steam vent with a cookie cutter or make 2 diagonal slashes in the center of the crust with a knife to expose the filling. Brush crust lightly with the egg glaze. If you have any extra dough, use to make a decoration on the crust. Use some of the glaze to "glue" the decoration to the crust.

8. Bake the pie at 425° F for 10 minutes, then reduce the heat to 350° F and bake for 20 minutes more, or until the crust is golden brown.

FREEZING TIPS

Follow recipe through step 7 but omit egg glaze. Carefully wrap, seal, and label. Freeze up to 2 months.
To Serve: Thaw. Brush pie with glaze. Place in a preheated 425° F oven and follow step 8.

COOK'S NOTE

Purchasing tips: Always buy kidneys that are firm, with no soft spots, and odor-free. Kidneys are usually trimmed upon purchase. If they are not, ask your butcher to remove the outer membrane and the core. At home, remove any excess fat, gristle, and tubes.

Lard is a great old-fashioned ingredient that makes a superlative crust with maximum flakiness. If you adore the flavor of butter but want the flakiness that lard gives crust, then use half lard and half butter for the total amount needed.

Yorkshire Pudding Pies

SERVES 4 (2 PIES EACH)

Traditionally, Yorkshire pudding was baked under a roast beef to catch the drippings, which gave it a distinctive flavor. The British Yorkshire pudding was adapted slightly by Americans, who used beef drippings to grease tins for baking popovers from a batter similar to that for Yorkshire pudding. (Popovers derive their name from their tendency to "pop over" the muffin tin while baking.) This recipe is a variation on both themes: Light, airy popovers are slit open and served with a roast beef filling.

FILLING:

- 2 tablespoons unsalted butter or margarine
- 1 medium yellow onion, finely chopped
- 10 ounces fresh brussels sprouts, trimmed, tough outer leaves removed, and quartered, or 1 10-ounce package frozen, thawed
- 1 medium boiling potato, preferably red-skinned, scrubbed but unpeeled, cut into 1/4-inch dice
- 2 medium carrots, cut into 1/4-inch dice
- 2 medium cloves garlic, minced
- 3/4 cup beef stock (page 185-186) or canned low-sodium beef broth
- 1/4 cup dry red wine
- 1/4 cup heavy cream
- 1 tablespoon tomato paste, preferably Italian
- 2 teaspoons finely chopped fresh marjoram, or 1-1/2 teaspoons dried, crumbled
- 1 pound cooked rare roast beef, cut into 1/2-inch dice (about 3 cups)

POPOVERS:

- 2 eggs, lightly beaten, at room temperature
- 1 cup milk, at room temperature
- 1 teaspoon unsalted butter or margarine, melted
- 1 cup all-purpose flour
- 1/4 teaspoon salt

PREPARATION

1. To make the beef filling: In a large skillet over medium-high heat, melt the butter. Add the onion, brussels sprouts, potatoes, and carrots. Cook, stirring often, about 5 to 6 minutes or until the vegetables are tender. Add the garlic and cook, stirring often, 2 minutes more.

2. Stir in the stock, wine, cream, tomato paste, and marjoram and cook for 5 minutes more. Add the beef and stir to coat evenly. Set aside and keep warm until ready to use.

3. To make the popovers: In a medium bowl combine the eggs, milk, and melted butter. Beat until blended, about 1 minute. Add the flour and salt, and beat about 2 minutes or until well blended and smooth. (This recipe can be made up to this point one day ahead. Wrap and refrigerate. Bring to room temperature before proceeding with recipe.)

4. Lightly grease 8 6-ounce custard cups. Arrange on a baking sheet and preheat for 2 minutes or until just hot. Fill each cup half full of batter. Replace on the baking sheet and transfer to an oven (**not preheated**) and turn heat to 425° F; bake 40 to 50 minutes or until puffed, crisp, and golden brown.

5. To serve, slit open popovers and fill with hot beef filling. Serve immediately.

- Have all the ingredients at room temperature before whisking.

- Preheat baking containers.
- Do not preheat the oven.
- Do not open oven door until baking time is completed.

Bollito Misto with Green Sauce

SERVES 6 TO 8

Bollito misto ("mixed boiled meats") is the triumphant dish originally from the region of Piedmont in Italy. The contents of *bollito misto* can vary regionally as well as from household to household. It is usually served with a sauce, sometimes a red sauce, perhaps a green sauce, or even pickled fruit with mustard. In this recipe I have included a piquant Italian green sauce made with parsley and capers that your guests can drizzle over the meat.

1 *pound beef brisket, trimmed*
1 *pound veal tongue, trimmed*
2 *cups dry red wine*
4 *medium carrots, cut into 1-inch pieces*
6 *ribs celery, cut into 1-inch pieces*
4 *medium yellow onions, thinly sliced*
2 *teaspoons dried oregano, crumbled*

1/4 *cup finely chopped fresh parsley, preferably Italian flat-leaf*
1 *16-1/2 ounce can crushed tomatoes*
2 *pounds chicken drumsticks (preferably skinned, rinsed, and dried from stewing chicken)*
1 *pound hot Italian sausage or other fresh hot sausage, pricked all over with a fork*

PREPARATION

1. In a heavy 8- to 10-quart pot over medium heat, place the brisket and veal tongue. Add the wine and half the carrots, celery, and onions. Add enough cold water to cover by 3 inches. Bring to a boil, using a skimmer or perforated spoon to skim the foam from surface frequently. Reduce the heat to low, and add the oregano, parsley and tomatoes. Simmer for 1-1/2 hours, skimming often.

2. Remove the tongue, and with a sharp paring knife, skin the tongue and return to the kettle along with the chicken drumsticks and the remaining carrots,

celery, and onions. Add the sausage and simmer for 1 hour more, or until all the meats are tender.

3. To serve, strain the broth, reserving the vegetables and broth and transferring the meats to a carving board. Slice all the meats very thinly. Transfer the meats to a warmed serving platter with the vegetables and pass with Green Sauce (recipe follows). Blot the surface of the broth with a single layer of paper towel to remove any grease. Strain the broth again, discarding all solid particles, and serve the broth separately.

1 medium clove garlic, halved
2 teaspoons capers, drained
2 anchovies, rinsed
6 scallions, including green part, quartered
1/4 cup finely chopped fresh parsley, preferably
    Italian flat-leaf
1 medium green bell pepper, cored, seeded, and
    quartered
1 teaspoon Dijon-style mustard

1/4 cup white wine vinegar
1/4 cup olive oil
Salt and freshly ground pepper to taste

In the bowl of a food processor fitted with a metal blade, combine the garlic, capers, and anchovies and pulse until coarsely chopped, about 3 times. Add the scallions, parsley, bell pepper, mustard, vinegar and oil. Process about 1 minute more or until coarsely chopped and well blended. Season with salt and pepper. This sauce can be made 1 day in advance, stored in an airtight container, and refrigerated.

Oxtail Soup with Barley

SERVES 6 TO 8

Oxtail soup is an English dish, traditionally made with a clear broth. This rendition of the classic is a tomato-based soup with barley. I have used the oxtail only for the sweet, rich flavor it imparts to the soup, discarding the meat as it tends to have a chewy texture that does not appeal to most.

3/4 cup uncooked barley, picked over
4 pounds steer oxtail, trimmed and cut
    crosswise into 1-1/2- to 2-inch long pieces
2 tablespoons olive oil
3 ribs celery, quartered
3 medium carrots, quartered
1 medium yellow onion, quartered
1/4 cup brandy or Madeira
1 46-ounce bottle tomato juice
1-3/4 cups beef stock (page 185-186) or canned
    low-sodium beef broth
2 tablespoons tomato paste, preferably
    Italian

2 medium leeks, green part included, tough
    outer leaves removed, washed thoroughly and
    thinly sliced
2 medium cloves garlic, minced
10 whole cloves
2 sprigs fresh oregano, or 1 teaspoon dried,
    crumbled
1 sprig fresh marjoram, or 1/2 teaspoon dried,
    crumbled
1 sprig fresh savory, or 1/2 teaspoon dried,
    crumbled
8 ounces smoked kielbasa, cut into 1/4-inch-thick
    slices

1. Preheat the oven to 400° F.

2. In a medium bowl place the barley and enough warm water to cover by 3 inches. Soak for 1 hour, then drain.

3. Meanwhile, place the oxtail sections into a deep roasting pan, sprinkle with the oil, and toss with the celery and carrots. Roast for 45 minutes. Remove the pan, add the onion, and return to oven for 30 minutes more, stirring once after 15 minutes. Remove the oxtail and vegetables and transfer to a 6- to 8-quart pot, reserve the pan with drippings.

4. Add the brandy to the roasting pan with oxtail drippings and set over medium heat. Bring the brandy mixture to a boil, and boil for 1 minute, scraping drippings from bottom and sides of pan.

5. Add the brandy mixture to the pot with the oxtail and vegetables and set over low heat. Add the tomato juice, stock, tomato paste, and leeks. Then add the garlic, cloves, oregano, marjoram, and savory. Bring to a boil, then simmer, partially covered, for 1-1/2 hours, stirring occasionally.

6. Strain the soup, discarding oxtail, vegetables, and all solid particles from broth.

7. Return the strained broth to the pot and set over medium-high heat. Bring to a boil, reduce the heat to low, and add the barley and kielbasa.

8. Simmer, covered, for 45 to 55 minutes or until barley is tender and grains are triple their original size.

COOK'S NOTE

When purchasing oxtail, buy steer oxtail with red flesh and fat that is white, not orange. Look for meaty pieces. Ask your butcher to trim the oxtail, removing the surface fat and connective tissue, and to cut oxtail into 1-1/2- to 2-inch-long sections.

Hungarian Beef Goulash

SERVES 4

The key ingredient in any goulash, contributing both a unique flavor and beautiful color, is paprika, the national spice of Hungary. It is available in three strengths—sweet, semisweet (a bit stronger), and hot, depending upon the number of veins and seeds removed from the peppers prior to milling. The amount of semisweet or hot paprika you use in this dish is a matter of personal taste, but be careful of the hot variety—a little goes a long way! Although the traditional recipes for goulash do not call for sour cream, I believe it adds a wonderfully creamy texture to the dish.

1 tablespoon vegetable oil
2 medium yellow onions, thinly sliced
2 cloves garlic, minced
1-1/2 pounds lean boneless beef, preferably chuck, trimmed and cut into 1-1/2-inch-long pieces
1 to 2 tablespoons Hungarian semisweet or hot paprika (see page 30)
1/2 teaspoon salt
1/4 teaspoon freshly ground pepper
1 tablespoon all-purpose flour
2 cups beef stock (page 183) or canned low-sodium beef broth

3 medium green bell peppers, cored, seeded, and cut into eighths, lengthwise
2 medium-sized ripe tomatoes, seeded and cut into eighths, lengthwise
1-1/2 teaspoons caraway seeds
3 medium boiling potatoes, preferably red-skinned, scrubbed but unpeeled, cut into 1/2-inch dice
8 ounces farfalle (bowtie–shaped pasta)
2/3 cup sour cream, at room temperature, optional

PREPARATION

1. In a heavy 6- to 8-quart pot over medium-high heat, heat the oil and cook the onion and garlic, stirring often, for 3 to 4 minutes or until onion is soft but not browned. Raise the heat to high, push the onion mixture to one side, and sear the beef in batches, turning pieces often so they brown evenly, about 7 to 9 minutes per batch. Transfer the meat as it is browned to a medium bowl and reserve.

2. Return the meat to the pot, stir in the paprika, salt, and pepper, and stir to coat meat evenly. Sprinkle the meat with the flour and stir to combine. Add the broth, bell pepper, tomatoes, and caraway. Bring to a boil, reduce heat to medium-low, cover, and simmer for 1 hour, stirring occasionally. Add the potatoes and simmer for 15 minutes more or until the meat and potatoes are tender but not soft.

3. Strain the goulash, returning the cooking liquid to the pot and keeping the meat and vegetables warm until ready to serve.

4. Add the farfalle to the pot with the strained cooking liquid. Cover, stirring often to prevent pasta from sticking to sides and bottom of the pot (there will only be a small amount of liquid), bring to boil, then cook pasta 7 to 9 minutes or until al dente (slightly firm to the bite).

5. To serve, remove the pot from the heat and gradually stir in the sour cream if using. Transfer the pasta to a serving dish and top with reserved warm beef and vegetables.

VARIATION

Substitute veal for the beef and/or Egg Dumplings (page 57) for the farfalle.

PAPRIKA STORAGE

Store paprika in airtight glass containers away from heat and light, preferably in the refrigerator. This will help paprika retain its strength.

Beef Tamale Pie

This colorful dish was probably inspired in the early eighteenth century by
the Mexican tamale, a dish in which beef is enclosed in steamed cornmeal dough.
Here the beef mixture is topped with a layer of cornmeal mush.

FILLING:

- 2 pounds lean boneless beef, preferably chuck, trimmed and cut into 2-inch cubes
- 1 cup beef stock (page 185-186) or canned low-sodium beef broth
- 3 medium cloves garlic, unpeeled
- 1-1/2 tablespoons vegetable oil
- 2 medium yellow onions, finely chopped
- 2 medium cloves garlic, minced
- 1 large red or green bell pepper, cored, seeded, and coarsely chopped
- 2-1/2 teaspoons chili powder (see page 30)
- 1 teaspoon ground cumin
- 1 tablespoon finely chopped fresh oregano, or 2 teaspoons dried, crumbled
- 1 14-1/2-ounce can whole peeled Italian plum tomatoes, chopped, with juice
- 1/4 cup dry red wine
- 2 cups fresh corn kernels, or 1 10-ounce package frozen, thawed
- 3 tablespoons chopped mild canned peeled green chilies
- 1/4 teaspoon salt
- 1/2 teaspoon freshly ground pepper

TOPPING:

- 2 cups yellow cornmeal
- 1 teaspoon salt
- 1 cup shredded sharp Cheddar cheese or Monterey Jack cheese

PREPARATION

1. To make the filling: Place the beef, stock, 1 cup water, and garlic cloves in a 6- to 8-quart pot over high heat. Bring to a boil, then reduce to medium-low. Simmer for 25 minutes or until beef is tender but not falling apart, skimming the surface often.

2. Remove the pot from the heat and strain, reserving 2 cups of the cooking liquid, adding water if needed to make the 2 cups. Discard the garlic and transfer the meat to the bowl of a food processor fitted with a metal blade. Pulse the meat 4 to 5 times or until meat is coarsely chopped.

3. Preheat the oven to 350°F.

4. In a large heavy skillet over medium heat, heat the oil. Add the onion, minced garlic, and bell pepper. Cook, stirring often, until onion is soft but not browned, about 4 minutes. Add the coarsely chopped beef, chili powder, cumin, oregano, tomatoes, wine, corn, chilies, salt, and pepper. Reduce the heat to medium-low and simmer 10 minutes, stirring often. Remove from the heat and drain fat. Ladle the filling into a 3- to 4-quart baking dish, spreading evenly, and reserve. (This recipe can be made up to this point 1 day ahead. Let cool, wrap, and refrigerate. Bring to room temperature before proceeding with recipe.)

5. To make the topping: In a 2- to 3-quart saucepan over medium heat, bring the 2 cups of reserved cooking liquid to a boil.

6. Stir the cornmeal and salt into 1 cup cold water (to help prevent lumping), then stir into the boiling cooking liquid. Cook mixture until thickened, stirring briskly and constantly with a wooden spoon. Cook the cornmeal mush until very thick, about 1 to 2 minutes, or until it pulls away from the sides of the pan. Mush will be difficult to stir. Be careful not to let the mush cool completely, or it will not be spreadable. Working very quickly, top the filling in the baking dish with all the mush, using a knife or spatula to smooth it over.

7. Bake for 40 to 45 minutes or until heated through and top is a light golden brown. Then sprinkle with the Cheddar cheese and bake for 5 to 10 minutes more or until cheese is melted. Let stand 10 minutes before serving.

FREEZING TIPS

Proceed with recipe through step 6. Let cool to room temperature, wrap, seal, and label. Freeze up to 2 months.

To Serve: Thaw. Bake according to step 7.

HOW TO PREPARE CHILI PEPPERS

FRESH CHILIES:
Oils from certain chilies can be very hot and act as an irritant. Try to wear rubber gloves when cooking with chilies, and don't touch your face! After handling chilies, wash you hands with warm soapy water. Before cutting the pepper, rinse it and pull out the stem under cold running water. Cut the pod in half lengthwise and brush out and discard the seeds. Using a sharp paring knife, cut out the fleshy ribs. The chili may be used right away, or soak it in lightly salted cold water to help reduce some of the hotness.

CANNED CHILIES:
Always drain canned chilies and rinse them to remove as much of the brine that they are packed in as possible.

DRIED CHILIES:
Small dried chili peppers should be stemmed and seeded before being used.

Sauerbraten with Braised Red Cabbage

SERVES 8 TO 10

Sauerbraten is a marinated beef pot roast, German style, typically accompanied by braised cabbage and apples. In this recipe the vegetables are braised together with the beef to create a spectacular winter meal. For the best flavor and optimal tenderness, marinate the beef one to two days.

1 *4-pound bottom round roast, trimmed*	3 *medium carrots, thinly sliced*
1 *cup red wine vinegar*	3 *ribs celery, cut into 1/2-inch dice*
1 *cup dry red wine*	4 *medium leeks, white part only, trimmed,*
1-1/2 *cups water*	*washed, and thinly sliced*
2 *medium yellow onions, thinly sliced and*	1 *tablespoon all-purpose flour*
rings separated	1/2 *teaspoon ground cloves*
4 *medium leeks, white part only, washed*	1/4 *teaspoon ground cinnamon*
thoroughly, and thinly sliced	1 *small red or green cabbage, tough outer*
2 *medium cloves garlic, minced*	*leaves removed, cored and shredded*
5 *black peppercorns, crushed*	1 *6-ounce package dried sliced apples*
8 *juniper berries, crushed*	1/2 *cup sour cream*
4 *sprigs fresh thyme, or 2 teaspoons dried*	1/2 *cup seedless raisins*
5 *sprigs fresh parsley*	7 *gingersnaps, crushed (about 1/2 cup),*
2 *teaspoons celery seed*	*or 2-1/2 teaspoons ground ginger and*
1 *bay leaf*	1 *tablespoon dark brown sugar*
3 *tablespoons vegetable oil*	*Salt and freshly ground pepper to taste*
1 *medium yellow onion, thinly sliced*	

PREPARATION

1. Place meat in a nonreactive 6- to 8-quart Dutch oven or flameproof casserole.

2. In a medium saucepan over medium-high heat, combine the marinade ingredients: the vinegar, wine, 1-1/2 cups water, onions, leeks, and garlic. Then stir in the peppercorns, juniper berries, thyme, parsley, celery seed, and bay leaf. Bring to a boil. Remove saucepan from heat and let cool. Pour the marinade over the beef in the Dutch oven, cover tightly, and refrigerate. Marinate for 1 to 2 days, turning once each day.

3. Strain meat and vegetables but reserve marinade. Discard vegetables. Pat meat dry with paper towels.

4. Transfer the Dutch oven to medium-high heat, heat the oil, and sear beef until browned evenly on all sides, about 3 to 4 minutes per side. Remove the Dutch oven from heat and transfer meat to a plate and reserve. Carefully pour off fat.

5. Return the Dutch oven to medium-high heat and add the onion, carrots, celery, and leeks. Cook 3 to 4 minutes, stirring often, or until vegetables are tender but not browned. Stir in the flour, cloves, cinnamon, and reserved marinade.

6. Return meat to Dutch oven and add the cabbage and apples. Lower heat and simmer, covered, about 2 to 3 hours or until meat is very tender but not falling apart. Transfer meat to a warmed serving platter.

7. Whisk 1/4 cup of the cooking liquid into the sour cream and then stir mixture back into the liquid in Dutch oven. Add raisins and crushed gingersnaps. Season with salt and pepper.

8. To serve, slice the meat thinly and serve alongside the vegetables and sauce.

Pot-Au-Feu with Horseradish Sauce

SERVES 6

Pot-au-feu, literally "pot on the fire," is a French dish traditionally served
with coarse salt, cornichons (brine-packed small gherkins), mustard, and grated horseradish.
I enjoy the boiled beef sliced and topped with an alabaster horseradish-cream sauce.
It is also customary to scoop out the marrow from the bones and spread it on bread.
The broth can be served with toasted French bread topped with shredded Gruyère.
A hearty red wine beautifully complements this dish.

1 *4-pound boneless, trimmed bottom round roast of beef*
2 *pounds veal knuckles or bones with marrow*
4 *medium yellow onions, roasted in a 500°F oven for 20 to 25 minutes, then studded with 2 whole cloves each*
8 *whole cloves*
Bouquet garni (place ingredients in cheesecloth and tie bundle with string):
- *8 sprigs fresh parsley*
- *1 bay leaf*
- *2 teaspoons black peppercorns*
- *4 medium cloves garlic*
- *6 sprigs fresh thyme*

6 *medium carrots, cut into 2-inch-long pieces*
6 *ribs celery, cut into 2-inch-long pieces*
6 *medium leeks, with 2 inches of green part, tough outer leaves removed, slit lengthwise almost to base and washed thoroughly*
4 *medium parsnips, peeled and quartered lengthwise*
8 *small white turnips, peeled and quartered*
2 *teaspoons salt*
2-1/2 *teaspoons freshly ground pepper*
Horseradish Cream Sauce (recipe follows)
French bread
Gruyère cheese

1. In a heavy 8- to 10-quart pot over medium-high heat, add the beef, veal knuckles, onions, and enough cold water to cover by about 3 inches. Bring to a boil. When liquid comes to a full boil, using a perforated spoon or skimmer, remove any foam that has risen to the surface. Reduce heat to low and simmer 1 hour, skimming often.

2. Add the bouquet garni. Cook, partially covered, for 1 hour. Then add the carrots, celery, leeks, parsnips, turnips, salt, and pepper. Cook for 30 minutes more, covered, or until the beef and vegetables are tender but not falling apart.

3. Remove the beef and veal knuckles; set aside the beef, but discard the knuckles. Strain the broth, reserving broth and vegetables, but discard bouquet garni. Blot with a sheet of paper towel any grease that has risen to the surface. (This recipe can be prepared up to this point 1 day ahead. Cool, cover, and refrigerate. The next day, skim off solidified fat from surface and reheat.)

4. To serve, slice the meat and place in the center of a warmed serving platter alongside the Horseradish Cream Sauce and surround with vegetables. Strain the broth, and serve in mugs topped with toasted French bread sprinkled with shredded Gruyère cheese.

HORSERADISH CREAM SAUCE

MAKES 1 CUP

1 cup sour cream
1-1/2 tablespoons prepared horseradish, drained
1/2 teaspoon Dijon-style mustard
1/8 teaspoon cayenne pepper
Salt and freshly ground white pepper to taste

In a small bowl combine sour cream, horseradish, mustard, and cayenne. Whisk together until well blended and season with salt and pepper. Chill until ready to serve.

Extra-Spicy Sloppy Joes

SERVES 4

These skillet sandwiches require a knife and fork; that's why they are called Sloppy Joes. They can be served open-faced or capped with the bun top, and make a complete meal along with a light salad. Children love them, and they're ideal for informal entertaining: try serving them the next time friends come over to watch a game on TV. You may add a can of drained kidney beans to the meat mixture if you like. And be sure to use a dark imported ale with a strong malt flavor to balance the extra-spicy seasonings.

1 tablespoon vegetable oil
1 medium yellow onion
1 pound extra-lean ground beef
2 large cloves garlic, minced
1 medium green bell pepper, cored, seeded, and finely chopped
3 scallions, including green part, thinly sliced
1/2 cup dark ale or beer
1/2 cup unsulfured blackstrap molasses
1 14-1/2-ounce can stewed tomatoes

2-1/2 tablespoons tomato paste, preferably Italian
3 tablespoons white vinegar
1 tablespoon chili powder
1 teaspoon ground allspice
1/4 teaspoon ground cloves
1/2 teaspoon salt
1/2 teaspoon freshly ground pepper
4 split hamburger buns, warmed

PREPARATION

1. In a large heavy skillet over medium-high heat, heat the oil. Add the onion and cook, stirring often, 3 to 4 minutes or until soft but not browned. Add the ground beef, stirring often to break up the clumps. Cook for 4 minutes or just until beef begins to brown. Carefully pour off the fat.

2. Add the garlic, bell pepper, and scallions. Cook for 5 minutes, stirring occasionally, or until the vegetables are just tender. Stir in the ale, molasses, tomatoes, and tomato paste, stirring often to break up the tomatoes. Cook for 5 minutes more.

3. Add the vinegar and bring to a boil. Reduce the heat to very low and stir in the chili powder, allspice, cloves, salt, and pepper. Simmer, partially covered, stirring occasionally, for 20 to 25 minutes or until slightly thickened. *Note:* The mixture will have a fair amount of liquid. (This recipe can be made 1 day ahead. Cool, wrap, and refrigerate.)

4. To serve, ladle the hot Sloppy Joe mixture over the bottom half of warmed rolls. Serve open-faced or cap with the top of the bun.

TO MICROWAVE

1. In a 2-quart microproof dish add the oil and the onion. Microcook on HIGH, uncovered, for 3 minutes. Add the meat and cook 2 minutes more on HIGH, covered and vented. Stir once. Cook 2 minutes more on HIGH, covered and vented. Add garlic, bell pepper, and scallions. Cover, vent, and cook 2 minutes on HIGH.

2. Add ale, molasses, tomatoes, tomato paste, vinegar, and seasonings. Cover and cook on HIGH 4 minutes. Stir once. Re-cover and cook 4 minutes on HIGH or until hot throughout. Let stand 2 minutes before ladling mixture onto rolls.

FREEZING TIPS

Follow recipe through step 3. Let cool, wrap, seal, label, and freeze up to 1 month.
To Serve: Thaw. Reheat over very low heat, stirring often, until heated through. Adjust seasoning with salt and pepper and proceed with step 4.

Fragrant Shepherd's Pie

Recipes for this traditional rustic dish range from basic meat and potatoes to eccentric versions with as many as seven different herbs and spices. My recipe accents the flavor of the lamb with buttery, nutty, roasted garlic, marjoram, and zucchini. It's a great dish to take to a pot-luck dinner—an easy to transport, inviting, and distinctive version of a favorite standby.

FILLING:

- 2 tablespoons unsalted butter or margarine, or vegetable oil
- 1 cup finely chopped red onion
- 1 pound lean ground lamb
- 1 pound extra-lean ground beef
- 1/2 cup dry red wine
- 1 14-1/2-ounce can whole peeled Italian plum tomatoes, drained and chopped
- 2 tablespoons tomato paste, preferably Italian
- 1 small head roasted garlic (see following page), peeled and mashed with a fork
- 5 ounces mushrooms, preferably short-stem, wiped clean with a damp paper towel, trimmed, and thinly sliced
- 1 small zucchini, cut into 1/4-inch dice
- 1/4 cup finely chopped fresh parsley, preferably Italian flat-leaf
- 1 tablespoon finely chopped fresh marjoram, or 2 teaspoons dried, crumbled
- 2-1/2 teaspoons finely chopped fresh oregano, or 2 teaspoons dried, crumbled
- Salt and freshly ground pepper to taste

TOPPING:

- 5 cups mashed potatoes, at room temperature (made from about 7 medium potatoes)
- 1/4 cup half-and-half (plus more, depending on consistency needed to pipe)
- 1/2 teaspoon freshly grated nutmeg
- 1/4 teaspoon salt
- 1/4 teaspoon freshly ground pepper
- 1 egg, beaten
- 1/2 cup freshly grated Parmesan cheese or shredded Gruyère cheese

PREPARATION

1. Preheat the oven to 375° F.

2. To make the filling: In a large skillet over high heat, melt the butter and add the onion. Cook the onion, stirring often, until soft but not browned, about 3 to 4 minutes. Add the lamb and beef, breaking it up with a wooden spoon, and cook 7 to 9 minutes, stirring often, until meat just begins to brown. Remove the skillet from heat and carefully pour off the fat.

3. Return the skillet to medium-high heat and add the wine, tomatoes, and tomato paste. Then stir in the garlic, mushrooms, zucchini, parsley, marjoram, and oregano. Season with salt and pepper. Bring the mixture to a boil, stirring constantly. Then reduce the heat to very low and simmer for 5 to 7 minutes or until mushrooms are tender and flavors are melded, stirring occasionally.

4. Remove the skillet from heat and strain the meat mixture, discarding all excess liquid. Transfer the meat mixture to a 3- to 4-quart baking dish, spreading evenly.

5. To prepare the topping: In a medium bowl combine the mashed potatoes, half-and-half, nutmeg, salt, and pepper. Transfer the topping to a pastry bag fitted with a large star tip. Pipe a crisscross or large rosette pattern evenly over the meat. If you prefer, spread the topping evenly over the meat with a knife. Then, with the tines of a fork, make decorative crosshatch marks. (This recipe can be made up to this point 1 day ahead. Cool, wrap, and refrigerate. Bring to room temperature before proceeding with recipe.)

6. Lightly brush the surface of the topping with the beaten egg, then sprinkle with the grated Parmesan. Bake for 40 to 50 minutes or until heated through and top is a light golden brown and crisp. Let stand 10 minutes before serving.

VARIATION

You can substitute sweet potatoes for the white potatoes. Follow the recipe and sprinkle with 2 tablespoons brown sugar (instead of the Parmesan cheese) just before baking.

COOK'S NOTE

To prevent discoloration of potatoes while you're preparing them for cooking, just place them in a bowl of cold water to cover after peeling.

The best tool to make flawless mashed potatoes is still the old-fashioned "potato masher." Not only is it simple to use, but the vertical movements of a masher do not make gluey potatoes the way the circular motion of a food processor or blender does.

TO ROAST GARLIC

Rub a whole, unpeeled head of garlic with 1 teaspoon olive oil. Wrap loosely with aluminum foil (but seal tightly to catch juices) and place on a shallow baking pan. Bake in a preheated 375° F oven for 35 to 45 minutes or until a fork can be inserted easily into garlic. (Be careful! Slash foil packet with a knife to release steam before opening so as not to burn yourself.) Unwrap and let cool. When cool enough to handle, peel apart garlic head and pinch cloves at root base to "pop" cloves out of skin.

Olla Podrida with Root Vegetables and Chick-Peas

SERVES 8 TO 10

Olla podrida means literally "rotten pot," but do not let that scare you, for this is a glorious meal. The country cuisine of Spain is renowned for its stews that are always on the fire, their flavors constantly changing with the addition of still another ingredient. Although quite simple to prepare, the varied ingredients create a complex flavor as multifaceted as it is delicious. Though it can be made and eaten the same day, this recipe is at its best if prepared ahead. Soak the chick-peas two days before serving, prepare the stew the day before and refrigerate, then reheat just before serving.

1 cup dried chick-peas (garbanzos), picked over
2 tablespoons olive oil
1 pound beef brisket, cut into 1-1/2-inch cubes
2 large red onions, finely chopped
2-1/2 quarts beef stock (page 185-186) or canned low-sodium beef broth
1-1/2 pounds stewing chicken parts, preferably drumsticks, skinned
1 pound pork spareribs, cut into individual ribs
1 pound whole chorizo (spicy Spanish pork sausage), pricked all over with a fork, or other spicy and/or hot fresh sausage

4 ribs celery, cut into eighths
3 medium carrots, cut into eighths
3 large leeks, including green part, tough outer leaves removed, trimmed, washed thoroughly, and thinly sliced
1 medium unpeeled head garlic, trimmed
4 medium sweet potatoes, peeled and cut crosswise into 1/2-inch-thick slices
4 small white turnips, peeled and quartered
1 lightly packed teaspoon saffron threads
1/2 to 1 teaspoon dried hot red pepper flakes, crushed
1 teaspoon salt
1 teaspoon freshly ground pepper

PREPARATION

1. Soak the chick-peas in enough cold water to cover by about 2 inches; cover and let stand overnight at room temperature. Or place the chick-peas in a saucepan with enough cold water to cover by 2 inches and bring to a boil. Remove the saucepan from the heat, cover, and let stand 1 hour at room temperature. Drain and rinse.

2. In a 10- to 12-quart stockpot over high heat, heat the oil and add the beef. Sear the meat until browned evenly on all sides, about 7 to 9 minutes. Remove the meat and set aside.

3. Reduce the heat to medium-high, add the onions, and cook for 3 to 4 minutes, stirring often, until soft but not browned. Add the reserved meat, stock, chick-peas, chicken, spareribs, chorizo, and 4 cups water. Then stir in the celery, carrots, leeks, garlic, sweet potatoes, turnips, saffron, red pepper flakes,

salt and pepper. Bring to a boil, skimming off foam from surface, then reduce heat to low and simmer for 1 hour, stirring and skimming occasionally.

4. Remove and discard the garlic. Remove the chicken and spareribs. Trim away the meat and discard the bones. Return the chicken and sparerib meat to the stockpot. Remove the chorizo and slice crosswise into 1/2-inch-thick slices and return to the stockpot. Serve hot directly from the stockpot.

FREEZING TIPS

Follow recipe. Let cool, wrap, seal, and label. Freeze up to 3 months.

To Serve: Thaw. Reheat gently over a low flame, stirring occasionally until heated through.

Hometown New England Boiled Dinner

SERVES 8

Even though I was an avowed vegetable-hater as a child, my mother used to make this meal for our family. I was always surprised that those "yucky" vegetables tasted marvelous and sweet. The exchange of flavors between the corned beef and vegetables is true culinary magic. This is my favorite of all international boiled dinners, but of course as a Bostonian, I'm biased. The secret to a terrific boiled dinner is that all the vegetables should be cooked perfectly at the same time. Many New Englanders drizzle the meat and vegetables with apple cider vinegar before serving. If you wish, you can serve this with Horseradish Cream Sauce (page 112) or a hearty coarse-grain mustard and an assortment of sweet and sour pickles.

4- to 5-pound uncooked whole corned beef
1 large head green cabbage, tough outer leaves removed, cored and quartered
8 medium boiling potatoes, preferably red-skinned, scrubbed but unpeeled, quartered
1 medium rutabaga, peeled and cut into eighths
7 medium carrots, quartered

4 medium white onions, halved
6 medium beets, peeled and cut into eighths
1/2 teaspoon salt
1/4 teaspoon freshly ground pepper
1/4 cup finely chopped fresh parsley, preferably Italian flat-leaf, to garnish
Apple cider vinegar

PREPARATION

1. Place the corned beef in a heavy 10- to 12-quart stockpot with enough cold water to cover by 3 inches. Bring to a boil, then reduce heat to low and simmer, partially covered, for 2 hours or until very tender but not falling apart. Skim the fat from the surface occasionally. If necessary, add *hot* water to the pot to keep the meat covered.

2. Add the cabbage, potatoes, rutabaga, carrots, onions, beets, salt, and pepper and simmer, partially covered, for 1 hour more.

3. To serve, drain the beef and vegetables, discard-ing the cooking liquid. Transfer the beef to the center of a warmed serving platter, surround with the vegetables, and sprinkle with the parsley. Drizzle with apple cider vinegar or pass with condiments.

COOK'S NOTE

If the uncooked corned beef appears overly salty, soak covered in cold water for 30 minutes, then drain and discard water. Proceed with the recipe.

Beef Bourguignon with Morels

There is nothing like the fragrance of *boeuf bourguignon*, the supreme match of Burgundy wine and beef, simmering on the stove. The meat cooks until it is buttery and melts in your mouth, while the morels make a perfect addition to this earthy dish. You'll want to serve a crusty French bread to dip into the sauce.

2-1/2 pounds lean boneless beef, preferably
    chuck, cut into 1-inch cubes
1/2 teaspoon salt
1/4 teaspoon freshly ground pepper
4 strips lean slab bacon, cut into 1/4-inch dice
2 medium yellow onions, finely chopped
12 ounces mushrooms, preferably short-stem,
    wiped clean with a damp paper towel and
    trimmed, larger mushrooms quartered
3 cups beef stock (page 185-186) or canned
    low-sodium beef broth
1-2/3 cups Burgundy wine
2 tablespoons tomato paste, preferably
    Italian

4 medium carrots, cut into 1-inch julienne
1-1/2 teaspoons finely chopped fresh rosemary,
    or 1/2 teaspoon dried, crushed
2 tablespoons sugar
1 10-ounce basket white pearl onions, peeled
    (for peeling hint, see page 48)
4 ounces fresh whole morels or other fresh
    wild mushrooms, wiped clean with a damp
    paper towel and trimmed
Salt and freshly ground pepper to taste
1/4 cup finely chopped fresh parsley, preferably
    Italian flat-leaf, to garnish

PREPARATION

1. Season the beef lightly with the salt and pepper and reserve.

2. In a heavy 6- to 8-quart Dutch oven or flameproof casserole over high heat, fry the bacon until browned and crisp, about 5 to 6 minutes. Using a slotted spoon, transfer to a paper-towel-lined plate to drain.

3. Carefully pour off all but 1 tablespoon of the excess fat. Reduce the heat to medium-high and add the onions and domestic mushrooms and cook, stirring often, for 5 to 6 minutes or until the onion is soft and the mushrooms are wilted and lightly

browned. Transfer the onion mixture to a medium bowl and reserve.

4. Add the beef to the Dutch oven and sear in batches, turning often so all sides brown evenly, about 4 to 6 minutes per batch. Transfer the beef to the bowl with the onion mixture as it is browned.

5. Add the stock, wine, and tomato paste to the Dutch oven and stir, scraping up the browned bits across the bottom and around the sides.

6. Reduce the heat to low and add the bacon, carrots, rosemary, and the reserved beef and onion mixture. Cover and simmer for 2 hours, stirring occasionally.

7. Meanwhile, in a large skillet over high heat, combine the sugar and pearl onions. Stir constantly until the sugar dissolves and turns a light golden brown, about 3 to 4 minutes. Immediately stir into the mixture in the Dutch oven.

8. After the beef mixture has cooked for 2 hours, stir in the morels and cook, uncovered, stirring occasionally, for 10 to 15 minutes more, or until the morels are tender and the beef is very tender but not falling apart. (This recipe can be prepared up to this point 1 day ahead. Let cool, cover, and refrigerate. Reheat gently over low heat, stirring occasionally until heated through, before proceeding with recipe.)

9. Season with salt and pepper and transfer to a warmed serving tureen or serve directly from the Dutch oven. Sprinkle with parsley.

Swedish-Style Meatballs

SERVES 4 TO 6

The hallmark of Swedish-style meatballs is their resplendent brown gravy. These flavorful meatballs composed of three kinds of ground meat also contain mashed potato, nutmeg, and a hint of fresh sage, and are served on a bed of egg noodles, all cloaked in that splendid gravy.

MEATBALLS:
- 8 ounces extra-lean ground beef
- 4 ounces extra-lean ground veal
- 4 ounces ground lamb
- 1 egg, lightly beaten
- 1 medium yellow onion, minced
- 1/2 cup mashed potatoes (made from 1 medium boiling potato)
- 1/2 cup unseasoned dried bread crumbs
- 1 tablespoon tomato paste, preferably Italian
- 1-1/2 teaspoons finely chopped fresh sage, or 1 teaspoon dried, crumbled
- 1/4 teaspoon ground nutmeg, preferably freshly grated
- 1/2 teaspoon salt
- 1/4 teaspoon freshly ground pepper
- 2 tablespoons safflower oil or olive oil
- 3 tablespoons finely chopped parsley, preferably Italian flat-leaf, to garnish

PASTA:

1 pound wide egg noodles

GRAVY:

3 tablespoons unsalted butter or margarine
3 tablespoons all-purpose flour
*1-1/2 cups beef stock (page 185-186), or canned
low-sodium beef broth, heated*
1/2 cup milk, heated
Salt and freshly ground pepper to taste

PREPARATION

1. Preheat the oven to 350° F.

2. To prepare the meatballs: In a medium bowl combine the beef, veal, lamb, egg, onion, potato, bread crumbs, tomato paste, sage, nutmeg, salt, and pepper and mix thoroughly. Using your hands, spoon a tablespoon of the mixture and shape into tight balls about 1 inch in diameter. There should be about 4 dozen meatballs.

3. In a large heavy skillet over medium-high heat, heat the safflower oil and add the meatballs in batches. Cook each batch, turning meatballs frequently, so they brown evenly, about 5 to 6 minutes. Transfer the meatballs as they are browned to a 2- to 3-quart baking dish. Reserve the skillet. Cover and bake for 15 minutes or until the meatballs are cooked and no trace of pink remains when tested.

4. Meanwhile, prepare the pasta: To a 6- to 8-quart pot of boiling water, add the noodles. Return to a

boil, stirring occasionally, and cook for 7 to 9 minutes or until al dente (slightly firm to the bite). Drain, transfer to a warmed serving platter, cover, and keep warm until ready to serve.

5. Meanwhile, prepare the gravy: Carefully wipe out the skillet, place over low heat, and melt the butter. Add the flour and cook, whisking vigorously until large bubbles appear, about 3 minutes. Cook 2 minutes more, whisking constantly; do not let the roux brown. Remove the skillet from the heat and gradually pour in the heated stock and then the heated milk while whisking constantly across the bottom and along the sides of the skillet until blended and smooth. Return the skillet to low heat, and cook, whisking constantly for about 5 minutes or until thickened. Season with salt and pepper.

6. Ladle the gravy over the meatballs, stir to combine, and then spoon the meatballs over the warm noodles, sprinkle with parsley, and serve immediately.

Herbed Salad Burgers

SERVES 4

What do you get when you combine a hamburger with a salad? Herbed Salad Burgers! Peppery arugula and feather-light bean sprouts are tossed in a salad that tops basil- and caper-spiked burgers.

SALAD:
- 2 tablespoons red wine vinegar
- 1/4 cup olive oil
- 1/4 teaspoon salt
- 1/8 teaspoon freshly ground pepper
- 1 small red onion, minced
- 2 ounces assorted fresh bean sprouts, such as alfalfa, sunflower, radish, and clover
- 1 bunch arugula, stemmed
- 1/2 pint ripe cherry tomatoes

BURGERS:
- 1 pound extra-lean ground beef
- 2 tablespoons ketchup
- 1 teaspoon Dijon-style mustard
- 1/4 cup drained capers, rinsed
- 3 tablespoons finely chopped fresh basil
- 1/2 teaspoon salt
- 1/4 teaspoon freshly ground pepper
- 4 rolls, about 5 inches in diameter

PREPARATION

1. To prepare the salad: In a medium non-metal bowl whisk together the vinegar, olive oil, salt, pepper, and onion. Stir in the sprouts, arugula, and cherry tomatoes until well coated. Cover and refrigerate until ready to serve.

2. Preheat the grill or broiler.

3. To prepare the burgers: In a medium bowl gently stir together the beef, ketchup, mustard, capers, basil, salt, and pepper until well blended. Shape into 4 flat 4-inch patties. Reserve at room temperature until ready to use.

4. For the grill: Over hot coals, grill 3 to 4 minutes per side for rare, 4 to 5 minutes per side for medium-rare, and 5 to 6 minutes per side for well-done. For the broiler: Broil 4 to 5 minutes per side for rare, 5 to 6 minutes per side for medium-rare, and 6 to 7 minutes per side for well-done. (*Note:* Both grill and broiler times are approximate. Cook to desired doneness and remember that the meat will still cook a bit more even after removed from the heat.)

5. To serve, drain the salad. Slit open the rolls, place a burger on the bottom half, top with drained salad, and cover with the roll top. Serve immediately.

Meatloaf Country-Style

Meatloaf is synonymous with the comforts of home, whether served hot or cold, or in a sandwich (one of my fondest culinary memories). The secret to a light texture, as in any dish made with ground beef, is to avoid kneading or mixing it excessively: The more you handle it, the more dense and heavy the dish.

MEATLOAF:
- 2 eggs
- 1/2 cup skim milk
- 1-1/2 teaspoons finely chopped fresh sage, or 1 teaspoon dried, crumbled
- 2 tablespoons chili powder
- 2 tablespoons finely chopped fresh chives or scallion, green part included
- 1/4 cup finely chopped fresh parsley, preferably Italian flat-leaf
- 1/2 teaspoon salt
- 1/2 teaspoon freshly ground pepper
- 1/8 teaspoon cayenne pepper
- 1-1/2 pounds extra-lean ground beef
- 1 cup unseasoned dried bread crumbs
- 1 medium yellow onion, minced
- 1 medium yellow or red bell pepper, cored, seeded, and minced
- 1 medium-sized tart apple such as Granny Smith, peeled, cored, and cut into 1/2-inch dice

GLAZE:
- 1/3 cup ketchup
- 2 tablespoons unsulfured dark molasses
- 1-1/2 teaspoons firmly packed dark brown sugar
- 1 teaspoon dry mustard
- 1/2 teaspoon ground ginger

PREPARATION

1. Preheat the oven to 350°F.

2. To prepare the meatloaf: In a large bowl beat the eggs, milk, sage, chili powder, chives, parsley, salt, pepper, and cayenne together until well blended. Stir in the beef, bread crumbs, onion, bell pepper, and apple until well blended.

3. Firmly pack the mixture into a 9-by-5-by-3-inch loaf pan and bake for 1 to 1-1/4 hours or until the meatloaf starts to shrink away from the sides of the pan and the top is well browned.

4. Meanwhile, prepare the glaze: in a small bowl, combine the ketchup, molasses, brown sugar, dry mustard, and ginger and mix until well blended.

5. Remove the pan from the oven and carefully pour off the excess fat surrounding the meatloaf. Spread the top with the glaze and return the meatloaf to the oven for 15 minutes more.

6. To serve, let stand for 10 minutes before slicing. Serve hot or at room temperature.

COOK'S NOTE

The recipe can be made up to 2 days ahead. Let cool, cover, and refrigerate. Reheat, covered, until heated through or serve at room temperature.

Mara's Veal Meatloaf

SERVES 8

Marjoram is a much-neglected seasoning, and my favorite herb. It is a superb complement to this veal-based loaf studded with robust soppressata and tender vegetables that keep the interior moist. The light flavor and delicate, herb-flecked texture make this meatloaf perfect for spring entertaining, but you'll want to serve it year-round!

2 eggs
1/2 cup skim milk
1/3 cup freshly grated Parmesan cheese
1/4 cup finely chopped fresh parsley, preferably Italian flat-leaf
1 tablespoon finely chopped fresh marjoram, or 1 teaspoon dried, crumbled
1/2 teaspoon salt

1/2 teaspoon freshly ground pepper
1-1/2 pounds extra-lean ground veal
1 medium zucchini, shredded
3 ounces Italian soppressata or Genoa salami, minced (about 3/4 cup)
1 medium red onion, minced
1 cup unseasoned dried bread crumbs

PREPARATION

1. Preheat the oven to 350° F.

2. In a large bowl beat the eggs, milk, Parmesan cheese, parsley, marjoram, salt, and pepper together until well blended. Stir in the veal, zucchini, soppressata, onion, and bread crumbs until well blended.

3. Firmly pack the mixture into a 9-by-5-by-3-inch loaf pan and bake for 1 to 1-1/4 hours or until the meatloaf starts to shrink away from the sides of the pan and the top is well browned.

4. To serve, carefully pour off the excess fat surrounding the meatloaf and let stand for 10 minutes before slicing. Serve hot or at room temperature.

COOK'S NOTE

The recipe can be made up to 2 days ahead. Let cool, cover, and refrigerate. Reheat, covered, until heated through or serve at room temperature.

Savory Venison Stew

Cooking with venison is no longer dependent on the largesse of the hunter, since it is now available commercially year-round. Farm-raised venison is in fact more tender and less "gamey" than its wild counterpart, and is even lower in fat and cholesterol than chicken!

1/3 cup all-purpose flour
1/4 teaspoon salt
1/2 teaspoon freshly ground pepper
  2 pounds lean boneless venison, preferably from the loin or rump, trimmed and cut into 1-inch cubes
  2 tablespoons safflower oil or corn oil
  2 cups beef stock (page 185-186) or canned low-sodium beef broth
  2 medium boiling potatoes, preferably red-skinned, scrubbed but unpeeled, cut into 1/2-inch dice

  1 large rutabaga, peeled and cut into 1-inch cubes
  3 medium carrots, cut into 1/2-inch-thick slices
2/3 cup red currant jelly
1/2 cup brandy
  8 juniper berries, crushed
 10 allspice berries, crushed
 10 black peppercorns, crushed
1/2 cup finely chopped pitted dried dates
Salt and freshly ground pepper to taste

PREPARATION

1. Preheat the oven to 350° F.

2. In a large bowl combine the flour, salt, and pepper and mix until well blended. Dredge the venison pieces in the flour mixture until evenly coated, shaking off excess flour.

3. In a heavy 3- to 4-quart flameproof casserole over medium-high heat, heat the safflower oil. Add the venison in batches and sear, turning the cubes so they brown evenly on all sides, about 5 to 6 minutes per batch. Transfer venison to a medium bowl as it is browned.

4. Pour the stock into the casserole (be careful—liquid may splatter) and stir, scraping across the bottom and around the sides of the casse-

role to release the browned bits. Stir in the potatoes, rutabaga, carrots, red currant jelly, brandy, juniper berries, allspice berries, peppercorns, dates, and reserved venison. Bring to a boil.

5. Remove the casserole from the heat, cover, and bake for 1-1/2 hours or until the venison is cooked (no trace of pink remains when tested) and tender. Season with salt and pepper. Serve directly from the casserole.

FREEZING TIPS

Follow the recipe. Let cool, wrap, seal, and label. Freeze up to 2 months.

MAIL-ORDER SOURCES FOR VENISON

D'ARTAGNAN, INC.
399-419 St. Paul Avenue
Jersey City, NJ 07306
201-792-0748

WORLD SAFARI, INC.
2563 South Shirlington Road
Arlington, VA 22206
703-979-3208

TEXAS WILD GAME COOPERATIVE
P.O. Box 530
Ingram, TX 78025
1-800-962-4263

ROBINIA HILL FALLOW DEER FARM
R.D. 2 Box 251
Moravia, NY 13118
315-496-2121

CAPOLI RANCH
Lansing, IA 52151
319-586-2590
319-538-4888

GAME EXCHANGE
107 Quint Street
San Francisco, CA 94124
1-800-426-3872
415-282-7878

Rabbit Ragout with Eggplant and Pine Nuts

SERVES 8

Rabbit is almost fat-free and can be substituted for chicken in many recipes.
As with chicken, the flavor of domesticated rabbit depends on age and type of feed:
The older the rabbit, generally, the more flavorful the meat. For a ragout, a light stew with a small amount of sauce, I prefer a more mature rabbit, weighing 3 to 3-1/2 pounds, which takes well to slow simmering.

3 tablespoons olive oil or safflower oil
2 cups long-grain white rice
1/3 cup pine nuts (pignoli)
1/3 cup all-purpose flour
1/2 teaspoon salt
1/2 teaspoon freshly ground pepper
1 3- to 3-1/2-pound rabbit (ask your butcher to cut it into 3-inch serving pieces), rinsed and dried
3 medium shallots, finely chopped
2 medium cloves garlic, minced
2/3 cup dry red wine

4 cups beef stock (page 185-186) or canned low-sodium beef broth
1 teaspoon finely chopped fresh rosemary, or 1/2 teaspoon dried, crushed and soaked in 1 tablespoon warm water
2 medium eggplants, unpeeled, cut into 1/2-inch dice
3 medium zucchini, cut into 1-inch cubes
1-1/2 cups drained Greek Kalamata olives or other brine-cured black olive, rinsed and pitted
Salt and freshly ground pepper to taste

PREPARATION

1. In a heavy 4- to 6-quart pot over medium-high heat, heat 1 tablespoon of the olive oil. Stir in the rice and pine nuts and cook, stirring frequently, about 5 to 6 minutes or until pine nuts are toasted a light golden brown. Remove the pot from the heat, and using a slotted spoon, transfer the rice and pine nuts to a paper-towel-lined plate to drain. Carefully wipe the oil from the pot with paper towels.

2. In a large bowl combine the flour, salt, and pepper and mix until well blended. Add the rabbit pieces and dredge until evenly coated, shaking off excess flour. Heat the remaining 2 tablespoons of olive oil in the pot over medium-high heat. Add the rabbit pieces in batches and sear, turning pieces so they brown evenly, about 3 minutes per side. Transfer the rabbit pieces to a large bowl and reserve until ready to use.

3. Add the shallots and the garlic and cook, stirring often, about 2 minutes or until softened but not browned.

4. Raise the heat to high. Pour in the wine and stock and bring to a boil. Boil for 1 minute.

5. Reduce the heat to low. Add the rosemary and reserved rabbit pieces. Cook, covered, stirring occasionally, for 1 hour or until the rabbit is just tender but cooked through and no trace of pink remains when tested. (This recipe can be made up to this point 1 day ahead. Let cool, cover, and refrigerate. Bring to room temperature before proceeding. Reserve the toasted rice mixture separately at room temperature.)

6. Stir in the eggplant and zucchini and cook, covered, for 10 minutes. Stir in the olives and the rice mixture and cook, covered, stirring occasionally, for 20 to 25 minutes more, or until the rabbit is very tender but not falling apart and the rice is tender. Season with salt and pepper. Transfer to a warmed serving platter and serve.

CHAPTER FOUR

PORK AND LAMB

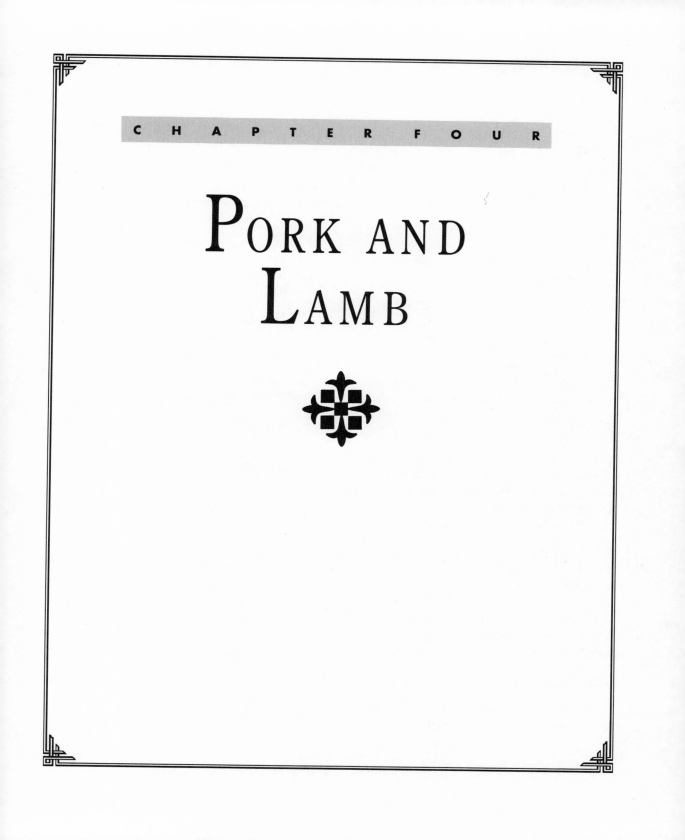

Trinidad Pepperpot

This West Indian dish traditionally is made with cassareep juice from the cassava root, which gives pepperpot a bittersweet touch that sets it apart from other stews. In this recipe I have replaced the hard-to-find cassara, which is actually toxic when raw, with a combination of maple syrup, dark ale, and vinegar. This recipe calls for okra to be cooked along with the stew, rather than served separately.

2 tablespoons olive oil or safflower oil
2 pounds lean boneless pork, preferably from the shoulder, trimmed and cut into 1-1/2-inch chunks
1 large red onion, finely chopped
1 medium clove garlic, minced
3 cups beef stock (page 185-186) or canned low-sodium beef broth
1 12-ounce bottle dark ale or beer
2 tablespoons maple syrup or 1-1/2 tablespoons firmly packed dark brown sugar

1/3 cup balsamic vinegar or red wine vinegar
3 tablespoons quick-cooking tapioca
1 2-inch-long cinnamon stick, or 1 teaspoon ground cinnamon
1 teaspoon finely chopped fresh thyme, or 1/2 teaspoon dried, crumbled
1 teaspoon dried hot red pepper flakes, crushed
1/2 teaspoon cayenne pepper
2 cups fresh okra, cut into 1/2-inch-thick slices, or 1 10-ounce package frozen sliced okra, thawed
Freshly ground pepper to taste

PREPARATION

1. In a heavy 6- to 8-quart pot over medium-high heat, heat the olive oil. Add the pork in batches and sear, turning until browned evenly on all sides, about 4 to 5 minutes per batch. Transfer the pork chunks to a medium bowl as they are browned.

2. Carefully pour off excess fat. Add the onion and garlic and cook, stirring often, 3 to 4 minutes or until soft but not browned. Add the stock (be careful—liquid may splatter) and scrape across the bottom and around the sides of the pot to release any browned bits. Stir in the ale, maple syrup, vinegar, tapioca, cinnamon stick, thyme, red pepper flakes, cayenne, and reserved pork. Bring to a boil, then reduce the heat to low and simmer, covered, 1 hour, stirring occasionally.

3. Remove and discard the cinnamon stick. Stir in the okra, re-cover, and cook 20 to 25 minutes if using fresh

okra or 15 minutes for frozen, until the okra is tender and the pork is cooked (no pink remains when tested) and tender. Adjust seasoning with black pepper and additional red pepper flakes; the stew should be peppery. Transfer to a warmed soup tureen or individual soup plates.

FREEZING TIPS

Follow the recipe. Let cool, wrap, seal, and label. Freeze up to 2 months.

To Serve: Thaw. Reheat gently over low heat, stirring occasionally until heated through.

COOK'S NOTE

This dish can be made up to 2 days in advance and refrigerated. Reheat gently over low heat, stirring occasionally, until heated through.

Sweet Potato and Ham Casserole

SERVES 4

Both the sweet potato and the yam (an unrelated tuber originating in Africa) have long been staple foods among the Southern states, where they are commonly used both in vegetable dishes and as the basis for pie. This traditional casserole, although sweet and with seasonings very similar to those used for sweet-potato or pumpkin pie, still appears as a favored main-course dish on tables throughout the South.

4 medium unpeeled sweet potatoes
1/2 cup maple syrup
1/2 teaspoon salt
1/2 teaspoon freshly ground pepper
2 eggs, lightly beaten
4 tablespoons (1/2 stick) unsalted butter or margarine, melted
1/4 cup milk
1/4 cup lowfat buttermilk

1-1/2 tablespoons bourbon
1/3 cup all-purpose flour
1/2 teaspoon ground cloves
1/2 teaspoon ground cinnamon
1/2 teaspoon grated orange zest
2 cups cooked ham, preferably Virginia ham, cut into 1/4-inch dice
1 cup finely chopped pecans

PREPARATION

1. Place the sweet potatoes in a 2- to 3-quart saucepan over high heat and add enough cold water to cover by 3 inches. Bring to a boil, then reduce the heat to medium and cook for about 25 minutes or until potatoes test tender when pierced with a fork. Drain, then rinse under cold running water and peel.

2. Transfer the sweet potatoes to a medium bowl and mash with a potato masher or fork. Measure 3-1/2 cups mashed sweet potatoes and reserve.

3. Preheat the oven to 350° F.

4. Combine the maple syrup, salt, pepper, eggs, butter, milk, buttermilk, bourbon, flour, cloves, cinnamon, orange zest, and ham with the mashed sweet potatoes. Stir until well blended. Ladle the mixture into a 13-by-9-by-2-inch baking dish.

5. Sprinkle the casserole with the pecans and bake for 35 to 40 minutes or until lightly browned. Serve hot directly from the baking dish.

Indonesian Pork Saté

Traditionally, saté (or satay) refers to a style of cooking: skewers of marinated beef, pork, or chicken are grilled, then dipped into a spicy peanut sauce. In this recipe the pork is braised, which makes it tender and succulent. I have tasted many types of meats paired with peanut sauces, and pork is definitely the winner!

1-1/2 tablespoons peanut oil or corn oil
2 medium cloves garlic, minced
1 medium yellow onion, minced
2 pounds lean boneless pork loin, trimmed and cut into 1/2-inch-wide strips
1 cup long-grain white rice
1 pound fresh spinach, stemmed and washed thoroughly
3/4 cup chunky peanut butter, preferably homemade, available at a health food store

1/4 cup canned coconut milk, available at a health food store, or cream of coconut
2 tablespoons dark sesame oil, available in Oriental markets or Oriental section of supermarket
3 tablespoons fresh lemon juice
1 tablespoon grated fresh ginger, or 1 teaspoon ground ginger
1/2 teaspoon dried hot red pepper flakes, crushed
Salt and freshly ground pepper to taste

PREPARATION

1. In a heavy 2- to 3-quart saucepan over medium-high heat, heat the oil. Add the garlic and onion and cook, stirring occasionally, for 3 to 4 minutes or until the onion is soft but not browned. Reduce the heat to medium-low. Add the pork and cook, covered, stirring occasionally, for 35 to 40 minutes or until the pork is cooked and there is no trace of pink when tested.

2. Raise the heat to medium-high, stir in the rice and 2 cups water, and bring to a boil. Reduce the heat to low and simmer, covered, for 20 to 25 minutes or until the rice is done and pork is tender, stirring once after 15 minutes.

3. Meanwhile, in another heavy 2- to 3-quart saucepan over medium-high heat, add the spinach and 1/4 cup water. Cook, covered, for 2 minutes or until the spinach is just wilted. Reduce the heat to low and stir in the peanut butter, coconut milk, sesame oil, lemon juice, ginger, and red pepper flakes. Cook, stirring, for 5 minutes. Season with salt and pepper.

4. To serve, transfer the pork mixture to a warmed serving platter, and the sauce to a warmed sauce-boat or small bowl. Serve immediately, passing the sauce separately.

Romanian Layered Pork and Noodle Casserole

SERVES 6

This layered pork dish is accented by the sweet green peas and by the flavors of fresh ginger and fennel. Everyone will fight over the crispy crust formed by the baked vermicelli.

8 ounces vermicelli (very thin spaghetti)
3 eggs, lightly beaten
3 medium cloves garlic, minced
1/2 teaspoon salt
1/4 teaspoon freshly ground pepper
1 cup shredded lowfat Gouda cheese or other lowfat cheese such as meunster or Monterey Jack
1 pound lean ground pork
2 medium yellow onions, finely chopped

2 medium carrots, grated
2 cups shelled fresh green peas, or 1 10-ounce package frozen, thawed
1 10-ounce package frozen chopped spinach, thawed and squeezed dry
3 tablespoons finely chopped fresh parsley, preferably Italian flat-leaf
1 cup finely chopped fresh fennel
1-1/2 teaspoons peeled fresh grated fresh gingerroot

PREPARATION

1. To prepare the pasta: To a 6- to 8-quart pot of boiling water, add the vermicelli and stir occasionally to separate. Return to a boil and boil for 4 to 5 minutes or until al dente (slightly firm to the bite). Drain.

2. Preheat the oven to 350° F. Liberally grease the bottom and sides of a deep 3- to 4-quart round ovenproof soufflé dish or casserole.

3. In a medium bowl beat together the eggs, garlic, salt, and pepper until just blended. Gently stir in the vermicelli and 1/2 cup of the cheese until the pasta is thoroughly coated. Reserve.

4. In another medium bowl combine the pork, onions, carrots, green peas, spinach, parsley, fennel, and ginger and mix with a fork until thoroughly blended.

5. Transfer one third of the pasta mixture to the bottom of the soufflé dish and spread evenly. Top with half the pork mixture. Repeat process with the second third of the pasta, the remaining pork mixture, and end with a layer of pasta. Sprinkle evenly with the remaining 1/2 cup of cheese.

6. Bake for 2-1/4 hours, or until there is no trace of pink when tested.

7. To serve, run a narrow spatula around the edge and sides of the casserole. Place a serving plate on top of the soufflé dish, and in one swift movement, holding the dish and plate together, invert both at once. Place the plate on the table and remove the dish. Serve immediately.

Biscuit-Topped Lamb Stew

SERVES 4, WITH 3 BISCUITS PER SERVING

Peppery sour-cream biscuits are the perfect complement to this slightly sweet and minty ragout-style stew. This recipe once again demonstrates the centuries-old affinity of lamb and mint.

STEW:
- 3 tablespoons all-purpose flour
- 1/4 teaspoon salt
- 1/2 teaspoon freshly ground pepper
- 2 pounds lean boneless lamb, preferably from the shoulder, trimmed and cut into 1-inch cubes
- 2 tablespoons safflower or olive oil
- 10 ounces mushrooms, preferably short-stem, wiped clean with a damp paper towel and trimmed, larger mushrooms quartered
- 1-3/4 cups beef stock (page 185-186) or canned low-sodium beef broth
- 1 10-ounce basket white pearl onions, peeled (for peeling hint, see page 48)
- 2 medium cloves garlic, minced
- 3 medium carrots, cut into 1/2-inch-thick slices
- 1/2 cup mint jelly
- 1/2 teaspoon dried thyme, crumbled
- Salt and freshly ground pepper to taste

BISCUITS:
- 1 cup all-purpose flour
- 2 teaspoons baking powder
- 1/2 teaspoon salt
- 1/4 teaspoon dried thyme, crumbled
- 3/4 teaspoon freshly ground pepper
- 1/3 cup unsalted butter or margarine, diced and chilled
- 1/2 cup sour cream or plain lowfat yogurt

PREPARATION

1. To prepare the stew: In a large bowl combine the flour, salt, and pepper and mix until well blended. Dredge the lamb in the flour mixture until evenly coated, shaking off excess flour.

2. In a heavy 6-quart ovenproof Dutch oven over medium-high heat, heat the oil. Add the mushrooms and cook, stirring occasionally, for 4 to 5 minutes or until lightly browned. Remove with a slotted spoon and transfer to a medium bowl and reserve. Add the lamb in batches and sear, turning often so cubes brown evenly on all sides, about 4 to 6 minutes per batch. Transfer the lamb to another medium bowl as it is browned.

3. Preheat the oven to 375° F.

4. Pour the stock into the Dutch oven (be careful—liquid may splatter) and stir, scraping up the browned bits from the bottom and around the sides of the Dutch oven. Add the onions, garlic, carrots, and lamb. Bring to a boil.

5. Remove the Dutch oven from the heat and stir in the mint jelly, thyme, and mushrooms. Cover and bake for 40 to 45 minutes or until the lamb is cooked (no trace of pink should remain when tested) and the vegetables are tender. Season with salt and pepper.

6. Meanwhile, make the biscuits: In a medium bowl combine the flour, baking powder, salt, thyme, and pepper. Using a pastry blender or fork, cut in the butter until the mixture has the consistency of coarse cornmeal. Stir in the sour cream until the dough holds together.

7. On a lightly floured work surface, knead the dough gently about 5 strokes. Pat or roll out to a uniform 1/4-inch thickness. Cut the dough into rounds using a floured 2-inch biscuit cutter. Reroll scraps of dough and repeat process until you have 12 rounds. Lightly wrap and refrigerate until ready to use.

8. Remove the Dutch oven from the oven and arrange the biscuits around the edge of the stew, leaving the center open; allow the edges of the biscuits to touch but not overlap. (*Note:* The biscuits should lie directly on top of the meat and vegetables, not in the broth, or the biscuits will become too soggy. If there is too much liquid in order to do this, place the Dutch oven over high heat and boil, uncovered, until liquid is about 1/2 inch below the meat and vegetables.) Bake, uncovered, for 20 to 25 minutes more or until the biscuits are lightly golden brown.

9. Serve at once, spooning the stew directly from the center of the Dutch oven into soup plates. Top with 3 biscuits per serving.

Moroccan-Style Lamb Stew

SERVES 6

Inspired by the flavors of Morocco, this lamb stew is an adventure for the senses, with its fruity orange juice, sweet, brightly colored apricots, and aromatic spices.

1/4 cup all-purpose flour
1/4 teaspoon salt
1/2 teaspoon freshly ground pepper
  2 pounds lean boneless lamb, preferably from the shoulder, trimmed and cut into 1-inch cubes
  2 tablespoons safflower oil or olive oil
  2 cups beef stock (page 185-186) or canned low-sodium beef broth
1/4 cup fresh orange juice

  2 medium boiling potatoes, cut into 1/2-inch dice
  3 medium carrots, cut into 1/4-inch-thick slices
1-1/2 cups pitted dried apricots, quartered
  2 tablespoons honey
  1 teaspoon ground coriander
  1 teaspoon ground allspice
  1 teaspoon ground ginger
1/2 teaspoon ground cumin
Salt and freshly ground pepper to taste

1. Preheat the oven to 350° F.

2. In a large bowl combine the flour, salt, and pepper and mix until well blended. Dredge the lamb in the flour mixture until evenly coated, shaking off excess flour.

3. In a heavy 3- to 4-quart flameproof casserole over medium-high heat, heat the oil. Add the lamb in batches and sear, turning often so cubes brown evenly on all sides, about 4 to 5 minutes per batch. Transfer the lamb to a medium bowl as it is browned.

4. Pour the stock into the casserole (be careful—liquid may splatter) and stir, scraping up the browned bits from the bottom and around the sides of the casserole. Stir in the orange juice, potatoes, carrots, apricots, honey, coriander, allspice, ginger, cumin, and lamb. Bring to a boil.

5. Remove the casserole from the heat, cover, and

bake for 1 hour or until the lamb is cooked (no trace of pink should remain when tested) and tender. Season with salt and pepper. Serve hot directly from the casserole.

FREEZING TIPS

Follow the recipe, let cool, wrap, seal, and label. Freeze up to 2 months.

To Serve: Thaw. Reheat gently over low heat, stirring occasionally until heated through.

COOK'S NOTE

This dish can be made up to 2 days ahead. Let cool, wrap, and refrigerate. Reheat gently over low heat, stirring occasionally until heated through.

Moussaka

SERVES 8

Feta is a tangy, crumbly cheese made from goat's or sheep's milk that is a staple of Greek cooking. Because it ripens in brine, feta tends to be salty, so I store it immersed in milk to help draw out some of the salt, then drain, rinse, and discard the soaking liquid. Since the eggplant slices are baked, not fried, this moussaka is made with far less oil than other versions.

FILLING:

- 3 medium eggplants, unpeeled, cut crosswise into 1/2-inch-thick slices
- 1 tablespoon olive oil, plus more to brush on eggplant
- 2 medium yellow onions, finely chopped
- 2 medium cloves garlic, minced
- 2 pounds lean ground lamb
- 1 16-ounce can Italian peeled whole plum tomatoes, drained and finely chopped
- 1 tablespoon tomato paste, preferably Italian
- 1/2 cup brandy
- 1 teaspoon ground cinnamon
- 1/2 teaspoon ground allspice
- 1 tablespoon finely chopped fresh oregano, or 1 teaspoon dried, crumbled
- 1/2 teaspoon salt
- 1/2 teaspoon freshly ground pepper
- 12 ounces feta cheese, rinsed and crumbled

TOPPING:

- 6 eggs
- 3 cups milk
- 1 cup plain lowfat yogurt
- 1/2 teaspoon ground nutmeg, preferably freshly grated
- 1/4 teaspoon grated orange zest

PREPARATION

1. To make the filling: Spread the eggplant on a work surface covered with paper towels. Lightly salt both sides of the slices and transfer them to a rack in a shallow baking pan. Cover the eggplant slices with more paper towels and place a heavy wooden cutting board on top as a weight. Let drain at least 30 minutes, preferably 1 hour.

2. Preheat the oven to 350°F.

3. Lightly rinse the eggplant slices and pat dry with paper towels. Lightly brush both sides of the eggplant slices with olive oil and transfer to 2 or 3 shallow baking pans, arranging them in a single layer so slices touch but do not overlap. Bake for 30 to 35 minutes or until tender when pierced with a fork and the edges are slightly puckered.

4. Meanwhile, in a large skillet over medium heat, heat the olive oil. Add the onions and garlic and cook, stirring often, for 3 to 4 minutes or until soft but not browned. Add the lamb and cook, breaking up the meat with the back of a wooden spoon, until no pink remains and lamb begins to brown, about 7 to 9 minutes. Carefully pour off excess fat.

5. Return the skillet to medium heat and stir in the tomatoes, tomato paste, brandy, cinnamon, allspice, oregano, salt, and pepper. Cook for 10 minutes more. Remove the skillet from the heat and stir in the feta cheese. Reserve until ready to use.

6. Lightly grease a shallow 4- to 6-quart baking dish, preferably an oval, earthenware dish. Arrange half the eggplant slices in a single layer, working in one direction and overlapping them. Ladle all of the lamb mixture on top of the eggplant. Top with remaining eggplant slices. (This recipe can be prepared up to this point 1 day ahead. Let cool, wrap and refrigerate. Bring to room temperature before proceeding.)

7. To make the topping: In a small bowl whisk together the eggs, milk, yogurt, nutmeg, and orange zest until well blended. Gradually pour over the eggplant slices.

8. Bake for 50 to 60 minutes or until the custard is set.

9. To serve, let stand for 10 minutes, then serve directly from the baking dish.

Spicy Lamb Bobotie

Bobotie is a curried lamb dish, supposedly of Malayan origin, made with fruit. In this adaptation, which is spicy but not hot, I have used mango chutney, currants, and orange zest.

FILLING:
- 3 slices white bread, crusts trimmed, cut into 1/2-inch cubes
- 1/2 cup skim milk
- 2 tablespoons olive oil
- 1 medium yellow onion, finely chopped
- 1/4 cup fresh lemon juice
- 3 tablespoons curry powder
- 1 tablespoon firmly packed dark brown sugar
- 1/2 teaspoon salt
- 1 teaspoon freshly ground black pepper
- 2 pounds lean ground lamb
- 1/2 cup mango chutney
- 2 medium carrots, shredded
- 2 cups cooked long-grain white rice (made from 2/3 cup raw rice)
- 1/3 cup dried currants or seedless raisins
- 1 tablespoon grated orange zest
- 1 egg, lightly beaten

CUSTARD:
- 2 eggs
- 2 cups plain lowfat yogurt
- 2 medium cloves garlic, minced
- 1/4 teaspoon salt
- 1/4 teaspoon freshly ground white pepper
- 1/2 cup blanched, slivered almonds

PREPARATION

1. Preheat the oven to 375° F. In a small bowl combine the diced bread and milk and let soak until ready to use.

2. To make the filling: In a large heavy skillet over medium-high heat, heat the olive oil. Add the onion and cook, stirring often, for 3 to 4 minutes or until soft but not browned. Stir in the lemon juice, curry powder, brown sugar, salt, and black pepper. Cook, stirring constantly, for 1 minute more.

3. Add the lamb, breaking it up with a wooden spoon. Cook, stirring often, for 7 to 9 minutes or until lamb begins to brown. Stir in the chutney, carrots, rice, currants, orange zest, egg, and the bread and milk mixture until well blended. Using a slotted spoon, spoon the lamb mixture into a 13-by-9-by-2-inch baking dish, smoothing the top with a spatula. (This recipe can be made up to this point 1 day ahead. Let cool, wrap, and refrigerate. Bring to room temperature before proceeding with recipe.)

4. To make the custard: In a medium bowl whisk together the eggs with the yogurt, garlic, salt, and white pepper until well blended.

5. Pour the custard mixture evenly over the lamb. Sprinkle evenly with the slivered almonds. Bake for 50 to 60 minutes or until the custard is set. Let stand for 5 minutes before serving. Serve hot directly from the baking dish.

Pasta, Grains, and Beans

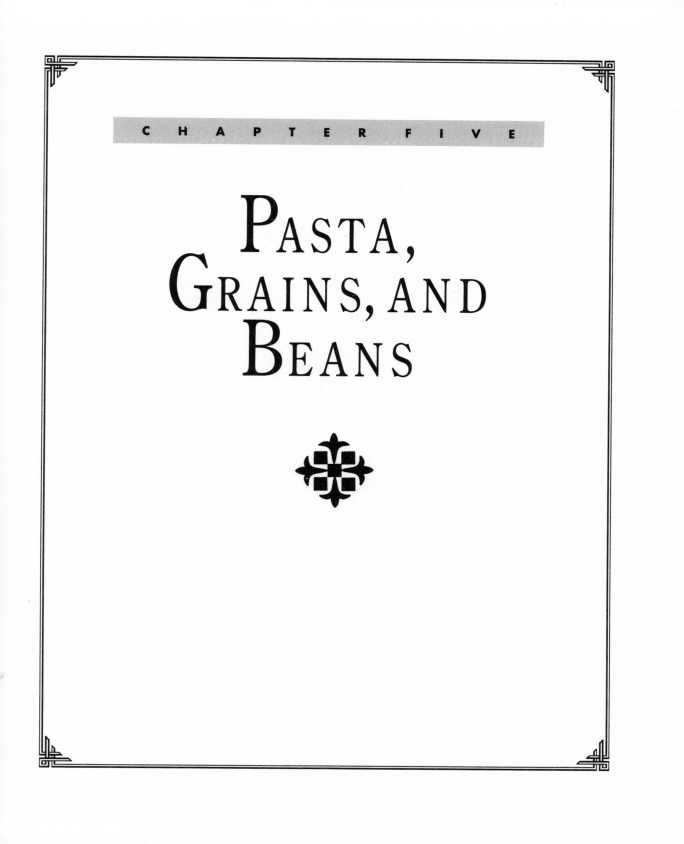

Pesto Minestrone

SERVES 8

Minestrone literally means "a big soup." Usually made with beef stock, this recipe uses a hearty vegetable stock instead. In this recipe, a spoonful of pesto in each bowl adds the characteristic flavor of Genoa.

SOUP:

- 2 tablespoons unsalted butter or margarine
- 1 medium red onion, finely chopped
- 2 medium carrots, cut into 1/4-inch dice
- 3 ribs celery, finely chopped
- 2 medium cloves garlic, minced
- 1 cup finely chopped fresh fennel
- 2 quarts vegetable stock (page 184) or water
- 1 large ripe tomato, seeded, and coarsely chopped
- 1/2 medium head green cabbage, tough outer leaves removed, cored and shredded
- 1 pound butternut squash, peeled and cut into 1/2-inch dice
- 2 medium red or yellow bell peppers, cored, seeded, and coarsely chopped
- 2 medium zucchini, thinly sliced
- 1 cup tubetti or other small pasta such as rotini (corkscrews) or elbow macaroni
- 1 15-1/2-ounce can cannellini beans, drained and rinsed
- 1 recipe Pesto (page 139)

PREPARATION

1. In a heavy 6- to 8-quart pot over medium-high heat, melt the butter. Add the onion, carrots, celery, garlic, and fennel. Cook, stirring often, about 7 to 8 minutes or until the vegetables are soft but not browned.

2. Stir in the stock. Raise heat to high and bring to a boil. Reduce the heat to low and stir in the tomato, cabbage, butternut squash, bell peppers, zucchini, and pasta. Simmer, stirring occasionally, for 5 to 6 minutes or until the vegetables are just tender and the pasta is al dente (slightly firm to the bite).

3. Stir in the cannellini beans and simmer for 1 to 2 minutes more or until the beans are just heated through. (This recipe can be prepared to this point up to 2 days ahead. Let cool, cover, and refrigerate.

Gently reheat over low heat, stirring often, and proceed with recipe.)

4. To serve, transfer to a warmed soup tureen, and pass the pesto separately.

FREEZING TIPS

Follow the minestrone recipe through step 2. Let cool, wrap, seal, and label. Freeze up to 3 months.

Pesto freezes well too. Prepare the entire recipe and spoon into a small freezer container, seal, and label. Freeze up to 2 months.

To Serve. Thaw. Reheat vegetables (not pesto) gently over low heat, stirring occasionally, until heated through. Follow step 3 and serve according to step 4.

PESTO
MAKES 1 CUP

4 medium cloves garlic
1/4 cup pine nuts (pignoli)
3 bunches fresh basil stemmed
1/2 cup freshly grated Parmesan cheese
1/4 cup freshly grated Romano cheese
1/2 cup olive oil
Salt and freshly ground pepper to taste

1. In a bowl of a food processor fitted with a metal blade or in a blender, pulse the garlic and pine nuts for about 1 minute or until very finely chopped. Add the basil, Parmesan and Romano cheese, and process until well blended, scraping down the sides of the bowl as necessary.

2. With the machine running, gradually pour in the olive oil through the feed tube in a slow steady stream until completely incorporated, scraping down the sides of the bowl as necessary. Season with salt and pepper.

Quintessential Macaroni and Cheese
SERVES 4

This perennial favorite may not be fancy or sophisticated, but it's always a crowd-pleaser!

8 ounces elbow macaroni
Olive oil

SAUCE:
3 tablespoons unsalted butter or margarine
3 tablespoons all-purpose flour

2-1/2 cups milk, heated
2 cups shredded extra-sharp Cheddar cheese
1/4 teaspoon ground nutmeg, preferably freshly grated
1/8 teaspoon cayenne pepper
Salt and freshly ground pepper to taste

PREPARATION

1. Preheat the oven to 375° F.

2. To a 6- to 8-quart pot of boiling water, add the elbow macaroni and stir occasionally. Return to a boil and boil for 5 minutes or until al dente (slightly firm to the bite). Drain and transfer to a 13-by-9-by-2-inch baking dish, toss lightly with some olive oil, and reserve at room temperature.

3. To make the sauce: In a heavy 2- to 3-quart saucepan over low heat, melt the butter. Add the flour, and whisk until large bubbles appear, about 3 minutes. Cook for 2 minutes more, whisking constantly; do not let the roux brown. Remove the saucepan from the heat and gradually pour in the hot milk, whisking constantly across the bottom and along the sides of the saucepan until blended and smooth. Return the saucepan to low heat and stir constantly until thickened, about 4 to 5 minutes.

4. Stir in the Cheddar cheese until just melted and smooth. Do not let the sauce come to a simmer. Stir in the nutmeg and cayenne, and season with salt and pepper.

5. Combine the sauce with the macaroni in the bak-ing dish and gently toss until the macaroni is well coated. (This recipe can be made up to this point 1 day ahead. Let cool, wrap, and refrigerate. Bring to room temperature and stir gently before proceeding with recipe.)

6. Bake for 30 to 40 minutes or until bubbly and the top is golden brown. Serve hot directly from the baking dish.

Macaroni and Cheese Deluxe

SERVES 4

Family and friends will rave over this updated classic made with Gorgonzola, a sweet, creamy blue cheese. Not only is this dish delicious, but it is red, white, and green—the colors of the Italian flag!

8 ounces fusilli (corkscrew-shaped pasta)
Olive oil
1 medium green bell pepper, cored, seeded, and finely chopped
1 medium red bell pepper, cored, seeded, and finely chopped

SAUCE:
2 tablespoons unsalted butter or margarine
2 tablespoons all-purpose flour

1-1/2 cups milk, heated
1/2 cup dry white wine
2 ounces Gorgonzola dolce (sweet Italian blue cheese), crumbled
4 ounces Asiago (Italian hard cheese), grated
4 ounces Fontina D'Aosta (Italian Fontina cheese), shredded
1/2 teaspoon celery seeds
Salt and freshly ground white pepper to taste

PREPARATION

1. Preheat the oven to 375° F.

2. To a 6- to 8-quart pot of boiling water, add the fusilli and stir occasionally. Return to a boil and boil for 5 to 7 minutes or until al dente (slightly firm to the bite). Drain and transfer to a 13-by-9-by-2-inch baking dish and toss lightly with some olive oil. Stir in the green and red bell peppers. Reserve at room temperature.

3. To make the sauce: In a heavy 2- to 3-quart saucepan over low heat, melt the butter. Add the flour, and whisk until large bubbles appear, about 3 minutes. Cook for 2 minutes more, whisking constantly; do not let the roux brown. Remove the saucepan from the heat and gradually pour in the hot milk, whisking constantly across the bottom and along the sides of the saucepan until blended and smooth. Return the saucepan to low heat and stir constantly, about 4 to 5 minutes or until slightly thickened. Stir in the wine and cook for 2 minutes more, stirring constantly until thickened.

4. Remove the saucepan from the heat. Stir in the Gorgonzola, Asiago, and Fontina cheese until just melted and smooth. Stir in the celery seeds and season with salt and pepper.

5. Ladle the sauce over the pasta mixture in the baking dish and toss gently until pasta is well coated. (This recipe can be made up to this point 1 day ahead. Let cool, wrap, and refrigerate. Bring to room temperature and stir gently before proceeding with recipe.)

6. Bake for 30 to 40 minutes or until bubbly and the top is golden brown. Serve directly from the baking dish.

Papajohn's Pastitsio

SERVES 6

My friend Michèle grew up with her father's famous pastitsio. Until now, the recipe has been a secret known only to its creator. Roger Papajohn was kind enough to reveal to us his beloved recipe for this Greek pasta dish, which is steeped in Middle Eastern tradition. We all thank you, Roger.

FILLING:

   1 *pound ziti or other medium-sized,*
     shaped pasta
Olive Oil
   2 *tablespoons olive oil*
   1 *medium clove garlic, minced*
   1 *medium yellow onion, finely chopped*
   1 *pound extra-lean ground beef*
   1 *teaspoon salt*
1/2 *teaspoon freshly ground pepper*
   1 *tablespoon dried mint, crumbled*
   1 *teaspoon dried oregano, crumbled*
   1 *teaspoon ground cinnamon*
   1 *cup freshly grated Parmesan cheese or*
     Romano cheese

SAUCE:

   4 *tablespoons (1/2 stick) unsalted butter*
     or margarine
   6 *tablespoons all-purpose flour*
   4 *cups milk, heated*
   2 *egg yolks, lightly beaten, at room temperature*
1/4 *teaspoon salt*
1/8 *teaspoon freshly ground white pepper*
1/8 *teaspoon ground nutmeg, preferably freshly*
     grated
   2 *tablespoons freshly grated Parmesan cheese*

1. To make the filling: To a 6- to 8-quart pot of boiling water, add the ziti, stirring often. Return to a boil and cook for 5 to 6 minutes or until just al dente (slightly firm to the bite). Drain, toss with a little olive oil and set aside to cool.

2. In a large skillet over medium-high heat, heat the 2 tablespoons olive oil, add the garlic and onion, and cook 3 to 4 minutes, stirring often, until onion is soft but not browned. Add the ground beef, breaking it up with the back of a wooden spoon, and cook 3 to 4 minutes, just until the meat begins to brown. Carefully pour off the fat.

3. Add the salt, pepper, mint, oregano, cinnamon, and Parmesan cheese. Cook, stirring, 2 minutes more. Set aside until ready to use.

4. Lightly grease the bottom and sides of a 13-by-9-by-2-inch baking dish. Spread half the cooked ziti in neat side-by-side rows, going in one direction; this will allow the pastitsio to cut neatly. Carefully cover them with all the meat mixture; then top with remaining ziti, arranging them in the same direction in neat rows. Set aside until ready to use. (This recipe can be prepared up to this point 1 day ahead. Let cool, wrap and refrigerate. Bring to room temperature before proceeding with recipe.)

5. Preheat the oven to 350° F.

6. To make the sauce: In a 2- to 3-quart saucepan over low heat, melt the butter, then whisk in the flour until large bubbles appear, about 3 minutes. Cook, whisking constantly, 2 minutes more; do not let the roux brown. Remove the saucepan from the heat and gradually add the hot milk, whisking constantly over the bottom and sides of the saucepan until well blended and smooth. Return saucepan to low heat and cook, whisking constantly, 3 to 4 minutes more or until slightly thickened.

7. Whisk one third of the milk mixture into the beaten eggs and then whisk mixture back into the saucepan. Cook, stirring vigorously, 3 minutes; the sauce will already be very thick. Do not let the sauce boil. Stir in the salt, pepper, and nutmeg.

8. Ladle the sauce evenly over the ziti, starting from one end and working your way to the opposite, spreading with a spoon as you pour. (*Note:* Ziti must be completely covered by sauce or the exposed pasta will burn.) Gently tap bottom of the dish against the kitchen counter to help pasta settle. Sprinkle with Parmesan cheese.

9. Bake for 50 to 60 minutes or until top is a light golden brown. Let stand 15 minutes before serving. To serve, cut into squares and transfer to a warmed serving platter.

Linguine al Ragù Bolognese

SERVES 6
MAKES 7 CUPS SAUCE

In Italy, a ragù is a thick, long-simmered meat and tomato sauce, and one of the best versions comes from Bologna. It takes a long time to cook, but those hours on the stove are critical to the rich flavor of this sauce. It's important not to "oversauce" the pasta; you want a proper balance of flavor and texture. A hearty red wine is the perfect accompaniment to this meal, with possibly a salad afterward.

BOLOGNESE SAUCE:
- *2 tablespoons olive oil*
- *3 medium cloves garlic, minced*
- *1 medium yellow onion, minced*
- *2 ribs celery, minced*
- *3 medium carrots, minced*
- *8 ounces extra-lean ground beef*
- *8 ounces extra-lean ground veal*
- *4 ounces lean ground pork*
- *2 cups beef stock (page 185-186) or canned low-sodium beef broth*
- *1 28-ounce can peeled whole Italian plum tomatoes, crushed, with their juice*
- *1/3 cup dry sherry*
- *3 tablespoons tomato paste, preferably Italian*
- *2 teaspoons dried marjoram, crumbled*
- *1/2 teaspoon ground nutmeg, preferably freshly grated*
- *2 chicken livers (about 2 ounces), rinsed, dried, and finely chopped*
- *1/4 cup half-and-half*
- *Salt and freshly ground pepper to taste*

PASTA:
- *1-1/2 pounds linguine*
- *Freshly grated Parmesan cheese*

PREPARATION

1. To make the sauce: In a heavy 6- to 8-quart pot over medium-high heat, heat the olive oil. Add the garlic, onion, celery, and carrots and cook, stirring often, for 7 to 8 minutes or until the vegetables are soft but not browned.

2. Stir in the beef, veal, and pork. Cook, stirring, breaking up the ground meats with the back of a wooden spoon, for 5 to 7 minutes or just until there is no trace of pink.

3. Stir in the stock, tomatoes, sherry, tomato paste, marjoram, and nutmeg. Bring to a boil. Reduce the heat to low and simmer partially covered, stirring occasionally, for 3-1/2 to 4 hours, or until the sauce has thickened, barely any liquid remains, and the flavors are well blended.

4. Stir in the chicken livers and half-and-half and simmer, uncovered, for 10 minutes more, stirring often. Season with salt and pepper.

5. Force the warm sauce in batches through the medium blade of a food mill into a large bowl until pureed. Alternatively, process in batches in the bowl of a food processor fitted with a metal blade until pureed. (This recipe can be prepared to this point up to 2 days ahead. Let cool, wrap, and refrigerate. Reheat gently over very low heat before serving.)

6. Return the pureed sauce to the pot and keep warm over very low heat until the pasta is cooked.

7. Meanwhile, to prepare the pasta: To a 6- to 8-quart pot of boiling water, add the linguine. Return to a boil, stirring the pasta occasionally, and cook for 7 to 9 minutes or until al dente (slightly firm to the bite). Drain, transfer to a warmed serving platter, and top with the sauce. Serve immediately. Pass the grated Parmesan cheese separately.

FREEZING TIPS

Follow the recipe through step 5. Let cool, wrap, seal, and label. Freeze up to 1 month.

To Serve: Thaw. Reheat gently over low heat, stirring occasionally until heated through. Proceed with step 7.

COOK'S NOTE

When purchasing chicken livers, look for livers that are odor-free and firm, not spongy. Chicken livers are very perishable and should be used the day of purchase. If a liver is tinged with yellow or green, discard it.

Doubly Delicious Meat Lasagne with Tomato-Olive Sauce

SERVES 8 TO 10

Though meat lasagne would seem to be familiar territory, the time-worn adage,
"if you've tasted one, you've tasted them all" is definitely not true here. This recipe is fortified
with both a Bolognese sauce and a lemony, olive-flecked tomato sauce.
One plateful and you'll be back for more!

LASAGNE:

1 pound curly-edged lasagne noodles
Olive oil
1 cup freshly grated Parmesan or Romano
  cheese
12 ounces part skim-milk mozzarella cheese,
  shredded
2 cups part skim-milk ricotta cheese
1 recipe Bolognese Sauce (page 143)

TOMATO-OLIVE SAUCE:
MAKES 4 CUPS

1 28-ounce can whole peeled Italian plum
  tomatoes, crushed, including their juice
1 medium carrot, grated
1 medium yellow onion
2 medium cloves garlic, minced
1/2 teaspoon grated lemon zest
1-1/2 teaspoons finely chopped fresh oregano,
  or 1 teaspoon dried, crumbled
1/2 cup drained Gaeta (Italian) olives or
  other brine-cured olives, rinsed, pitted,
  and halved lengthwise
Salt and freshly ground pepper to taste

PREPARATION

1. To prepare the lasagne: To a 10- to 12-quart stockpot of boiling water, add the lasagne noodles. Return to a boil, stirring occasionally. Cook for 7 to 9 minutes or until al dente (slightly firm to the bite). Drain, rinse briefly under cold running water, and lightly toss with some olive oil. Reserve at room temperature until ready to use.

2. Preheat the oven to 375° F.

3. To prepare the sauce: In a heavy 2- to 3-quart saucepan over medium-high heat, add the tomatoes, carrot, onion, garlic, lemon zest, oregano, and olives. Bring to a boil, then reduce the heat to medium-low and simmer, stirring occasionally, for 15 minutes or until the carrot is very tender. Season with salt and pepper and reserve until ready to use.

4. Ladle one third of the tomato-olive sauce evenly over the bottom of a 13-by-9-by-2-inch baking dish. Arrange one third of the lasagne noodles in a flat double layer, parallel to the longer side of the baking dish.

Sprinkle with half the Parmesan cheese and half the mozzarella cheese. Dot with half the ricotta cheese, then spread with half the Bolognese Sauce. Arrange the second third of the noodles in a flat double layer, spread with the second third of the tomato sauce, and dot with the remaining ricotta. Spread with the remaining Bolognese sauce. Spread with the remaining lasagne noodles, gently pressing down with your palms to flatten. Drizzle with the remaining tomato-olive sauce and sprinkle with the remaining Parmesan and mozzarella. (This recipe can be prepared to this point up to 2 days ahead. Let cool, wrap, and refrigerate. Bring to room temperature before proceeding.)

5. Bake for 1-1/2 hours or until cheese is bubbling and top is golden brown. (*Note:* If the top browns more than to your taste, cover loosely with aluminum foil and continue baking until done.) Let stand for 10 minutes before serving.

6. To serve, cut the lasagne into 8 or 10 equal portions and serve hot directly from the baking dish.

Vegetarian Lasagne

SERVES 8 TO 10

Slice into this pasta creation and you will discover vivid layers of crisp-tender carrots, mushrooms, red bell pepper, and zucchini, plus the old favorites—ricotta and mozzarella. All are nestled in the curves of tender spinach pasta ribbons.

LASAGNE:

1 pound curly-edged spinach lasagne noodles (whole-wheat lasagne noodles, also available at specialty food shops and Italian grocery stores, are a tasty alternative)

Olive oil

2 cups part skim-milk ricotta cheese

1 cup freshly grated Parmesan cheese or Romano cheese

12 ounces part skim-milk mozzarella cheese, shredded

FILLINGS:

4 eggs, lightly beaten

1 cup plain lowfat yogurt

8 tablespoons (1 stick) unsalted butter or margarine, melted

1 tablespoon finely chopped fresh thyme, or 2 teaspoons dried, crumbled

1/2 teaspoon salt

1/2 teaspoon freshly ground white pepper

4 cups 1/2-inch cubes cut from fresh bread, preferably Italian semolina bread (about half a 13-ounce loaf)

4 medium carrots, cut into 1/2-inch julienne, steamed until just tender

3 medium zucchini, cut into 1/2-inch julienne, steamed until just tender

10 ounces mushrooms, preferably short-stem, wiped clean with a damp paper towel, trimmed, and minced

2 medium red bell peppers, cored, seeded, and finely chopped

SAUCE:

1 recipe Tomato-Olive Sauce (page 145)

PREPARATION

1. To prepare the lasagne: To a 10- to 12-quart stockpot of boiling water, add the lasagne noodles. Return to a boil, stirring occasionally, and cook for 7 to 9 minutes or until al dente (slightly firm to the bite). Drain, rinse briefly under cold running water, and toss lightly with some olive oil. Reserve at room temperature until ready to use.

2. Preheat the oven to 375°F.

3. To prepare the fillings: In a large bowl combine the eggs, yogurt, melted butter, thyme, salt, and pepper. Stir in the diced bread until well blended. Divide the mixture equally between two large bowls. Stir the steamed carrots and zucchini into one bowl, the mushrooms and bell peppers into the second bowl.

4. Ladle half the Tomato-Olive Sauce evenly over

the bottom of a 13-by-9-by-2-inch baking dish. Arrange one third of the lasagne noodles in a flat double layer going in one direction, parallel to the longer side of the dish. Dot with half the ricotta cheese. Sprinkle with one third of the Parmesan cheese and one third of the mozzarella cheese. Spread with all of the mushroom-pepper filling. Arrange the second third of the noodles in a flat double layer. Dot with the remaining ricotta. Sprinkle with the second third of the Parmesan and second third of the mozzarella. Spread with all the carrot-zucchini filling. Arrange the remaining lasagne noodles, gently pressing down with your palms to flatten. Top with the remaining tomato sauce and the remaining Parmesan and mozzarella. (This recipe can be prepared to this point up to 2 days ahead. Let cool, wrap, and refrigerate. Bring to room temperature before proceeding.)

5. Bake for 1-1/2 hours or until the cheese is bubbling and the top is golden brown. (*Note:* If the top browns more than to your taste, cover loosely with aluminum foil and continue baking until done.) Let stand for 10 minutes before serving.

6. To serve, cut the lasagne into 8 or 10 equal portions and serve hot directly from the baking dish.

The Ultimate Spaghetti and Meatballs

SERVES 4 TO 6

My first plate of spaghetti with meatballs was served to me at a friend's birthday party, amidst balloons and party hats, in the middle of a raucous round of "pin the tail on the donkey." There it was, glorious spaghetti that seemed to have no end, an entangled mass that went on . . . forever, and all of it drenched in a zesty tomato sauce. I don't think I ever did finish that plate of spaghetti and meatballs, but here are the makings of some other child's fondest memories.

MEATBALLS:
1 pound extra-lean ground beef
1 egg, lightly beaten
1/2 cup unseasoned dried bread crumbs
1/4 cup skim milk
1 medium yellow onion, minced
1 medium clove garlic, minced
2 tablespoons finely chopped fresh parsley, preferably Italian flat-leaf
1 tablespoon finely chopped fresh oregano, or 1 teaspoon dried, crumbled

1/2 teaspoon salt
1/4 teaspoon freshly ground pepper
1/2 teaspoon paprika, preferably Hungarian semisweet (See page 30)
2 tablespoons olive oil
4 cups tomato sauce, preferably homemade

PASTA:
1 pound spaghetti
Freshly grated Parmesan cheese or Romano cheese

1. To prepare the meatballs: In a medium bowl combine the beef, egg, bread crumbs, skim milk, onion, garlic, parsley, oregano, salt, pepper, and paprika and mix thoroughly. Using your hands, spoon a tablespoon of the mixture and shape into tight balls about 1 inch in diameter. There should be about 3-1/2 dozen meatballs.

2. In a large heavy skillet over medium-high heat, heat the olive oil and add the meatballs in batches. Cook each batch, turning meatballs frequently so they brown evenly, about 4 to 6 minutes. Transfer meatballs to a large bowl as they are browned and reserve.

3. Meanwhile, in a 2- to 3-quart saucepan over medium heat, heat the tomato sauce, stirring occasionally. Reduce the heat to low, add the meatballs, and simmer, occasionally stirring gently, for 10 minutes or until the meatballs are cooked and there is no trace of pink when tested. Keep warm over a very low flame, occasionally stirring gently, until ready to serve.

4. To prepare the pasta: To a 6- to 8-quart pot of boiling water, add the spaghetti. Return to a boil, stirring occasionally, and cook for 7 to 9 minutes or until al dente (slightly firm to the bite). Drain, transfer to a warmed serving platter, and top with the tomato sauce and meatballs. Pass the grated Parmesan cheese separately.

Risotto with Wild Mushrooms and Asparagus

SERVES 4

Risotto is one of the most famous of all Italian dishes. It is an extremely versatile dish, allowing for the addition of many different ingredients. Although it is not difficult to prepare, it must be stirred constantly to attain the proper consistency. The texture of the cooked rice should be tender and creamy, not dry or sticky. I think it is imperative to use Arborio, an Italian short-grain rice available in specialty food stores and Italian markets, and frequently in supermarkets. Risotto can also be made successfully in a microwave (page 149). This is one of the few recipes in which I do not recommend substituting margarine for the butter.

1 ounce dried porcini (wild mushrooms)
3 tablespoons unsalted butter
1 medium yellow onion, minced
1 cup Arborio rice
1-1/2 cups chicken stock (page 186-187) or
    canned low-sodium chicken broth, heated

1/2 cup dry white wine, heated
8 ounces asparagus, cut into 1-inch-long pieces,
    steamed until just tender
2 tablespoons unsalted butter
1/2 cup freshly grated Parmesan cheese
Salt and freshly ground pepper to taste

PREPARATION

1. Soak the dried mushrooms in 1 cup boiling water until soft, at least 20 minutes, preferably 30. Remove mushrooms and discard any woody stems. Strain the soaking liquid through a paper-towel-lined sieve (squeeze the towel when done to obtain all liquid) and reserve. Finely chop the mushrooms and reserve.

2. In a heavy 3- to 4-quart saucepan over medium-high heat, melt the butter. Add the onion and cook, stirring often, 3 to 4 minutes or until soft but not browned. Stir in the rice and cook, stirring often, 2 minutes or until well coated.

3. Stir in 1/2 cup of the hot stock, the hot wine, and the reserved mushrooms and their soaking liquid. Cook, stirring often, 4 to 5 minutes or until the liquid has been completely absorbed.

4. Reduce the heat to medium. Add 1/2 cup hot stock and cook, stirring often, about 5 minutes or until most of the liquid has been absorbed, all but a few tablespoons. Repeat the process of adding stock in 1/2 cup amounts and then cooking, stirring frequently, until it is nearly absorbed. This will take a total of about 20 to 25 minutes cooking time. The rice should be creamy and al dente (slightly firm to the bite). (*Note:* Each addition of stock will take slightly longer to be absorbed. The more the rice cooks, the longer it takes to absorb liquid.)

5. Remove the saucepan from the heat and stir in the asparagus pieces, butter, and Parmesan cheese. Cook, stirring often, about 2 minutes or until the butter is melted and the asparagus pieces are heated through. (*Note:* The butter should just melt; do not allow it to cook.) Season with salt and pepper.

6. To serve, transfer to a warmed serving platter and serve immediately.

TO MICROWAVE

In an 8- or 9-inch-square microproof dish, heat the butter, uncovered, on HIGH 1 minute. Add the onion and rice and stir to coat. Microcook on HIGH, uncovered, for 2 minutes more. Stir in the stock, wine, and reserved mushrooms and microcook, uncovered, on HIGH 16 minutes, stirring once after 8 minutes. Let stand, covered, for 3 minutes. Stir in the steamed asparagus, butter, and Parmesan cheese and season with salt and pepper. Serve immediately.

COOK'S NOTE

Never rinse Arborio rice before cooking.

The King of Jambalaya

I like to believe the origin of jambalaya is as John F. Mariani describes it in *The Dictionary of American Food and Drink* (1983): According to legend, a gentleman stopped at a Louisiana inn very late one evening to have dinner. Finding that there was no food left to eat, the owner of the inn instructed the cook, whose name was Jean, to *balayez*, which translates as "mix some things together." Upon tasting the dish, the appreciative guest not only proclaimed it delectable, but named it "Jean Balayez."

2 tablespoons bacon fat or corn oil or safflower oil

2 medium yellow onions, finely chopped

2 medium cloves garlic, minced

1 medium green bell pepper, cored, seeded, and finely chopped

1 pound chorizo (spicy Spanish sausage) or hot Italian sausage, thinly sliced

1 pound skinless, boneless chicken breasts, cut into 1-1/2-inch-wide strips

4 ounces cooked reduced-sodium ham, cut into 1/2-inch dice

2 tablespoons all-purpose flour

3 medium-sized ripe tomatoes, seeded and coarsely chopped

3 cups chicken stock (page 186-187) or canned low-sodium chicken broth

1 teaspoon finely chopped fresh thyme, or 1/2 teaspoon dried, crumbled

2 cups long-grain white rice

8 ounces medium shrimp, shelled and deveined, and rinsed thoroughly

2 or 3 dashes Tabasco sauce, or more to taste

Salt and freshly ground pepper to taste

PREPARATION

1. In a heavy 6- to 8-quart pot over high heat, heat the bacon fat. Add the onions, garlic, bell pepper, sausage, chicken, and ham and cook, stirring often, for 5 to 6 minutes or until the chicken is lightly browned. Using a slotted spoon, transfer ingredients to a medium bowl and reserve.

2. Stir the flour into the fat remaining in the pot and cook, stirring vigorously, for 3 to 4 minutes or until the roux has turned an orangy-brown (similar in color to peanut butter).

3. Reduce the heat to low. Stir in the reserved veg-etable and meat mixture, the tomatoes, stock, and thyme. Cover tightly and simmer for 30 minutes.

4. Add the rice, re-cover, and cook undisturbed for 20 to 25 minutes more, or until the rice is tender but not mushy and the chicken and sausage is cooked (showing no trace of pink when tested).

5. Remove the pot from the heat and stir in the shrimp until completely covered by the rice. Let stand, covered, for 3 minutes more or until the shrimp turn pink. Season with Tabasco, salt, and pepper.

Tuscan White Bean Soup with Rosemary

SERVES 4

The Tuscans are known as *mangiafagioli:* bean-eaters. They adore beans and pay tribute with a variety of recipes that attest to their devotion. Cannellini beans make a spectacular soup, and the addition of Parmesan cheese and rosemary enhance their delicate flavor and light, almost fluffy texture.

1 *pound dried cannellini (white beans), picked over*
2 *tablespoons olive oil or safflower oil*
2 *medium yellow onions, minced*
3 *ribs celery, minced*
4 *cups chicken stock (page 186-187) or canned low-sodium chicken broth*
1/2 *cup skim milk*

2 *tablespoons freshly grated Parmesan cheese or Romano cheese*
1/2 *teaspoon dried rosemary, crushed and soaked in 1 tablespoon warm water*
1/4 *cup finely chopped fresh parsley, preferably Italian flat-leaf*
Salt and freshly ground pepper to taste

PREPARATION

1. Soak the cannellini in cold water to cover by 2 inches overnight, covered, at room temperature. Drain and rinse. Alternatively, place the beans in a heavy 3- to 4-quart saucepan over medium-high heat with enough cold water to cover by 2 inches and bring to a boil. Remove the saucepan from the heat, cover, and let stand for 1 hour. Drain the beans and rinse under cold running water.

2. In a heavy 6- to 8-quart pot over medium heat, heat the olive oil. Stir in the onions and celery and cook, stirring often, for 4 to 5 minutes or until the vegetables are soft but not browned.

3. Raise the heat to high. Stir in the stock (be careful—liquid may splatter), 2 cups water, and the beans. Bring to a boil, then reduce the heat to low and simmer, partially covered, stirring occasionally,

for 40 to 45 minutes, or until the beans are very tender but still hold their shape.

4. Using a slotted spoon, transfer half the warm bean mixture to a food mill fitted with a fine blade, and force through into a large bowl. Alternatively, transfer half the warm bean mixture to the bowl of a food processor fitted with a metal blade and process until pureed. Return the bean puree to the pot with the remaining beans. (This recipe can be prepared to this point up to 3 days ahead. Let cool, cover, and refrigerate. Bring to room temperature before proceeding.)

5. Return the pot to low heat and stir in the milk, Parmesan cheese, rosemary, and parsley. Season with salt and pepper.

6. To serve, transfer to a warmed soup tureen or individual soup bowls.

Best-Ever Red Beans and Rice

SERVES 8 TO 10

This traditional Louisiana dish is customarily served on Monday after a Sunday feast of ham, so that the ham bone may be used to flavor the beans. I prefer using red chili rather than kidney beans and baking rather than boiling them, to obtain a creamier texture.

1 pound dried red chili beans or red kidney beans, picked over
8 strips lean slab bacon
2 medium yellow onions, finely chopped
3 medium cloves garlic, minced
2 medium green bell peppers, cored, seeded, and finely chopped
1/4 cup unsulfured blackstrap molasses
3-1/2 tablespoons white vinegar

3 tablespoons finely chopped fresh chives, or more to taste
1 tablespoon finely chopped fresh thyme, or 2 teaspoons dried, crumbled, or more to taste
2 teaspoons dry mustard
1/2 teaspoon dried hot red pepper flakes, crushed, or more to taste
2 cups long-grain white rice
2 or 3 dashes Tabasco sauce, or more to taste
Salt and freshly ground pepper to taste

PREPARATION

1. Soak the beans in cold water to cover by 2 inches overnight, covered, at room temperature. Drain and rinse. Alternatively, place the beans in a heavy 3- to 4-quart saucepan over medium-high heat with enough cold water to cover by 2 inches and bring to a boil. Remove the saucepan from the heat, cover, and let stand for 1 hour. Drain the beans and rinse under cold running water.

2. In a heavy 6- to 8-quart flameproof casserole or ovenproof Dutch oven over medium-high heat, add the bacon and fry until browned and crisp, about 6 to 7 minutes. Using a slotted spoon, transfer the slices to a paper-towel-lined plate to drain. When the bacon is cool enough to handle, crumble it and reserve.

3. Add the beans to the bacon fat in the casserole. Add the onions, garlic, bell peppers, molasses, vinegar, chives, thyme, mustard, red pepper flakes, and reserved crumbled bacon. Add enough cold water to cover by 3 inches and bring to a boil. Reduce the heat to low and simmer until the beans are just tender, about 1 hour.

4. Preheat the oven to 350° F.

5. Meanwhile, in a heavy 3- to 4-quart saucepan over high heat, bring 4 cups of water to a boil. Reduce the heat to medium-low, add the rice, and simmer, covered, stirring occasionally, for 10 minutes. (The rice will only be partially cooked).

6. Drain the beans, reserving 2 cups of the cooking liquid. Return the beans and reserved cooking liquid to the casserole, and stir in the partially cooked rice. (This recipe can be prepared to this point up to 2 days ahead. Let cool, cover, and refrigerate. Bring to room temperature before proceeding.)

7. Bake, covered, for 30 minutes or until the rice is tender.

8. To serve, season with Tobasco, salt and pepper.

Adjust seasoning with more fresh chives, thyme, and Tabasco. Remember—both beans and rice absorb a lot of flavor. Serve hot directly from the casserole and pass the Tabasco sauce.

Robust Cuban Bean Soup

The coffee, rum, and lime juice make this a particularly piquant and rich-tasting version of black bean soup. The contrast of the black beans with the spring green of the limas makes for a beautiful as well as nutritious dish.

1 pound dried black beans, picked over
4 cups vegetable stock (page 184) or canned low-sodium chicken broth
1 medium yellow onion, finely chopped
3 medium cloves garlic, minced
1 cup freshly brewed coffee
2/3 cup dark rum
3 tablespoons fresh lime juice or lemon juice
1-1/2 teaspoons dry mustard

1/2 teaspoon dried hot red pepper flakes, crushed
1/4 pound cooked ham, preferably Virginia, julienned
1 10-ounce package frozen lima beans, thawed
4 medium scallions, green part included, thinly sliced
1 tablespoon finely chopped fresh cilantro
Salt and freshly ground pepper to taste

PREPARATION

1. Soak the black beans in cold water to cover by 2 inches overnight, covered, at room temperature. Drain and rinse. Alternatively, place the beans in a heavy 3- to 4-quart saucepan over medium-high heat with enough cold water to cover by 2 inches and bring to a boil. Remove the saucepan from the heat, cover, and let stand for 1 hour. Drain the beans and rinse under cold running water.

2. Place the beans in a heavy 3- to 4-quart saucepan, set over low heat, and stir in the stock, 1 cup water, the onion, garlic, coffee, and rum. Then add the lime juice, mustard, and red pepper flakes. Bring to a boil, then reduce the heat to low and simmer, partially covered, about 1 to 1-1/4 hours or until the beans are soft. Stir occasionally.

3. Remove the saucepan from the heat and force the soup, in batches, through the finest blade of a food mill set over a large bowl, until pureed and smooth. Alternatively, process in batches in the bowl of a food processor fitted with a metal blade until pureed. (This recipe can be prepared to this point up to 2 days ahead. Let cool, wrap, and refrigerate.)

4. Transfer the soup back to the saucepan and set over low heat. Stir in the ham, lima beans, and scallions and reheat, uncovered, stirring occasionally, about 5 to 7 minutes or until heated through. Stir in the cilantro. Season with salt and pepper.

5. To serve, transfer to a warmed soup tureen or individual soup bowls.

TO MICROWAVE

Follow step 1. In a 3-quart microproof dish with a tight-fitting lid, combine the drained beans, 1-1/3 cups stock, the onion, garlic, coffee, rum, lime juice, mustard, and red pepper flakes. Cover and micro-cook on HIGH 10 to 15 minutes or until it boils.

Stir in the remaining 2-2/3 cups stock and 1 cup water. Re-cover and microcook on MEDIUM 40 to 45 minutes or until beans are very tender. Let stand for 5 minutes. Follow step 3. Return mixture to microproof bowl and stir in the ham, lima beans, and scallions. Microcook on HIGH 2 minutes or until heated through.

Stir in the cilantro and season with salt and pepper. Transfer to a warmed soup tureen or individual soup bowls.

HOW TO "SOAK" DRIED BEANS IN THE MICROWAVE

In a 3-quart microproof casserole with a tight-fitting lid, combine 1-1/2 cups water and 1 pound dried beans that have been picked over and rinsed. Cover tightly and microcook on HIGH 7 to 15 minutes or until it reaches a boil. Stir once. Re-cover and micro-cook on MEDIUM 2 minutes. Let stand, covered, 1 hour. Drain, rinse under cold running water, and proceed with the recipe.

CHAPTER SIX

VEGETABLES

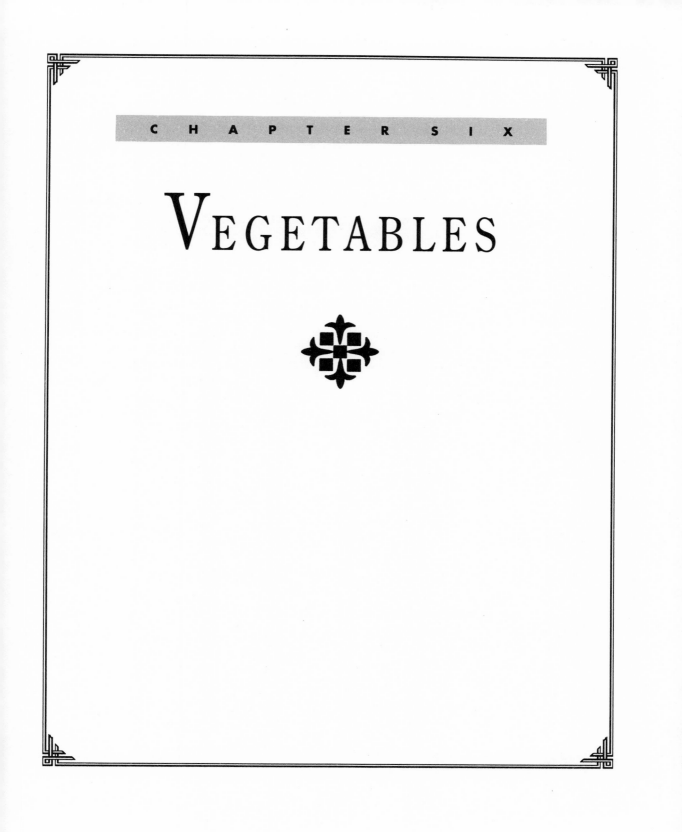

Tangy Hot-or-Cold Meatless Borscht

SERVES 8 TO 10

There are many versions of borscht, but the one ingredient common to them all is fresh beets, which gives this soup its characteristic robust flavor and beautiful ruby-red color. Borscht is usually served topped with a dollop of sour cream, and in Eastern Europe a meatless borscht is traditionally served on Christmas Eve. I like to serve it with whole-wheat pita pockets stuffed with goat cheese and fresh dillweed.

2 pounds beets, scrubbed but unpeeled, with
  1 inch of stem left on
2 medium yellow onions, finely chopped
2 medium cloves garlic, minced
1 medium head green cabbage, tough outer
  leaves removed, cored and shredded
3 medium carrots, peeled and thinly sliced
2 medium parsnips, peeled and thinly sliced
3 medium boiling potatoes, preferably
  red-skinned, scrubbed but unpeeled, cut into
  1/2-inch dice
1 14-1/2-ounce can peeled whole Italian plum
  tomatoes, crushed, with their juice
2 medium Granny Smith apples, peeled, cored,
  and finely chopped

1/4 cup red wine vinegar
1/4 cup fresh lemon juice
3 tablespoons firmly packed dark brown sugar
2 teaspoons caraway seeds
2 tablespoons finely chopped fresh dillweed
  or 2 teaspoons dried, crumbled
1 19-ounce can navy beans or cannellini,
  drained and rinsed
Salt and freshly ground pepper to taste
1 cup sour cream or plain lowfat yogurt,
  at room temperature
2 medium cucumbers, peeled, seeded, and cut
  into 1/4-inch dice, to garnish

PREPARATION

1. Place the beets in a heavy 8- to 10-quart pot over medium-high heat with enough cold water to cover by 2 inches. Bring to a boil, then reduce the heat to low and simmer, covered, for 25 to 30 minutes or until beets are just tender. Remove the pot from the heat and remove the beets with a slotted spoon and reserve. Strain the cooking liquid through a sieve lined with 2 layers of paper towel, and return to the pot.

2. When the beets are cool enough to handle, "rub" off the skins with your fingertips (this is easier than using a knife or vegetable peeler). Using a food processor fitted with a shredding disk or the coarse side of a box grater, shred the beets coarsely and reserve.

3. Add the onions, garlic, cabbage, carrots, parsnips, potatoes, tomatoes to the pot. Then stir in the apples, vinegar, lemon juice, and brown sugar. Bring to a boil, then reduce the heat to low and simmer, partially covered, for 7 to 8 minutes or until the potatoes and cabbage are tender.

4. Add the caraway seeds, 1 tablespoon of the dill-weed, the beans, and the reserved grated beets. Simmer, uncovered, for 5 to 6 minutes more. Season with salt and pepper.

5. To serve hot, transfer to a warmed soup tureen. If to be served cold, let cool at room temperature, cover, and refrigerate for at least 2 hours or until thoroughly chilled, then transfer to a chilled tureen. Garnish with the cucumbers and remaining table-spoon of dillweed. Pass the sour cream separately to be spooned on top of each serving.

FREEZING TIPS

Make recipe through step 4. Let cool, wrap, seal, and label. Freeze up to 2 months.

To Serve: Thaw. If serving cold, proceed with step 5. If serving hot, reheat gently over low heat, stirring occasionally until heated through. Proceed with step 5.

COOK'S NOTE

Leaving an inch of stem on the beets prevents them from "bleeding" into the cooking water.

This recipe can be made through step 4 the day before serving. Cool, cover, and refrigerate. If to be served chilled, proceed with recipe. If to be served hot, reheat gently over low heat, stirring occasionally until heated through and proceed with recipe.

Caramelized Onion Soup with Sherry

SERVES 4

This recipe demonstrates the onion being used to its fullest. The natural sugar of the onion caramelizes and provides the base for a golden, soothing soup. Although simple and inexpensive to make, the interaction of the ingredients lends a pungent yet delicate complexity to this French favorite. I advise against substituting margarine for butter in this particular recipe because the success of the recipe depends on the "crowning touch" of the flavor of sweet creamery butter at the end.

SOUP:
2 tablespoons unsalted butter
4 medium yellow onions, thinly sliced
3 tablespoons all-purpose flour
4 cups beef stock (page 185-186) or canned low-sodium beef broth

3 tablespoons dry sherry
1 teaspoon finely chopped fresh thyme, or 1/2 teaspoon dried, crumbled
Salt and freshly ground pepper to taste

CROÛTES:

8 1-inch-thick slices of whole-wheat bread
2 tablespoons olive oil, or more if needed
1 medium clove garlic, halved lengthwise

TOPPING:

2 cups shredded French (Comté) or Swiss
   Gruyère cheese or a low-sodium cheese of your
   choice, preferably "nutty" in flavor
1 tablespoon unsalted butter, diced

PREPARATION

1. Preheat the oven to 400° F.

2. In a heavy 4- to 6-quart pot over low heat, melt the butter and stir in the onions. Cook, stirring occasionally, for 30 to 35 minutes or until the onions are a deep golden brown. Sprinkle the flour over the onions and cook, stirring often, for 2 minutes. Stir in 2 cups water, then add the stock, sherry, and thyme. Cook for 20 minutes, stirring occasionally. Season with salt and pepper.

3. Meanwhile, make the croûtes: Using a pastry brush, lightly coat both sides of the bread slices with the olive oil. Arrange the bread slices in a single layer on a baking sheet and bake for 5 minutes per side or until completely dry and lightly golden brown. When the croûtes are cool enough to handle, rub both sides of each slice with the halved clove of garlic and reserve.

4. Preheat the broiler.

5. To serve, ladle the soup into individual oven-proof soup bowls, top each with 2 croûtes, pressing them into the soup so their edges will not burn, sprinkle with the Gruyère cheese, and dot with the butter. Place 5 to 6 inches from the heat source of a preheated broiler and broil for 1 to 2 minutes or until the top is lightly golden brown. Serve immediately.

Watercress-Mint Spanakopita

SERVES 8

This famous Greek pie is frequently cut into small squares and served as an appetizer. The flaky, crisp phyllo dough layered with spinach and cheese makes a wonderfully satisfying one-dish meal.

1 tablespoon olive oil or safflower oil
2 medium yellow onions, finely chopped
3 medium scallions, including green part,
   thinly sliced
4 pounds fresh spinach, stemmed, washed
   thoroughly, and finely chopped
2 bunches watercress, coarsely chopped
1 tablespoon grated orange zest
1-1/2 tablespoons finely chopped fresh mint,
   or 2 tablespoons dried, crumbled
1 teaspoon ground nutmeg, preferably freshly
   grated

1/2 teaspoon salt
1/2 teaspoon freshly ground pepper
5 eggs, lightly beaten
1 cup milk
1 pound feta cheese, crumbled (if very salty,
   soak briefly in milk before crumbling)
1 cup freshly grated Romano cheese or
   Parmesan cheese
1 1-pound package frozen phyllo dough
   (28 to 32 17-by-12-inch sheets), thawed
8 tablespoons (1 stick) unsalted butter or
   margarine, melted

PREPARATION

1. Preheat the oven to 375° F. Lightly grease a 13-by-9-by-2-inch baking dish.

2. In a heavy 6- to 8-quart pot over medium-high heat, heat the olive oil. Add the onions and scallions and cook, stirring often for 4 minutes or until soft but not browned. Stir in the spinach, watercress, orange zest, mint, nutmeg, salt, and pepper. Cook, covered, for 10 minutes or until the spinach is soft, stirring occasionally. Remove the cover, raise heat to high, and continue to cook, stirring often, until about half the liquid has evaporated. Remove from the heat and, using a slotted spoon, transfer the spinach mixture to a medium bowl to cool.

3. In a small bowl combine the eggs, milk, feta cheese, and Romano cheese and stir until blended. Stir into the cooled spinach mixture until well blended.

4. On a dry work surface, stack the phyllo dough and cover with a slightly damp cloth to prevent the sheets from drying out as you work. Working quickly with a pastry brush, evenly brush some melted butter onto the top sheet. Carefully fit the sheet into the baking dish, allowing the edges to drape over the sides. (*Note:* The phyllo sheets will extend quite a bit over the edges.) Repeat this pro-cess with all but 5 of the phyllo sheets, buttering each sheet and fitting it into the dish at a slight angle so that the corners fan out around the dish rather than being stacked evenly one on top of the other.

5. Ladle the filling into the phyllo-lined baking dish, spreading it evenly. Fold the edges of the phyllo dough on top of the filling. Cover with remaining phyllo dough, brushing each sheet with butter. Tuck the edges of the top sheets into the sides of the dish to form a neat edge. Brush the top sheet with any remaining butter.

6. With the dull edge of a knife, score the pie into squares but do not cut through the crust.

7. Bake for 45 to 55 minutes or until the top is crisp and lightly golden brown.

8. To serve, let stand for 5 minutes, then finish cutting into squares and serve hot or at room temperature.

VARIATION

Substitute fresh arugula for the watercress and fresh dillweed, *not* dried, for the mint.

Mushroom Stroganoff

Beef stroganoff is said to have been invented in honor of the Russian Count Pavel Stroganov. This contemporary version replaces the original beef with a flavorful combination of mushrooms, along with yogurt and Marsala.

1 *ounce dried porcini or cepes (wild mushrooms)*
2 *tablespoons Marsala*
8 *ounces extra-wide egg noodles*
Olive oil
2 *tablespoons unsalted butter or margarine*
1 *medium yellow onion, thinly sliced*
12 *ounces mushrooms, preferably short-stem, wiped clean with a damp paper towel, trimmed, and thinly sliced*

2/3 *cup plain lowfat yogurt, at room temperature*
1-1/2 *teaspoons Dijon-style mustard*
1-1/2 *teaspoons poppy seeds*
1 *tablespoon finely chopped fresh chives*
Salt and freshly ground pepper to taste

PREPARATION

1. Soak the dried mushrooms in the Marsala plus 1/4 cup boiling water until soft, at least 30 minutes. Remove mushrooms and discard any woody stems. Strain the soaking liquid through a paper-towel-lined sieve (squeeze the towel when done to obtain all liquid) and reserve. Finely chop the mushrooms.

2. Meanwhile, prepare the noodles. To a 6- to 8-quart pot of boiling water, add the noodles and stir occasionally. Return to a boil and boil 5 to 6 minutes or until al dente (slightly firm to the bite). Drain noodles and transfer to a medium bowl. Lightly toss with some olive oil and reserve at room temperature.

3. In a heavy 6- to 8-quart pot over medium-high heat, melt the butter. Raise the heat to high and add the onion, the fresh mushrooms, and the dried

mushrooms and their soaking liquid. Cook the onion mixture, stirring frequently, about 7 to 9 minutes or until the fresh mushrooms are wilted and a light golden brown.

4. Reduce the heat to low and simmer for 5 minutes, stirring often. Stir 1/4 cup of the warm mushroom mixture into the yogurt, then return this mixture to the pot.

5. Stir in the mustard, poppy seeds, chives, and reserved noodles. Stir gently until noodles are coated evenly. Season with salt and pepper.

6. Simmer for 2 minutes more, stirring gently, until heated through. Transfer to a warmed serving platter and serve immediately.

Festive Cheese Fondue

SERVES 4

Fondue originated in Switzerland, where legend has it that a Swiss shepherd,
bored with his usual meal of bread, wine, and cheese, one evening lit a fire beneath his
iron pot and proceeded to dunk his bread into the newly melted mixture of cheese and wine.
Fondue makes a perfect meal for an informal gathering of friends after skiing,
after the theater or any time you want to get to know people better. Everything can be
prepared ahead, and the foods you choose for dipping set out in baskets on the table.
I recommend serving no more than four people per fondue pot: If you are serving
five or more, start a second pot. Remember, this is a main course, so choose at least
four ingredients from the list of dipping foods below and have plenty on hand.
Just wash the vegetables thoroughly, trim, and then blanch.
Make sure your bread is dry; one-day-old bread is a must!

DIPPING FOODS:

Day-old bread, cut into 1-inch cubes, such
as French baguette, or homemade-style
whole-wheat or oatmeal
Long, thin breadsticks
Cooked tortellini with various flavors of pasta
wrappings and fillings, such as cheese
or chicken and prosciutto
Whole red radishes, washed thoroughly and
trimmed
Whole string beans, trimmed
Broccoli florets
Whole mushrooms, preferably short-stem,
wiped clean with a damp paper towel and
trimmed
Red bell pepper strips
Cauliflower florets
Yellow crookneck squash, cut into 1-inch
cubes
Zucchini, cut into 1/2-inch-thick slices
Dried sausage, sliced thinly
Asparagus spears, cut into 1-inch-long
pieces

Whole snow peas
Brussels sprouts, halved lengthwise
Miniature vegetables such as baby zucchini, corn,
squash
Jicama, cut into 1-inch cubes

FONDUE:

1/4 cup all-purpose flour
8 ounces Swiss Emmenthaler or Swiss
Appenzeller cheese, shredded
8 ounces Swiss Gruyère or French Gruyère
cheese, shredded
1 medium clove garlic, halved
1 cup dry white wine
3 tablespoons kirsch (a dry, colorless brandy
distilled from the juice of the black morello
cherry)
1/2 teaspoon ground nutmeg, preferably freshly
grated
1/4 teaspoon paprika, preferably Hungarian
semisweet (page 30)

1. In a medium bowl combine the flour and cheeses and toss until the cheese is thoroughly coated.

2. Set the fondue pot over medium heat, rub with the garlic clove, and add the wine. Bring the wine to a simmer but do not let boil. Stir in the flour-coated cheese. Using a wooden spoon, stir constantly in a figure-eight motion until the cheese is just melted. Stir in the kirsch, nutmeg, and paprika until just blended.

3. Carefully set the fondue pot over the table burner and adjust the flame so the fondue will maintain a gentle simmer throughout the meal.

4. Serve immediately: Each guest spears the dipping foods with a fondue fork and dunks into the melted cheese mixture. (*Note:* The cheese will eventually form a thick crust on the bottom of the fondue pot as the fondue sits over the burner. This is a delicacy—try it!)

VARIATION

For a "diet" version, substitute the same quantity of low-sodium Gouda for the Swiss Emmenthaler and low-sodium Swiss Lorraine for the Swiss Gruyère.

CHEESE FONDUE CAUTIONS AND TIPS

1. Cheese fondue should always be kept just below a simmer in order to maintain a silky, saucelike consistency. Otherwise, it can become stringy or rubbery.

2. If the cheese fondue doesn't thicken or starts to separate, whisk together 1/2 teaspoon cornstarch with 1 teaspoon warm water in a small cup. Return the fondue pot to the stove over low heat and whisk in the cornstarch mixture. Whisk vigorously until the fondue begins to thicken or regains its smooth consistency.

3. If the cheese fondue is too thick, return the fondue pot to the stove over low heat and whisk in 1/2 cup of heated wine. Whisk vigorously until the fondue regains its saucelike consistency.

4. The wine should be a dry white wine. The kirsch should be of good quality or it will impart an astringent bite to the fondue.

FONDUE LORE

If a woman seated at the fondue table drops her piece of bread into the pot, she has to kiss the man seated nearest to her. If a man drops his piece of bread, he has to buy the next bottle of wine.

Eggplant and Polenta Parmesan

Polenta is the Italian name for cornmeal and for the pudding that is a specialty of Venice and northeastern Italy. After cooking, it is usually cooled, then sliced and grilled, fried, or baked, as in this recipe. You can find the appropriate cornmeal labeled "polenta" in your supermarket or in an Italian grocery store.

POLENTA:

1-1/2 teaspoons salt
1-1/2 cups polenta (Italian cornmeal)

EGGPLANT:

2 medium eggplants, unpeeled, cut crosswise
   into 1/2-inch-thick slices
2 eggs
1/3 cup freshly grated Parmesan cheese
1 cup unseasoned dried bread crumbs
3 tablespoons olive oil, plus more if needed
1 recipe Tomato Sauce (recipe follows)
1 cup part skim-milk ricotta cheese
1-1/2 cups shredded smoked mozzarella cheese
   or part skim-milk mozzarella

TOMATO SAUCE:
(MAKES 3 CUPS)

2 tablespoons olive oil
1 medium yellow onion, finely chopped
3 medium cloves garlic, minced
1 28-ounce can whole peeled Italian plum
   tomatoes, crushed, including their juice
2 tablespoons tomato paste, preferably
   Italian
1/2 cup dry white wine
3 tablespoons balsamic vinegar or red wine
   vinegar
1 bay leaf
1-1/2 tablespoons finely chopped fresh basil
2 teaspoons dried oregano, crumbled
1 tablespoon grated orange zest
1 teaspoon fennel seeds, crushed
1/2 teaspoon dried hot red pepper flakes,
   crushed
1/4 cup finely chopped fresh parsley, preferably
   Italian flat-leaf
Salt and freshly ground pepper to taste

PREPARATION

1. To make the polenta: Lightly grease a 13-by-9-by-2-inch baking dish.

2. In a heavy 6- to 8-quart pot over medium-high heat, bring 4-1/2 cups water and the salt to a boil.

Reduce the heat to low and gradually add the polenta, pouring in a thin, steady stream, whisking vigorously. Cook, stirring frequently, for 5 minutes or until the polenta is very thick and pulls away from the sides of the pan. Transfer to the prepared baking dish, pack down firmly, and smooth the top with a spatula. Reserve at room temperature until ready to use. *(This recipe can be prepared to this point up to 2 days ahead. Let cool, wrap, and refrigerate. Bring to room temperature before proceeding.)*

3. To prepare the eggplant: Spread the eggplant on a work surface covered with paper towels. Lightly salt both sides of the slices and transfer slices to a rack in a shallow baking pan. Cover the eggplant slices with more paper towels and place a heavy wooden cutting board on top as a weight. Let drain at least 30 minutes, preferably 1 hour. Lightly rinse the eggplant slices and pat dry with paper towels. Reserve until ready to use.

4. In a medium bowl beat the eggs lightly. In another medium bowl combine the Parmesan cheese and bread crumbs. With one hand, dip each eggplant slice into the eggs, then into the Parmesan mixture until evenly coated, shaking off excess. Repeat until all eggplant slices are coated.

5. In a large skillet over medium-high heat, heat the olive oil. Add the reserved eggplant slices in batches and sauté, turning only once, until both sides are lightly browned, about 4 minutes per side. Add more olive oil as needed. Transfer the sautéed eggplant slices to a large paper-towel-lined platter to drain; blot any excess oil.

6. Transfer the slices to the polenta-lined baking dish, letting slices touch but not overlap. Reserve at room temperature.

7. Preheat the oven to 375°F.

8. To make the tomato sauce: In a 3- to 4-quart saucepan over medium-high heat, heat the olive oil. Add the onion and garlic and cook, stirring often, for 3 to 4 minutes or until softened but not browned.

9. Add the tomatoes, tomato paste, wine, and vinegar, and stir to combine. Then stir in the bay leaf, basil, oregano, orange zest, fennel seeds, and red pepper flakes. Bring to a boil, then reduce heat to medium-low. Simmer for 25 to 30 minutes, stirring occasionally, until thickened. Remove and discard the bay leaf. Stir in the parsley and season with salt and pepper. (The tomato sauce can be made up to 3 days ahead. Let cool, cover, and refrigerate. Bring to room temperature before proceeding.)

10. Spread the ricotta cheese over the eggplant. Ladle the tomato sauce over the ricotta, sprinkle with the mozzarella cheese, and bake for 30 to 35 minutes or until cheese has melted and dish is heated through.

MICROWAVE "FIRM" POLENTA
CAN BE BAKED, FRIED, OR GRILLED
MAKES 16 1/2-INCH-THICK SLICES

1-1/2 cups polenta (Italian cornmeal)
1-1/2 teaspoons salt
2 tablespoons unsalted butter
1/8 teaspoon freshly ground white pepper

In a 3-quart microproof dish combine the polenta, salt, and 4-1/2 cups water. Cover tightly and microcook on HIGH 5 minutes. Stir once and microcook, uncovered, for 4 to 7 minutes more or until all the water is absorbed, stirring once after 3 minutes.

Stir in the butter and pepper, then transfer the polenta to a lightly greased 9-by-5-by-3-inch loaf pan (or utensil size specified in recipe), pack down firmly, and smooth the top. Let stand at room temperature until cool and set. If to be baked, follow recipe. If to be fried or grilled, slice the polenta about 1/2 inch thick, then fry or grill until lightly browned and heated through.

Vegetable Cobbler

SERVES 4

This vegetarian main-dish recipe is an adaptation of old-fashioned creamed onions,
a side dish frequently appearing at the family dinner table, especially at holidays.
The creamy pearl onions have been embellished with barley and potatoes, and flavored
with nutmeg. I like to dot the bread-crumb topping with butter; margarine is not a good
substitute in this recipe.

3 tablespoons unsalted butter
3 tablespoons all-purpose flour
2-1/2 cups milk, heated
2 cups cooked barley
2 medium boiling potatoes, cooked and cut
　　into 1/2-inch dice
1 10-ounce basket white pearl onions, peeled
　　(see page 48)

1 cup shredded Swiss Gruyère
1/2 teaspoon ground nutmeg, preferably freshly
　　grated
Salt and freshly ground white pepper to taste
1/2 cup fresh bread crumbs, preferably from a
　　French baguette
2 teaspoons unsalted butter

PREPARATION

1. Preheat the oven to 350° F.

2. In a heavy 2- to 3-quart saucepan over low heat,
melt the butter. Add the flour, whisking constantly
until large bubbles appear, about 3 minutes. Cook 2
minutes more, whisking constantly; do not let the
roux brown. Remove the saucepan from the heat
and gradually pour in the hot milk, whisking constantly across the bottom and around the sides
until well blended and smooth. Return the

saucepan to low heat and stir until thickened, about
5 to 6 minutes. Stir in the barley, diced potatoes,
onions, Gruyère, and nutmeg. Season with salt and
pepper.

3. Spoon the mixture into a 3- to 4-quart ovenproof
gratin dish or casserole, preferably oval. Sprinkle
with the bread crumbs and dot with the butter.
Bake for 20 to 25 minutes, or until bubbly and lightly golden brown.

Kasha Ratatouille

In this version of ratatouille, the eggplant and zucchini are baked rather than sautéed, using less oil than in traditional recipes. The kasha, or roasted buckwheat groats, provide an excellent source of protein, as do the cannellini beans.

2 medium eggplants, unpeeled, cut into 1/2-inch dice
2 tablespoons olive oil or safflower oil
2 medium cloves garlic, minced
1 large red onion, finely chopped
1/8 teaspoon fennel seeds, crushed
1/2 cup dry white wine
2 tablespoons tomato paste, preferably Italian
3 medium zucchini, cut into 1/2-inch dice

2 medium-sized ripe tomatoes, seeded and coarsely chopped
1 egg, lightly beaten
1/4 cup medium granulation kasha (roasted buckwheat groats)
2 tablespoons minced fresh basil
1 15-1/2-ounce can cannellini (white beans), drained and rinsed
Salt and freshly ground pepper

PREPARATION

1. Place the diced eggplant in a colander, lightly salt, and toss. Set the colander in a large bowl to catch the released liquid. Weight down eggplant with a second, heavier bowl and let eggplant stand for at least 30 minutes, preferably 1 hour. Rinse lightly, drain, and pat dry. Reserve until ready to use.

2. Preheat the oven to 400° F.

3. In a heavy 6- to 8-quart flameproof casserole or ovenproof Dutch oven over medium-high heat, heat the olive oil. Add the garlic, onion, and fennel seeds. Cook, stirring, for 3 to 4 minutes or until soft but not browned. Remove from the heat and stir in the wine, tomato paste, zucchini, tomatoes, and eggplant.

4. Cover and bake for 20 minutes. Remove, stir once, re-cover, and bake for 25 to 30 minutes more or until the vegetables are very tender but still hold their shape.

5. Meanwhile, in a small bowl combine the egg and kasha and stir until all the grains are well coated. Place the kasha in a large skillet over high heat. Using a wooden spoon, stir the kasha vigorously for 3 to 4 minutes or until the egg has dried and the grains separate. Remove from the heat and add 1/2 cup boiling water all at once (be careful—liquid may splatter). Return the skillet to low heat, cover, and cook the kasha mixture for 3 to 5 minutes or until tender and the liquid is absorbed. Remove from the heat and let stand, uncovered, until ready to use.

6. Remove the casserole from the oven and stir in the kasha, basil, and cannellini. (*Note:* The retained heat will warm the kasha, basil, and cannellini.) Season with salt and pepper.

7. Serve directly from the casserole, either hot or at room temperature.

Zucchini and Sun-Dried Tomato Skillet Pizza

MAKES 2 INDIVIDUAL SEVEN-INCH PIZZAS

These innovative pizzas with a very thinly rolled semolina crust are made individually in a 9- or10-inch skillet. For this reason, and because the zucchini slices for the topping must be cooked evenly in a large, uncrowded pan, the recipe yields just two pizzas. Since the recipe for the semolina dough (page 168) provides enough for four pizza crusts, you may either freeze the excess dough for use on another occasion, or simply double the recipe below to make four pizzas.

3 *small zucchini, cut into 1/4-inch-thick slices*
1 *teaspoon salt*
1 *tablespoon oil from oil-packed sun-dried tomatoes*
4 *sun-dried tomato halves packed in oil, minced*
3 *medium cloves garlic, lightly smashed*
Pinch dried hot red pepper flakes, crushed

1 *large ripe tomato, seeded and coarsely chopped*
1/4 *teaspoon freshly ground pepper*
2 *tablespoons minced fresh basil*
1/2 *recipe Quick Semolina Pizza Dough (see following page), at room temperature*
2/3 *cup shredded part-skim milk mozzarella cheese*

P R E P A R A T I O N

1. Put the zucchini in a colander inside a large bowl and sprinkle with 1/2 teaspoon of the salt; toss and let drain for 5 minutes. Lightly rinse, pat dry with paper towels, and reserve.

2. Meanwhile, in a large heavy skillet over medium heat, heat the oil from the sun-dried tomatoes. Add the sun-dried tomatoes, garlic, and red pepper flakes. Cook until the garlic begins to soften, about 2 minutes. Raise the heat to high, add the zucchini, and toss to coat with the oil. Cook, tossing frequently, until the zucchini is evenly browned, about 3 minutes. Remove from the heat, add the fresh tomato, and season with the remaining 1/2 teaspoon salt and all the black pepper. Discard the garlic. (This recipe can be prepared to this point up to 1 day ahead; let cool, cover, and refrigerate. Bring to room temperature before proceeding with the recipe.) Add the basil and stir.

3. Roll the pizza dough into a log 1-1/2 inches in diameter. Cut off a walnut-size piece of dough, flatten it into a 1/16-inch-thick round, and reserve. Cut remaining dough in half crosswise. On a lightly floured work surface, roll out each piece of dough into a 7-inch round about 1/16-inch thick. Roll gently; the dough will be soft. Cover the rounds with plastic wrap. Heat a 9- or 10-inch cast-iron skillet over medium-high heat until hot.

4. Test the temperature of the skillet: Place the reserved walnut-size piece of dough into the heated skillet. Bubbles should appear on the underside within the first 45 seconds; if they don't, increase the heat a little. If bubbles appear but then burn within the first three minutes, reduce the heat. The crust is cooked on one side only; it should be dark brown.

5. Carefully place one of the dough rounds into the hot skillet, reduce the heat to low, cover with aluminum foil, and cook until the crust is dark brown on the bottom, about 3 minutes. (*Note:* Check the heat after 2 minutes and adjust the heat, if necessary, to avoid burning.)

6. Remove the pizza crust from the skillet. Sprinkle half the mozzarella cheese evenly over the crust and top with about 1/2 of the zucchini mixture. Return the pizza to the skillet and cook, covered with aluminum foil, until the cheese melts, about 2 minutes. Keep warm until ready to serve. Repeat process with the remaining round of dough.

QUICK SEMOLINA PIZZA DOUGH
MAKES 4 7-INCH PIZZA CRUSTS

1 cup semolina flour, available at specialty food shops
1 teaspoon baking powder
1/2 teaspoon salt
1 tablespoon extra virgin olive oil

1. In the bowl of a food processor fitted with a metal blade, combine the semolina flour, 1/3 cup hot water, the baking powder, salt, and olive oil. Pulse until the dough is just blended, about 45 seconds.

2. Roll into a ball and cover with plastic wrap. Refrigerate for at least 15 minutes or up to 2 hours. Bring to room temperature before proceeding with the recipe.

CHAPTER SEVEN

COLD ONE-DISH MEALS

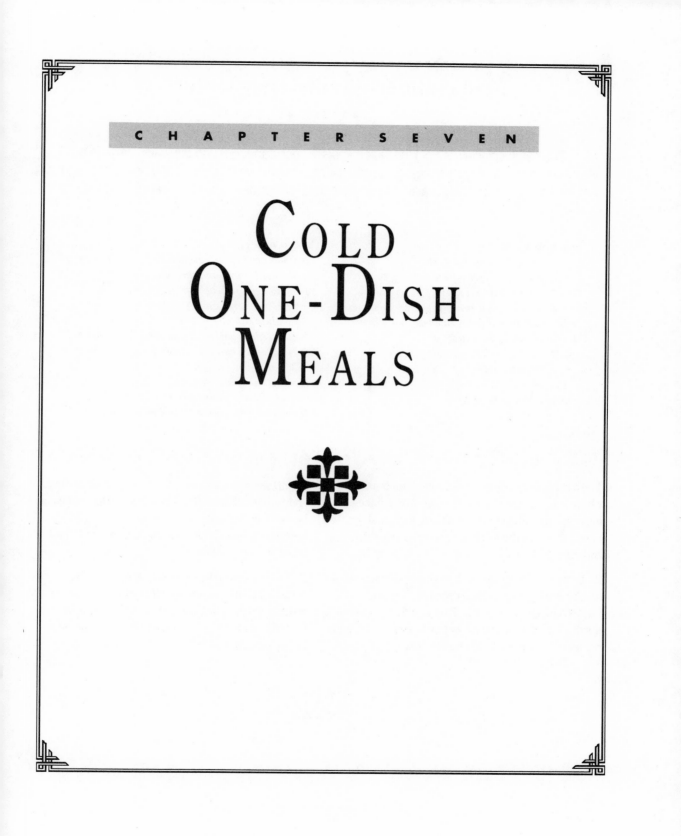

Midsummer Main-Dish Coleslaw

SERVES 4

The name coleslaw is from the Dutch *koolsla*: *kool* (cabbage) and *sla* (salad). This is a tantalizing and satisfying main-course salad. The orange carrots and red and green cabbage, along with the chicken, make for a spectacular dish certainly worthy of serving to guests.

DRESSING:

- 1 cup plain lowfat yogurt
- 1/4 cup apple cider vinegar
- 1/4 cup fresh lemon juice
- 2 tablespoons drained prepared horseradish
- 3 tablespoons finely chopped fresh dillweed
- 1-1/2 teaspoons mustard
- 1/4 cup finely chopped fresh parsley, preferably Italian flat-leaf
- 1/2 cup olive oil
- Salt and freshly ground pepper

SALAD:

- 1 small head green cabbage, tough outer leaves removed, cored and shredded
- 1 small head red cabbage, tough outer leaves removed, cored and shredded
- 2 medium carrots, grated
- 1 cup seedless golden raisins or dried currants
- 3 cups cooked chicken, preferably grilled, cut into 1/2-inch-wide strips
- 1 small red onion, minced
- Salt and freshly ground pepper to taste
- 1 cup finely chopped walnuts, to garnish

PREPARATION

1. To prepare the dressing: In a medium bowl whisk together the yogurt, vinegar, lemon juice, horseradish, dillweed, dry mustard, and parsley. Slowly whisk in the olive oil to form a fairly thick and creamy dressing. Adjust seasoning to taste.

2. To prepare the salad: In a large non-metal bowl combine the green and red cabbage, carrots, raisins, chicken, and onion. Toss together with two-thirds of the dressing until evenly coated. Cover and refrigerate at least 2 hours before serving. Transfer

the dressing to a non-metal storage container, cover, and refrigerate until ready to serve. (This recipe can be made up to 1 day ahead. Wrap and refrigerate. Refrigerate remaining dressing in a separate non-metal storage container.)

3. To serve, toss the salad with the remaining dressing, adjust seasoning with salt and pepper to taste, and toss again. Garnish with the chopped walnuts. Allow coleslaw to return to room temperature before serving.

Paella Salad

This dish is my own adaptation of one of the masterpieces of Spanish cuisine, paella, whose name is taken from the pan in which it is cooked, the *paellera*. For an extra-special presentation, you might serve this salad in a Spanish *paellera*. It is a stellar dish for buffet-style entertaining!

RICE:
- 1 tablespoon olive oil
- 1 medium yellow onion, minced
- 1 cup long-grain white rice
- 1/4 teaspoon salt
- 1 teaspoon lightly packed saffron threads, soaked in 2 cups water

DRESSING:
- 3 medium cloves garlic, halved
- 1 medium yellow onion, quartered
- 2 medium-sized ripe tomatoes, seeded and quartered
- 1/2 cup drained, chopped pimentos
- 1/4 cup balsamic vinegar or red wine vinegar
- 1-1/2 tablespoons finely chopped fresh oregano, or 1 teaspoon dried, crumbled
- 1/2 cup olive oil
- Tabasco sauce to taste
- Salt and freshly ground pepper to taste

SALAD:
- 2 cups cooked chicken (preferably breast meat), cut into 1-inch cubes
- 1 pound medium shrimp, shelled, deveined, rinsed thoroughly, and poached until just pink
- 1 cup cooked lobster meat (available at fish market), cut into bite-sized pieces
- 1 medium green bell pepper, cored, seeded, and finely chopped
- 1-1/4 cups fresh shelled green peas, cooked, or half a 10-ounce package frozen, thawed, uncooked
- 3 medium scallions, green part included, finely chopped
- 1/4 cup finely chopped fresh parsley, preferably Italian flat-leaf
- 12 ounces marinated whole artichoke hearts, drained and halved lengthwise
- Lemon wedges

PREPARATION

1. To prepare the rice: In a heavy 4- to 6-quart pot over medium-high heat, heat the olive oil. Add the onion and rice and cook, stirring frequently, for 4 to 5 minutes or until the onion is soft but not browned. (*Note:* Do not let the rice brown.) Add the salt and the saffron plus its soaking water and bring to a boil, stirring occasionally. Reduce the heat to low, cover, and simmer undisturbed for 12 to 15 minutes or until the rice is tender and all the liquid has been absorbed. Transfer the rice to a large serving platter, fluff with a fork, and let cool at room temperature.

2. To prepare the dressing: In the bowl of a food

processor fitted with a metal blade or in a blender, pulse the garlic until finely chopped. Add the onion, tomatoes, pimentos, vinegar, and oregano and process until puréed. With the machine running, gradually pour in the olive oil through the feed tube in a slow, steady stream. When all the oil has been incorporated, transfer the dressing to a small bowl. Season to taste with Tabasco, salt, and pepper. Reserve at room temperature until ready to use.

3. To prepare the salad: In a large bowl gently toss together the chicken, shrimp, lobster, bell pepper, green peas, scallions, parsley, and half the dressing. Refrigerate, but allow to return to room temperature before serving.

4. Just before serving, transfer the rice to a medium non-metal bowl and toss with the remaining dressing. (*Note:* The rice will absorb a lot of the dressing, so toss only before serving.) Place the rice in a mound in the center of the serving platter. Spoon the chicken and seafood mixture around the rice. Arrange the halved artichoke hearts, cut side up with tip outward, around the edge of the platter, alternating about every fifth one with a wedge of lemon. (Guests should squeeze lemon juice over the salad before eating it.)

COOK'S NOTE

The dressing may be made up to 2 days ahead. Transfer to a non-metal storage container, cover, and refrigerate. Whisk thoroughly before proceeding with recipe.

Avocado Gazpacho

SERVES 4

Sublime, buttery avocados provide a perfect contrast to the crunchy bell pepper in this refreshing chilled soup from Spain. Radishes and lime juice add extra gusto and a rosy pink hue.

SOUP:

3 eggs
1/2 cup olive oil
1/4 cup apple cider vinegar
1-1/2 cups canned tomato juice
2 medium cloves garlic, minced
3 tablespoons fresh lime juice or lemon juice
1 tablespoon firmly packed light brown sugar
1/2 teaspoon salt
1/4 teaspoon freshly ground pepper
1/4 teaspoon cayenne pepper

1 tablespoon finely chopped fresh dillweed
1 medium red onion, quartered
1 large cucumber, peeled, seeded, and quartered
1 medium green bell pepper, cored, seeded, and cut into eighths
1 bunch red radishes, halved
3 medium-sized ripe tomatoes, seeded, juice reserved
1 medium-sized ripe avocado, cut into 1/2-inch dice

PREPARATION

1. In a medium non-metal bowl whisk together the eggs, olive oil, vinegar, tomato juice, garlic, lime juice, brown sugar, salt, pepper, cayenne, dillweed, and reserved juice from the fresh tomatoes. Cover and refrigerate until ready to use.

2. Meanwhile, in the bowl of a food processor fitted with a metal blade, process the onion, cucumber, bell pepper, radishes, and tomatoes in batches, adding a bit of the tomato-juice mixture as needed to prevent

the blade from stopping. Do not process until smooth; the vegetables should just be finely chopped and still have some texture. Stir in the rest of the tomato-juice mixture and transfer the soup to a non-metal bowl, cover, and refrigerate for at least 2 hours. The gazpacho should be thoroughly chilled.

3. To serve, stir in the diced avocado and adjust seasoning to taste. Ladle into chilled soup bowls, and serve immediately.

Three-Bean Salad with Tuna and Sage

SERVES 4

This salad should be made the day before serving so that it can marinate.
Try kidney beans as a substitute for the cannellini for an even more colorful salad!

DRESSING:

- 1 egg yolk
- 1/3 cup white wine vinegar
- 2 medium cloves garlic, minced
- 2 teaspoons finely chopped fresh sage, or
  1 teaspoon dried, crumbled
- 2 tablespoons finely chopped fresh parsley,
  preferably Italian flat-leaf
- 2-1/2 teaspoons sugar
- 1/2 teaspoon salt
- 1/4 teaspoon freshly ground pepper
- 2/3 cup olive oil, preferably extra virgin

SALAD:

- 1 15-1/2-ounce can cannellini (white beans) or
  kidney or other type bean, drained and rinsed
- 4 ounces fresh green beans, cooked until crisp-
  tender and cut into 1-inch pieces
- 4 ounces fresh yellow wax beans, cooked until
  crisp-tender and cut into 1-inch pieces
- 1 medium red onion, minced
- 1 6-1/2-ounce can water-packed chunk light
  tuna, drained and flaked
- 1 bunch watercress, stemmed
- 3 medium scallions, including green part, thinly
  sliced, to garnish

PREPARATION

1. To make the dressing: In the bowl of a food processor fitted with a metal blade or in a blender, pulse the egg yolk, vinegar, garlic, sage, parsley, sugar, salt, and pepper just until blended. With the machine running, slowly pour the olive oil through the feed tube in a slow, steady stream until all the oil has been incorporated and is well blended. Transfer to a non-metal container and adjust seasoning to taste. (*Note:* Dressing will be slightly vinegary.) Cover and refrigerate until ready to use.

2. To make the salad: In a large non-metal bowl combine the cannellini, green beans, wax beans, onion, and tuna. Gently toss together with the dressing until well coated. Cover and refrigerate overnight before serving.

3. To serve, bring the salad to room temperature, stir to redistribute, and adjust seasoning to taste. Spoon into the center of the serving platter surrounded with watercress, garnish with scallions, and serve.

Potato Supper Salad

There are many notable potato salads—French, Scandinavian, German—but my favorite is still the American potato salad with hard-cooked eggs, relish, paprika, and with the savory addition of Westphalian ham. This salad is best made the day before you plan to serve it.

SALAD:
- 3-1/2 *pounds small new potatoes, unpeeled but scrubbed, cooked until tender but not mushy, quartered*
- 1/4 *cup apple cider vinegar*
- 3 *ribs celery, finely chopped*
- 1 *medium green bell pepper, cored, seeded, and finely chopped*
- 1 *large cucumber, peeled, seeded, and finely chopped*
- 1 *medium white onion, minced*

DRESSING:
- 1 *cup mayonnaise, preferably homemade*
- 2 *tablespoons apple cider vinegar*
- 1/4 *cup olive oil*
- 1/2 *cup prepared sweet relish*
- 1-1/2 *tablespoons honey*
- 1/2 *teaspoon celery seed*
- 1/2 *teaspoon salt*
- 1/4 *teaspoon freshly ground pepper*
- 2 *cups 1/2-inch juliennes of Westphalian ham or other smoked ham*
- 3 *hard-cooked eggs, coarsely chopped, to garnish*
- 1/4 *cup finely chopped fresh parsley, preferably Italian flat-leaf, to garnish*
- 3/4 *teaspoon paprika, preferably Hungarian semisweet (page 30), to garnish*

PREPARATION

1. To make the salad: In a large non-metal bowl combine the potatoes, vinegar, celery, bell pepper, cucumber, and onion.

2. To make the dressing: In a small non-metal bowl whisk together the mayonnaise, vinegar, olive oil, relish, honey, celery seed, salt, and pepper until well blended. Adjust seasoning to taste. Transfer half the dressing to a non-metal storage container and cover. Refrigerate until ready to use.

3. Add the remaining dressing to the bowl with the potato mixture and toss gently to combine. Cover and refrigerate overnight.

4. To serve, toss the potato mixture with the ham and adjust seasoning to taste with salt and pepper. Garnish with chopped egg, parsley, and paprika. Let stand at room temperature briefly before serving; it's best chilled but not too cold.

Greek Salad

I have two secrets to making a Greek salad. One is not to serve the anchovies whole, but to rinse them and then mash them with the garlic and other seasonings to make a paste, which helps rid the anchovies of their briny flavor. The second is to soak the onion slices in cold water, which helps draw out their astringency and makes them sweeter.

SALAD:
- 1 medium red onion, thinly sliced, rings separated
- 1 medium cucumber, thinly sliced
- 1 large green bell pepper, cored, seeded, and thinly sliced
- 1 large yellow or red bell pepper, cored, seeded, and thinly sliced
- 10 ounces feta cheese, rinsed (if very salty, soak briefly in milk before crumbling), and crumbled
- 2 medium-sized ripe tomatoes, cut into eighths
- 3/4 cup Greek Kalamata olives or other brine-cured olives, rinsed, pitted, and halved lengthwise

DRESSING:
- 4 anchovies, rinsed
- 2 medium cloves garlic, minced
- 1 tablespoon finely chopped fresh oregano
- 4-1/2 teaspoons finely chopped fresh mint
- 1/4 teaspoon salt
- 1/4 teaspoon freshly ground pepper
- 2 tablespoons fresh lemon juice
- 5 tablespoons red wine vinegar
- 1/3 cup olive oil

PREPARATION

1. In a medium bowl cover the onion rings with cold water and let soak for 20 minutes. Drain on paper towels and discard the water.

2. Meanwhile, make the dressing: In a medium non-metal bowl combine the anchovies, garlic, oregano, mint, salt, and pepper. Using a fork, mash the ingredients together until they form a paste.

Whisk in the lemon juice and vinegar until combined. Then whisk in the olive oil until well blended. Adjust seasoning to taste.

3. To prepare the salad: In a large non-metal bowl toss together the drained onion, cucumber, bell peppers, feta cheese, tomatoes, and olives. Toss together with the dressing and serve.

Italian Peasant Bread Salad

SERVES 4

This main-course salad should be made with day-old Italian-style dense wheat bread.
If the bread was baked in a brick oven, so much the better!
Try the light tomato-basil vinaigrette with other salads, too.

DRESSING:

1/4 cup balsamic vinegar or red wine vinegar
1 tablespoon tomato paste, preferably Italian
2 medium cloves garlic, minced
1/2 teaspoon salt
1/4 teaspoon freshly ground pepper
3 tablespoons finely chopped fresh basil
1/2 cup olive oil, preferably extra virgin
1 small red onion, minced

SALAD:

1/2 loaf day-old Italian-style wheat bread (about 7 ounces), cut into 1/2-inch cubes
1 medium head radicchio, tough outer leaves removed, cored and shredded
1 small head romaine lettuce, tough outer leaves removed, cored and shredded
10 ounces miniature mozzarella cheese balls, or plain or smoked mozzarella cheese, cut into 1/2-inch dice
3 ounces prosciutto, sliced 1/4-inch thick and julienned
1/4 cup drained, chopped pimento
1/4 cup freshly grated Parmesan cheese

PREPARATION

1. To prepare the dressing: In a medium non-metal bowl whisk together the vinegar, tomato paste, garlic, salt, pepper, and basil. Slowly whisk in the olive oil until well blended. Stir in the onion and adjust seasoning to taste.

2. To prepare the salad: In a medium non-metal bowl combine the diced bread and half the dressing. Cover and refrigerate for 1 hour.

3. In a large non-metal bowl combine the radicchio, romaine, mozzarella cheese, prosciutto, and pimento. Toss together with the remaining dressing until evenly coated. Cover and refrigerate for 1 hour.

4. To serve, allow the bread mixture and radicchio mixture to return to room temperature, then toss together with the Parmesan cheese. Adjust seasoning to taste and serve.

Chilled Lentil Soup

Lentils are one of the many foods cultivated particularly in the Pacific Northwest. The lentil, naturally high in protein, has long been valued as a substitute for meat. In this recipe its delicate flavor is enhanced by white wine and radishes, resulting in a truly memorable summer soup. A wedge of semi-soft cheese and crusty whole-wheat bread are the perfect accompaniments.

2 tablespoons unsalted butter or margarine	3 tablespoons tomato paste, preferably Italian
1 large red onion, finely chopped	2 teaspoons finely chopped fresh thyme, or 1/2
2 medium cloves garlic, minced	teaspoon dried, crumbled
2 quarts vegetable stock (page 184) or canned	Salt and freshly ground pepper to taste
low-sodium chicken broth	2 bunches red radishes, julienned
1/2 cup dry white wine	2 ounces toasted sliced almonds (page 96), to
1 pound dried lentils, picked over and rinsed	garnish

PREPARATION

1. In a heavy 3- to 4-quart saucepan over medium-high heat, melt the butter. Add the onion and garlic and cook, stirring often, for 3 to 4 minutes or until soft but not browned. Stir in the stock, wine, lentils, tomato paste, and thyme. Bring to a boil, then reduce the heat to low and simmer, partially covered, for 1 hour or until the lentils are very tender. Stir occasionally and skim off any foam that rises to the surface.

2. Force the hot lentil soup, in batches, through the finest blade of a food mill into a large bowl. Alternatively, process in batches in the bowl of a food processor fitted with a metal blade and process until puréed.

3. Cool the lentil soup to room temperature and season with salt and pepper. Cover and refrigerate for at least 2 hours or until thoroughly chilled. (This recipe can be prepared to this point up to 2 days ahead.)

4. To serve, stir the julienned radishes into the chilled soup. Ladle the soup into a chilled tureen or individual soup bowls, and garnish with toasted almonds.

TO MICROWAVE

In a 3-quart microproof dish with a tight-fitting lid, combine the butter, onion, and garlic and microcook uncovered, on HIGH 3 minutes or until soft.

Stir in 4 cups of the stock, the wine, lentils, tomato paste, and thyme. Cover tightly and microcook on HIGH 10 minutes more or until it reaches a boil. Then microcook, covered, on MEDIUM 40 to 45 minutes or until lentils are tender. Let stand 5 minutes. Stir in the remaining 4 cups stock. Then follow steps 2 through 4.

FREEZING TIPS

Follow the recipe through step 2. Let cool, wrap, seal, and label. Freeze up to 2 months.

To Serve: Thaw. Season with salt and pepper and proceed with step 4.

Cold Chicken and Pasta Primavera

SERVES 4

This salad is a treat for the eye as well as the palate, wonderfully colorful and also delicious. I like the simple mixture of pasta, chicken, and vegetables, but for a festive occasion you might want to toss in some cooked shrimp or scallops!

SALAD:
1 small head bibb lettuce, tough outer leaves removed, cored and leaves separated
8 ounces tricolor pasta (spinach, tomato, egg) in an interesting shape, such as shells or wagon wheels, cooked al dente (slightly firm to the bite)
3 cups cooked chicken (preferably breast meat), cut into 1/2-inch-wide strips
4 ounces green beans, cooked until crisp-tender and halved lengthwise

1 pint ripe cherry tomatoes, halved
1 medium yellow crookneck squash, halved lengthwise, sliced thinly crosswise, and steamed until just tender
1 medium zucchini, halved lengthwise, and steamed until just tender
Salt and freshly ground pepper to taste

DRESSING:
1 recipe Pesto (page 139), at room temperature

PREPARATION

1. To prepare the salad: Line a serving platter with the lettuce leaves. Cover with damp paper towels and wrap in plastic wrap. Refrigerate until ready to serve.

2. In a large bowl gently toss together the pasta and pesto dressing. Add the chicken, green beans, toma-toes, squash, and zucchini. Gently toss until well combined. Adjust seasoning to taste with salt and pepper.

3. To serve, spoon the pasta mixture on the lettuce-lined platter and serve immediately.

Grilled Tuna Niçoise

This supper salad can be prepared in advance and then beautifully composed on individual plates just before serving. The recipe calls for a garnish of goat cheese and a tarragon dressing that complements all the ingredients. To grill the tuna, prepare the grill or preheat the broiler, brush the tuna with a little olive oil, and grill over medium-hot coals (or broil) for 2 to 3 minutes per side, or until medium-rare (slightly pink in the center).

DRESSING:

1/4 cup white wine vinegar
1 tablespoon coarse-grain mustard
2 teaspoons finely chopped fresh tarragon, or 3/4 teaspoon dried, crumbled
1/2 teaspoon salt
1/8 teaspoon freshly ground pepper
1/4 teaspoon dried hot red pepper flakes, crushed
1/2 cup olive oil, preferably extra virgin
1 small red onion, minced

SALAD:

8 ounces fresh green beans, cooked until crisp-tender
1 medium head Boston lettuce, tough outer leaves removed, cored, and leaves separated
1 pint ripe cherry tomatoes
1-1/4 pounds grilled or broiled tuna steaks, about 3/4 inch thick, cut into 1/2-inch-wide strips
12 ounces small new potatoes, unpeeled but scrubbed, cooked until tender but not mushy, quartered
3/4 cup drained French Niçoise olives, rinsed
4 hard-cooked eggs, quartered
8 anchovies, rinsed
3 ounces goat cheese, crumbled, to garnish

PREPARATION

1. To make the dressing: In a small non-metal bowl whisk together the vinegar, mustard, tarragon, salt, pepper, and red pepper flakes until combined. Gradually pour in the olive oil in a slow, steady stream, whisking constantly until well blended. Stir in the onion and adjust seasoning to taste.

2. To serve, in a medium non-metal bowl toss together the green beans with several tablespoons of the dressing. Arrange the lettuce leaves on four plates. Decoratively arrange the beans, tomatoes, tuna, potatoes, olives, and eggs in individual sections. Drape the anchovies over the beans. Drizzle the remaining dressing over the composed salads and garnish with goat cheese. Serve immediately.

Armenian Bulgur Salad

I have used mint, peas, and honey to give a subtly sweet note to this refreshing salad, while walnut oil heightens the wheat flavor of the bulgur. I like to serve this salad with Armenian string cheese, a braided semisoft cheese with caraway seeds.

1 cup bulgur

DRESSING:
1/4 cup fresh lemon juice
1 tablespoon honey
3/4 teaspoon salt
1/2 teaspoon freshly ground pepper
1/3 cup finely chopped fresh mint
3-1/2 tablespoons finely chopped fresh parsley, preferably Italian flat-leaf
4 scallions, white part only, thinly sliced

2 teaspoons walnut oil (available at specialty food shops)
1/4 cup olive oil
1 medium cucumber, peeled, seeded, and finely chopped
1 medium yellow or red bell pepper, cored, seeded, and cut into 1/2-inch dice
1 cup shelled fresh green peas, cooked, or half a 10-ounce package frozen, thawed
1 large ripe tomato, seeded and finely chopped

PREPARATION

1. To prepare the bulgur: In a 2- to 3-quart saucepan over medium-high heat, bring 2 cups water to a boil. Stir in the bulgur and reduce the heat to medium-low. Cover and simmer the bulgur for 8 to 12 minutes or until all the water has been absorbed. Transfer to a large bowl and let cool to room temperature. When cool, cover and refrigerate until chilled.

2. Meanwhile, prepare the dressing: In a medium non-metal bowl whisk together the lemon juice, honey, salt, pepper, mint, parsley, scallions, walnut oil, and olive oil until well blended. Stir in the cucumber, bell pepper, peas, and tomato. Adjust sea-soning to taste. Cover and refrigerate until ready to serve.

3. To serve, fluff the chilled bulgur with a fork and toss together with the dressing mixture. Taste and adjust seasoning if necessary. Transfer to a serving bowl or platter and serve.

COOK'S NOTE

For this recipe it is unnecessary to cook the thawed frozen peas.

Vitello Tonnato with Bibb Lettuce and Sorrel

This is a knife-and-fork salad that makes a splendid summer dinner. The piquant tuna sauce and subtly seasoned veal of this famous dish make a superb combination of flavors, while the taste and texture of the buttery bibb lettuce and tangy sorrel add a light touch of the garden.

VEAL:

1-1/2 pounds veal scallops (8 very large scallops or 10 to 12 smaller scallops), pounded (see instructions for preparing chicken breasts, page 51)

Salt and freshly ground pepper to taste

   2 tablespoons unsalted butter, not margarine

   2 scallions, white part only, thinly sliced

   2 tablespoons fresh lemon juice

MAYONNAISE:

   1 egg yolk

   2 tablespoons fresh lemon juice, or more if needed

  1/2 teaspoon dry mustard

  1/4 cup dry white wine

  1/4 teaspoon salt

  1/2 teaspoon freshly ground pepper

  3/4 cup olive oil

   1 6-1/2-ounce can water-packed chunk light tuna, drained and pureed

   3 tablespoons minced sweet gherkins

   2 tablespoons drained capers, rinsed

   4 anchovies, rinsed and minced

Salt and freshly ground pepper to taste

Bibb lettuce leaves, washed, wrapped in damp paper towels, and refrigerated

Sorrel leaves or watercress, washed, stemmed, wrapped in damp paper towels, and refrigerated

PREPARATION

1. To prepare the veal: Lightly season both sides of the pounded veal scallops with salt and pepper.

2. In a large skillet over medium-high heat, melt the butter. Add the scallions and cook, stirring occasionally, for 4 to 5 minutes or until softened but not browned.

3. Add the veal in batches and cook for 1 minute on each side. (Note: The veal should be slightly pink in the center.) Transfer the veal to a platter, sprinkle with the lemon juice, and reserve at room temperature.

4. To prepare the mayonnaise: In a blender or in the bowl of a food processor fitted with a metal blade, blend the egg yolk, lemon juice, mustard, wine, salt and pepper briefly. With the blender on low speed, gradually pour in the olive oil in a slow, steady stream. When all the oil has been incorporated and you have a saucelike consistency, turn off the blender and transfer the mayonnaise to a medium non-metal bowl. Stir in the pureed tuna, gherkins, capers, and anchovies. Season with salt, pepper, and additional lemon juice if needed.

5. To serve, arrange the lettuce leaves and sorrel around the edge of a serving platter. Transfer the veal to the platter and spoon the tuna sauce over it, covering the surface of each piece. Garnish with lemon zest if desired.

STOCKS

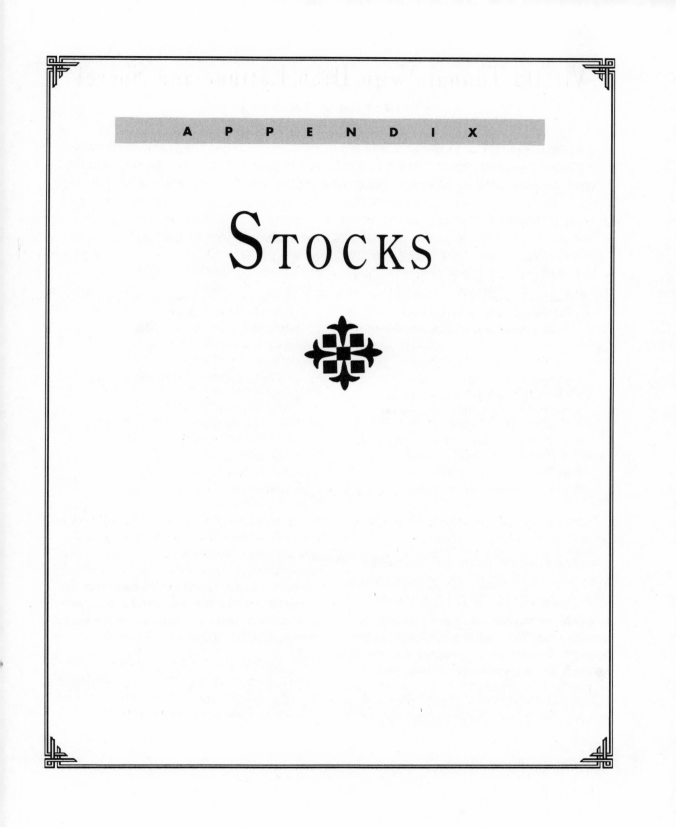

Vegetable Stock

Difficult as it may be to resist the temptation, the making of a good vegetable stock does not call for emptying the contents of your refrigerator into a stockpot. Basically, a good stock should be kept simple rather than muddied with too many competing flavors. In particular, avoid the use of strongly flavored vegetables such as turnips or cabbage or vegetables such as green bell pepper that will tend to make the stock bitter. Use only the stems of mushrooms, or else remove the glands located underneath the mushroom caps so that the stock will not turn brown. Above all, do not reduce this stock by allowing it to boil, as it will get cloudy and bitter; it must cook at a gentle simmer. You may want to experiment with making a stock sweeter by adding such vegetables as parsnips or sweet potatoes; or to match the stock to the meal you're preparing by making such additions as shiitake mushroom stems for an Oriental dish, jalapeño peppers for Mexican food, or fresh basil for an Italian meal.

3 medium carrots, quartered
3 ribs celery, quartered, leaves included
2 medium boiling potatoes, scrubbed but unpeeled, cut into eighths
2 medium leeks, green part included, washed thoroughly, and coarsely chopped
2 medium yellow onions, quartered
2 medium zucchini, cut into eighths

1 medium cucumber, peeled, seeded, and finely chopped
2 large cloves garlic, lightly crushed
Bouquet garni (place ingredients in cheesecloth and tie bundle with string):
• 5 sprigs fresh parsley
• 3 sprigs fresh thyme
• 2 bay leaves
• 10 peppercorns

PREPARATION

1. In a 6- to 8-quart nonreactive stockpot over medium-high heat, add the carrots, celery, potatoes, leeks, onions, zucchini, cucumber, garlic, the bouquet garni, and 2-1/2 quarts cold water. Add more water if needed to cover the contents of the stockpot by 1 inch. Slowly bring to a boil. Reduce the heat to very low and simmer gently for 1 hour, stirring occasionally and skimming the surface as needed. (*Note:* Do not let the stock boil, or it will turn cloudy.)

2. Let stock cool to room temperature. Carefully strain the stock through a fine mesh strainer or colander lined with a double layer of dampened cheesecloth, but do not press the contents or force it through. Discard all solid particles. Let stock cool completely, then transfer to nonreactive containers. Refrigerate up to 1 week, or wrap, seal, label, and freeze up to 4 months.

Beef Stock

The uses for beef stock are infinite, and once you make a homemade stock, you will never want to use the canned variety again. But gone are the days when the local meat market had bones available: you may need to place an order way in advance. So befriend a butcher and ask him to set aside some marrow-filled bones for you! Though a homemade beef stock takes longer than other types of stocks to prepare (10 hours, unattended), the superb results make it all worth while.

4 pounds beef bones, preferably marrow and knuckle, cut into 1-1/2- to 2-inch-long pieces (have your butcher do this)

3 pounds veal bones, preferably shin, knuckle, and feet, cut into 1-1/2- to 2-inch-long pieces (have your butcher do this)

3 medium yellow onions, coarsely chopped

3 medium carrots, coarsely chopped

3 ribs celery, coarsely chopped

2 leeks, including green part, washed thoroughly, and coarsely chopped

Bouquet garni (place ingredients in cheesecloth and tie bundle with string):
- 4 sprigs fresh parsley
- 3 sprigs fresh thyme
- 7 peppercorns
- 4 whole cloves
- 1 bay leaf

PREPARATION

1. Preheat the oven to 450° F.

2. Place the beef and veal bones in a single layer in a large deep roasting pan. Roast in the upper rack of the oven for 1 hour, turning them once after 30 minutes. Add the onions, carrots, and celery to the roasting pan and bake 30 minutes more, but do not let the vegetables brown.

3. Using a slotted spoon, transfer the bones and vegetables to an 8- to 10-quart nonreactive stockpot. Carefully pour off the fat from the roasting pan and set pan over medium heat. Add 1 cup water and bring to a boil, scraping the sides and bottom to loosen the browned bits. Boil for 1 minute. Pour the mixture over the bones and vegetables and add 3 quarts cold water, adding more if needed to cover the contents of the stockpot by 1 inch.

4. Slowly bring to a boil. Reduce the heat to very low and simmer gently for 1 hour, stirring occasionally and skimming the surface as needed. Remember to skim the surface of stocks diligently, especially beef; a well-skimmed stock will be clear when chilled. (*Note:* Do not let the stock boil for any length of time, or it will turn cloudy.) Add the leeks and the bouquet garni, and simmer gently for 10 hours.

5. Carefully remove and discard the large bones. Strain the stock through a fine mesh strainer or colander lined with a double layer of dampened cheesecloth, but do not press on the contents or force it through. Discard all solid particles.

6. Return the stock to the stockpot and boil until it is reduced to about 2 quarts. This is a delicately flavored stock. For a more concentrated flavor, boil strained stock until reduced to about 3 cups.

7. Let stock cool to room temperature, then transfer to nonreactive storage containers. Refrigerate up to 1 week, or wrap, seal, label, and freeze up to 4 months. (*Note:* A layer of fat will rise to the top of the containers and solidify when refrigerated. This fat acts as a protection against spoilage. Just lift it off and discard before using or freezing the stock.)

Chicken Stock

MAKES 4 TO 5 QUARTS

Chicken stock is an extremely versatile and therefore a very important stock. It may be used as a base not only for poultry dishes, but also for veal, vegetable dishes, and even for some of the stronger-flavored fish. Although chicken stock might overpower a delicate fish like sole, it is a perfect match for such oilier varieties as bluefish and fresh tuna.

4 pounds chicken parts, preferably necks and backs
3 ribs celery, quartered, leaves included
3 medium carrots, quartered
2 medium yellow onions, coarsely chopped
2 medium leeks, including green part, washed thoroughly, finely chopped

Bouquet garni (place ingredients in cheesecloth and tie bundle with string):
- *6 sprigs fresh parsley*
- *4 sprigs fresh thyme*
- *2 bay leaves*
- *5 peppercorns*

PREPARATION

1. In an 8- to 10-quart nonreactive stockpot over medium-high heat, combine the chicken parts and 2 quarts cold water, adding more water if needed to cover the chicken by 3 inches. Slowly bring to a boil. Reduce the heat to very low and simmer gently for 45 minutes, stirring occasionally and skimming the surface as needed. Remember to skim the surface of stocks diligently, especially chicken; a well-skimmed stock will be clear when chilled. (*Note:* Do not let the stock boil for any length of time, or it will turn cloudy.)

2. Add the celery, carrots, onions, leeks, and the bouquet garni. Return to a boil, then reduce the heat

to very low and simmer for 3 hours more, stirring occasionally and skimming the surface as needed.

3. Let stock cool to room temperature. Carefully remove and discard the large bones. Strain the stock through a fine mesh strainer or colander lined with a double layer of dampened cheesecloth, but do not press on the contents or force it through. Discard all solid particles.

4. Let stock cool completely, then transfer to nonreactive containers. Refrigerate up to 2 days, or wrap, seal, label, and freeze up to 3 months. (*Note:* A layer of fat will rise to the top of the containers and solidify when refrigerated. This fat acts as a protection against spoilage. Just lift it off and discard before using or freezing the stock.) This is a delicately flavored stock. For a more concentrated flavor, boil strained stock until reduced to about 3 cups.

Fish Stock

MAKES 2-1/2 TO 3 QUARTS

This is a quick and easy fish stock, enhanced by white wine and aromatics that complement fish wonderfully.

1 pound fish trimmings, such as heads, tails, skin, and bones, from a nonoily fish such as sole or flounder
1 cup dry white wine
4 ribs celery, finely chopped, leaves included
2 medium carrots, cut into eighths
1 medium yellow onion, cut into eighths
3 medium shallots, quartered

1 fresh fennel, finely chopped, or 1 teaspoon fennel seeds, crushed
Bouquet garni (place ingredients in cheesecloth and tie bundle with string):
  • *3 sprigs fresh parsley*
  • *2 sprigs fresh tarragon*
  • *2 teaspoons grated lemon zest*
1/2 teaspoon salt

PREPARATION

1. In a 6- to 8-quart nonreactive stockpot over medium-high heat, add the fish trimmings, white wine, celery, carrots, onion, shallots, fennel, the bouquet garni, the salt, and 2-1/2 quarts cold water. Add more water if needed to cover the contents of the stockpot by 1 inch. Slowly bring to a boil. Reduce the heat to very low and simmer gently for 30 minutes, stirring occasionally and skimming the surface as needed. (*Note:* Do not let the stock boil for any length of time, or it will turn cloudy.)

2. Let stock cool to room temperature. Carefully strain the stock through a fine mesh strainer or colander lined with a double layer of dampened cheesecloth, but do not press the contents or force it through. Discard all solid particles. Let stock cool completely, then transfer to nonreactive containers. Refrigerate up to 2 days, or wrap, seal, label, and freeze up to 2 months. (*Note:* A layer of fat will rise to the top of the containers and solidify when refrigerated. This fat acts as a protection against spoilage. Just lift it off and discard before using or freezing the stock.) This is a delicately flavored stock. For a more concentrated flavor, boil strained stock until reduced to about 3 cups.

U.S. Weights and Measures

Here are some of the most commonly used weights and measures:

1 tablespoon = 3 teaspoons

1/2 tablespoon = 1-1/2 teaspoons

1/3 tablespoon = 1 teaspoon

A pinch = less than 1/8 teaspoon (dry)

A dash = 3 drops to 1/4 teaspoon (liquid)

1 cup = 16 tablespoons

1/2 cup = 8 tablespoons

1/4 cup = 4 tablespoons

16 cups = 4 quarts (liquid) = 1 gallon

8 cups = 2 quarts (liquid) = 1/2 gallon

4 cups = 1 quart = 2 pints = 32 ounces (liquid)

2 cups = 1/2 quart = 1 pint = 16 ounces (liquid)

1 cup = 1/2 pint = 8 ounces (liquid)

Index

A

almonds, toasting of, 96
Armenian bulgur salad, 181
artichoke hearts, creamed chicken with wild
  rice and, 64
asparagus:
  lobster Newburg with, 90
  risotto with wild mushrooms and, 148–149
avocado gazpacho, 173

B

barley:
  oxtail soup with, 105–106
  vegetable cobbler, 165
basil-tomato vinaigrette, 177
bean(s):
  cassoulet with duck and garlic sausage, 71
  chili con carne tequila, 94–95
  pesto minestrone, 138–139
  red, and rice, best-ever, 152–153
  refried, chicken tortilla pie with tomatillo
    sauce and, 66
  "soaking" of, in microwave, 154
  soup, robust Cuban, 153–154
  three-, salad with tuna and sage, 174
  white, soup with rosemary, Tuscan, 151
beans, green:
  coq au vin avec legumes, 47
  grilled tuna niçoise, 180
beef:
  bollito misto with green sauce, 104–105
  bourguignon with morels, 118–119
  chili con carne tequila, 94–95
  doubly delicious meat lasagne with tomato-
    olive sauce, 144–145
  extra-spicy Sloppy Joes, 112–113
  fragrant shepherd's pie, 114–115
  goulash, Hungarian, 106–107
  herbed salad burgers, 121
  Kentucky burgoo, 67
  Mara's veal meatloaf, 123
  meatloaf country-style, 122
  olla podrida with root vegetables and chick-
    peas, 115–116
  oxtail soup with barley, 105–106
  Papajohn's pastitsio, 141–142
  Philadelphia cheese-steak supper
    sandwiches, 99–100
  picadillo-stuffed peppers, 95–96
  pot-au-feu with horseradish sauce, 111–112
  ragù Bolognese, 143
  sauerbraten with braised red cabbage,
    110–111
  savory steak and kidney pie, 101–102
  spaghetti and meatballs, the ultimate,
    147–148
  stew with quinoa, southwestern, 98–99
  stock, 185–186
  Swedish-style meatballs, 119–120
  tamale pie, 108–109
  Yorkshire pudding pies, 103–104
beef, corned, 98
  hash, red flannel, 97–98
  hometown New England boiled dinner, 117
beets, 157
  red flannel corned beef hash, 97–98
  tangy hot-or-cold meatless borscht, 156–157
biscuit-topped lamb stew, 132–133

O

okra, chicken filé gumbo with, 49
onion, caramelized, soup with sherry, 157–158
onions, pearl:
    peeling of, 48
    vegetable cobbler, 165
orzo, quick fish soup with, 82
oxtail, 106
    soup with barley, 105–106
oyster loaves, 83

P

paella salad, 171–172
Papajohn's pastitsio, 141–142
paprika, 106
pasta, 13
    and chicken primavera, cold, 179
    chicken-tortellini soup, 44
    classic tuna-noodle casserole, 76
    contemporary tuna noodle casserole, 77
    doubly delicious meat lasagne with tomato-olive sauce, 144–145
    fish soup, quick, with orzo, 82
    Hungarian beef goulash, 106–107
    linguine al ragù Bolognese, 143–144
    macaroni and cheese deluxe, 140–141
    mushroom stroganoff, 160
    Papajohn's pastitsio, 141–142
    pesto minestrone, 138–139
    quintessential macaroni and cheese, 139–140
    Romanian layered pork and noodle casserole, 131
    spaghetti and meatballs, the ultimate, 147–148
    turkey tetrazzini with corn bread topping, 63
    vegetarian lasagne, 146–147
    whole-wheat, chicken with pine nuts, saffron and, 70

pastitsio, Papajohn's, 141–142
pearl onions:
    peeling of, 48
    vegetable cobbler, 165
pepperpot, Trinidad, 128
peppers:
    chili, preparation of, 109
    picadillo-stuffed, 95–96
    roasting of, 92
pesto minestrone, 138–139
Philadelphia cheese-steak supper sandwiches, 99–100
phyllo:
    crust, chicken pot pie with, 61
    watercress-mint spanakopita, 158–159
picadillo-stuffed peppers, 95–96
pilau, saffron-shrimp, 88
pine nuts:
    chicken with saffron, whole-wheat pasta and, 70
    rabbit ragout with eggplant and, 125–126
pizza, skillet, zucchini and sun-dried tomato, 167–168
polenta and eggplant Parmesan, 163–164
popovers, 103
pork:
    cassoulet with duck and garlic sausage, 71
    doubly delicious meat lasagne with tomato-olive sauce, 144–145
    Kentucky burgoo, 67
    and noodle casserole, Romanian layered, 131
    olla podrida with root vegetables and chick-peas, 115–116
    picadillo-stuffed peppers, 95–96
    potato supper salad, 175
    ragù Bolognese, 143
    saté, Indonesian, 130
    sweet potato and ham casserole, 129
    Trinidad pepperpot, 128

potato(es):
    fragrant shepherd's pie, 114–115
    grilled tuna niçoise, 180
    preventing discoloration of, 115
    supper salad, 175
    vegetable cobbler, 165
pot-au-feu with horseradish sauce, 111–112
pot pie, chicken:
    creamy, with herbed crust, 58
    with phyllo crust, 61
poultry, 13
    cassoulet with duck and garlic sausage, 71
    turkey tetrazzini with corn bread topping, 63
    turkey with mole, 54
    see also chicken
preparation and storage, 19–20
presentation and garnishing, 31–32

Q

quiche, shrimp and crabmeat, 75
quinoa, southwestern beef stew with, 98–99
quintessential macaroni and cheese, 139–140

R

rabbit ragout with eggplant and pine nuts,
    125–126
ragù Bolognese, 143
ratatouille, kasha, 166–167
rice, 13
    basmati, preparation of, 89
    best-ever red beans and, 152–153
    king of jambalaya, 150
    paella salad, 171–172
    risotto with wild mushrooms and asparagus,
        148–149
    saffron-shrimp pilau, 88
    wild, creamed chicken with artichoke hearts
        and, 64

Romanian layered pork and noodle casserole,
    131
rouille, 91
Russian dressing, 100

S

saffron:
    chicken with pine nuts, whole-wheat pasta
        and, 70
    shrimp pilau, 88
salad burgers, herbed, 121
salads:
    Armenian bulgur, 181
    cold chicken and pasta primavera, 179
    Greek, 176
    grilled tuna niçoise, 180
    Italian peasant bread, 177
    midsummer main-dish coleslaw, 170
    paella, 171–172
    potato supper, 175
    three-bean, with tuna and sage, 174
    vitello tonnato with bibb lettuce and sorrel,
        182
salmon:
    coulibiac of, 79
    kedgeree, 80
salt, 13, 14
sandwiches:
    extra-spicy Sloppy Joes, 112–113
    herbed salad burgers, 121
    Philadelphia cheese-steak supper, 99–100
sauces:
    horseradish cream, 112
    mole, 54
    Mornay, 88
    ragù Bolognese, 143
sauerbraten with braised red cabbage, 110–111
sausage:
    bollito misto with green sauce, 104–105

T

tamale beef pie, 108–109
tomatillo sauce, chicken tortilla pie with refried beans and, 66
tomato(es):
    basil vinaigrette, 177
    olive sauce, doubly delicious meat lasagne with, 144–145
    peeling of, 92
    sun-dried, and zucchini skillet pizza, 167–168
tortellini chicken soup, 44
tortilla chicken pie with refried beans and tomatillo sauce, 66
Trinidad pepperpot, 128
tuna:
    grilled, niçoise, 180
    noodle casserole, classic, 76
    noodle casserole, contemporary, 77
    three-bean salad with sage and, 174
    vitello tonnato with bibb lettuce and sorrel, 182
turkey:
    with mole, 54
    tetrazzini with corn bread topping, 63
Tuscan white bean soup with rosemary, 151

V

veal:
    doubly delicious meat lasagne with tomato-olive sauce, 144–145
    Mara's meatloaf, 123
    ragù Bolognese, 143
    Swedish-style meatballs, 119–120
    vitello tonnato with bibb lettuce and sorrel, 182

vegetable(s), 12, 13
    caramelized onion soup with sherry, 157–158
    cobbler, 165
    eggplant and polenta Parmesan, 163–164
    festive cheese fondue, 161–162
    kasha ratatouille, 166–167
    mushroom stroganoff, 160
    pesto minestrone, 138–139
    root, olla podrida with chick-peas and, 115–116
    stock, 184
    stuffed chicken breasts, 51
    tangy hot-or-cold meatless borscht, 156–157
    vegetarian lasagne, 146–147
    watercress-mint spanakopita, 158–159
    zucchini and sun-dried tomato skillet pizza, 167–168
vegetarian lasagne, 146–147
venison:
    mail-order sources for, 125
    stew, savory, 124
vinaigrette, tomato-basil, 177
vitello tonnato with bibb lettuce and sorrel, 182

W

watercress-mint spanakopita, 158–159
weights and measures, 189

Y

Yorkshire pudding pies, 103–104

Z

zucchini:
    kasha ratatouille, 166–167
    and sun-dried tomato skillet pizza, 167–168

About the Author

Mara Reid Rogers grew up in the historic Beacon Hill section of Boston. After earning a degree in photography from the Parsons School of Design, she went on to receive a professional culinary degree from Peter Kump's New York Cooking School.

Ms. Rogers is a professional cook, food writer, and food stylist, most recently on the staff of *House Beautiful* magazine, where she wrote frequently for the Quick Cook column. She has also worked on projects for *Esquire*, *New Body*, and *Solutions*. She is the author of *The Fish Grill Book* (Michael Friedman Publishing Group, Inc., 1990) and the owner of First Class Productions, a production company specializing in food.

Ms. Rogers and her husband live in Summit, New Jersey.